power foods

from the editors of whole living magazine

power foods

150 delicious recipes with the 38 healthiest ingredients

foreword by martha stewart

Clarkson Potter/Publishers
New York

Some photographs and recipes originally appeared
in Martha Stewart Living Omnimedia publications.

Library of Congress Cataloging-in-Publication Data
Power Foods: 150 delicious recipes with the 38 healthiest ingredients /
the editors of *Whole Living* magazine. — 1st ed.
Includes index.
1. Cookery (Natural foods)   2. Nutrition.   3. Functional foods.
TX741.W474 2011
641.5′636 — dc22   2010003255

ISBN 978-0-307-46532-0

Printed in China

Design by Michele Outland
Cover design by William van Roden
Cover photograph by Sang An

Photograph credits appear on page 373.

10 9 8 7 6 5 4 3 2 1

First Edition

For all of us desiring a long, good life
of well-being.

acknowledgments

This book represents the dedication and hard work of many talented individuals.

Thank you to *Whole Living* editor-in-chief Alexandra Postman, as well as former *Body + Soul* editor-in-chief Alanna Fincke, publisher and managing director Janesse Thaw Bruce, and editors Donna Coco and Hillary Geronemus. To contributing food editors Sarah Carey and Anna Kovel and executive editorial director of food Lucinda Scala Quinn, who oversaw the development of these delicious recipes along with Kristen Evans, Sandra Rose Gluck, Emma Feigenbaum, Charlyne Mattox, and Caroline Wright. To *Whole Living* design director Matthew Axe, along with former *Body + Soul* design team Asya Palatova, Nancy M. Tassone, Lauren Sanders, and Lena Watts.

To the Special Projects Group at MSLO, headed by editor in chief Ellen Morrissey and art director William van Roden. To deputy editor Evelyn Battaglia and senior associate editor Christine Cyr Clisset, who collaborated with the magazine's editors to frame the content of the book and shepherd it through its many stages, and to managing editors Leigh Ann Boutwell and Sarah Rutledge Gorman. To contributing art director Michele Outland, who created the book's elegant design; to Jemme Aldridge, Jessi Blackham, and Sunny Stafford, who helped with design details; and to Catherine Gilbert, who organized and compiled the many photographs.

To Kathie Madonna Swift, MS, RD, LDN, for her expertise in vetting the nutritional information and the recipes, and to contributing writer Cheryl Redmond.

To photographers Johnny Miller and Romulo Yanes, and to many others for contributing their fine work (a complete list of photographers appears on page 373). Thank you to style director Ayesha Patel and stylists Tanya Graff, Allison Liebman, Dawn Sinkowski, Sarah Smart, and Michelle Wong.

As always, thank you to MSLO's editorial director Gael Towey and creative director Eric A. Pike. Others who provided ideas and support include: Carlene Bauer, Monita Buchwald, Mary Cahill, Denise Clappi, Rebecca Dalzell, Alison Vanek Devine, Stephanie Fletcher, Katie Goldberg, Heloise Goodman, Lisa Leonard Lee, Sari Lehrer, Nanette Maxim, Sara Parks, Lauren Piro, George D. Planding, Erika Preuss, Megan Rice, and Lindsey Stanberry.

Finally, we are grateful to our longtime partners at Clarkson Potter/Publishers, including Rica Allannic, Amy Boorstein, Angelin Borsics, Doris Cooper, Derek Gullino, Maya Mavjee, Mark McCauslin, Donna Passannante, Marysarah Quinn, Lauren Shakely, Jane Treuhaft, and Kate Tyler.

CONTENTS

foreword

I am especially happy that we are publishing *Power Foods* at this point in time. In the more than 30 years since we began writing about food and creating delicious, interesting, and inspired recipes for the home cook, our focus has often been on the underlying goodness of the food. We have always shopped for "clean," well-grown, carefully produced ingredients, and have always suggested that our readers buy organic, shop at food cooperatives and farmers' markets, grow as much for the table at home as possible, and cook simple, nutritious meals for loved ones, as often as time allows.

Today, I think we all know that a clean and thoughtful diet is essential to overall good health and well-being. I think we all know that daily use of artificial additives, chemicals, mass-produced ingredients, and factory-farmed meats, poultry, eggs, and dairy can lead to dietary imbalances, illness, and undesirable complications.

What we all desire for ourselves and our families is a good, long, healthy life, and what this book does in a very large and helpful way is clarify what we should be eating, why, and how.

Healthy eating doesn't have to be a challenge. It should be easy and it should be pleasurable. Our dishes center around seasonal produce, lean proteins, and whole grains. The recipes are clear and easy; the Basics portion of the book lists what we need in our pantry, refrigerator, and freezer; and the ingredients' nutritional information is clear and understandable.

Before you begin to read through the nutritional information and the recipes, pay close attention to the Golden Rules on page 11. Commit them to memory, then as a reminder, photocopy the page (or print a copy from wholeliving.com/golden-rules) and stick it to your refrigerator or your office bulletin board or in some other prominent place. Make copies of the Golden Rules for your family and your friends. These are commonsense guidelines for cooking and eating; they are easy to incorporate into any routine. And they will keep you healthier and happier in the long run.

introduction

The foods we eat have an enormous impact on our health, our well-being, and even our mood. In that sense, food has incredible power: the power to increase and sustain energy; the power to heal.

But "health food" has gotten a bad rap. People tend to think of it as bland and boring—good for you, but not good-tasting. In *Power Foods,* we'll show you how "delicious" and "nutritious" can actually go together, and that healthy eating doesn't have to be challenging. Simply centering your diet around seasonal produce, lean proteins, and whole grains—the foods our ancestors consumed for generations—will boost your vitality, change your body, and improve your well-being. Healthy eating will become less about rules and restrictions, and more about learning to approach cooking in a new way, so that you feel nourished and recharged.

Though all whole, seasonal foods are good for you, some are naturally better than others. The 38 foods and food groups covered in this book represent a selection of the most potent. Narrowing the list was no easy task. Ultimately, we settled on these 38 because they contain outstanding amounts of vitamins, minerals, phytonutrients, essential fatty acids, fiber, and more—with a proven track record of fighting disease and promoting good health. These foods are also easy to cook with and are widely available at most grocery stores, which means you can integrate them into your diet daily.

Whether you've been cooking this way for years or are just starting to incorporate more whole foods into your diet, you'll find inspiration and essential information in this book. First, we profile the 38 foods and food groups, with tips for selecting, storing, preparing,

and cooking them, followed by 150 power-packed recipes organized by breakfasts, starters and snacks, sandwiches and wraps, soups and stews, salads, main dishes, side dishes, and desserts. Then you'll find all you need to know to stock a healthy pantry, including information on healthful oils, alliums (such as onions and garlic), herbs, spices, and alternative sweeteners. A glossary explains vitamins, minerals, and other nutritional terms you'll encounter, followed by the Eating for Your Health section, which outlines the best dietary choices for a number of health issues, from heart disease to asthma. Finally, a nutritional index breaks down the key vitamins and minerals found in each power food, so you can put together daily menus that help you feel energized and whole.

To get the greatest benefit from your food, we suggest buying organic whenever possible. This goes beyond avoiding ingestion of chemical pesticides and hormones; organic food considers the health of the environment, which affects our collective well-being. Organics can be expensive, so if you need to watch your grocery dollars, start with the foods that are most heavily sprayed (see "When to Insist on Organic," right) or that you eat most often.

Don't forget: Part of the power of food comes from the pleasure it gives us. The dishes in this book have been crafted to maximize the ingredients' flavors while preserving their goodness. We hope this book turns you on to a delicious diet that will help you live a long, healthy life.

Alexandra Postman
Editor in Chief, *Whole Living*

the golden rules

1

Choose a wide variety of natural, unprocessed foods. A thoughtfully prepared whole foods diet will leave you feeling enriched, not deprived.

2

Buy organic—especially for the produce most heavily treated with pesticides (see below) as well as dairy products and meat.

3

Shop locally and eat seasonally. Check farmers' markets for produce at its peak, which will be more flavorful and healthful.

4

Think of fruits and vegetables in terms of the rainbow; if you eat a range of colors, you're assured of getting all the essential nutrients.

5

Limit salt intake; salt can increase your risk of hypertension and heart disease. Season with fresh herbs, spices, or lemon or lime juice instead.

6

Buy grains, nuts, and seeds in bulk, from a store with a rapid turnover, and replenish often.

7

Choose cooking oils that contain "good" mono-unsaturated and polyunsaturated fats, such as olive oil or neutral-flavored canola or safflower oil.

8

For cooking, use organic, low-sodium broth in cartons, or make chicken and vegetable broth from scratch and freeze small batches.

9

Plan ahead and shop wisely. If a salad calls for half a package of tofu, use the rest in a stir-fry.

10

Fill half your plate with vegetables, one quarter with whole grains, and one quarter with lean protein.

when to insist on organic

The Environmental Working Group (ewg.org), a nonprofit that aims to protect public health and the environment, determined you can reduce the amount of pesticides you ingest by 90 percent if you buy organic for these 12 fruits and vegetables: apples, celery, cherries, imported grapes, lettuce, nectarines, peaches, pears, potatoes, spinach, strawberries, and sweet bell peppers. Because milk fat can harbor traces of hormones (including rBGH) given to cows, it's also crucial to choose organic dairy products.

COMMON TERMS

Throughout this book you'll find many nutritional and health terms. Most nutrients are included in the glossary, starting on page 352, but these frequently repeated terms are also defined here, for easy reference.

AMINO ACIDS

Amino acids are chemical compounds found in plant and animal proteins. There are 20 different types of amino acids. About half of these the body synthesizes (or creates); they are called nonessential amino acids. The rest—called essential amino acids—must be acquired through diet. The body uses both nonessential and essential amino acids to make new proteins in the body. Proteins are an integral element in repair and growth of body tissue, immune protection, and the transmission of nerve impulses.

ANTIOXIDANTS

Antioxidants help protect the body against free radicals, which are unstable molecules that can damage cells and cause cancer. Many antioxidants are found in food while others are synthesized in the body. Some antioxidants come in the form of vitamins, such as vitamins A, C, and E, while others are phytonutrients, such as lycopene, beta-carotene, lutein, and selenium. Whole foods, such as fruits, vegetables, nuts, and grains, are among the best sources of antioxidants.

CARBOHYDRATES

Along with protein and fats, carbohydrates are one of the main dietary components the body needs in order to function. Carbohydrates come primarily in the form of sugars, starches, and fiber (the latter can't be digested). Once carbohydrates are consumed, the digestive system converts the sugars and starches into sugar molecules, which enter the bloodstream and provide energy for cells and tissue. Whole, minimally processed foods, such as vegetables, fruits, whole grains, and low-fat dairy, are the best kinds of carbohydrates; the fiber in these foods helps slow sugar absorption, resulting in an even, sustained level of energy. Heavily processed foods—including sugary cereals, white flour, and potato chips—contain little fiber and their starches and sugars rapidly turn into glucose in the body, spiking blood sugar, which can cause energy levels to quickly plummet. Excess glucose—what the body doesn't need for immediate energy, or for future reserves in the form of glycogen (stored in the liver and muscles)—turns to fat.

CAROTENOIDS

These fat-soluble plant pigments, ranging in color from yellow to orange to red, typically function as antioxidants; the body can even convert a few into vitamin A. The best-known carotenoid is carotene, from which the group gets its name.

CHOLESTEROL

A waxy fat compound, cholesterol is important for making some hormones and forming cell membranes. Cholesterol is found both in animal foods and in the body, which the liver manufactures from fatty foods. Cholesterol is transported through the body by molecules called lipoproteins: low-density lipoprotein (LDL) is known as "bad" cholesterol because it builds up on arterial walls and can lead to atherosclerosis; high-density lipoprotein (HDL) is considered "good" cholesterol because it helps move excess cholesterol from the arteries to the liver for disposal and may protect against heart disease.

FATS

Along with carbohydrates and protein, fats are one of the body's most basic nutrients. Just as amino acids make up protein molecules, so do fatty acids comprise fat molecules. Fats come in two forms: saturated and unsaturated.

SATURATED FATS Saturated fats are primarily found in animal products. In the diet, saturated fats tend to increase the body's production of LDL ("bad") cholesterol and reduce the production of HDL ("good") cholesterol. They have a higher melting point than similar unsaturated fats, and foods containing saturated fats (like butter) are often solid at room temperature.

UNSATURATED FATS Unsaturated fats are mostly found in plant products, and they tend to lower the body's production of LDL ("bad") cholesterol. There are two main types of unsaturated fats:

MONOUNSATURATED FATS Found in olive oil and nuts, monounsaturated fats tend to increase the body's production of HDL ("good") cholesterol and reduce the production of LDL ("bad") cholesterol.

POLYUNSATURATED FATS Polyunsaturated fats tend to reduce the body's production of cholesterol—both HDL ("good") cholesterol and LDL ("bad") cholesterol. Both omega-3 and omega-6 are polyunsaturated fats with myriad health benefits. Omega-3 fatty acids are found in walnuts, flaxseed, and many types of cold-water fish; they are crucial to brain and heart health, and may reduce inflammation and lower risk of some chronic diseases. Omega-6 fatty acids, which are also important to brain development, are plentiful in many types of vegetable oil, such as corn, soybean, and safflower. Unfortunately, many Americans get too many omega-6 fatty acids in their diets, which may promote inflammation.

FIBER (SOLUBLE AND INSOLUBLE)
The indigestible portion of plant foods, fiber passes through the body without being absorbed. There are two main types: insoluble fiber, which does not dissolve in water and helps prevent constipation; and soluble fiber, which forms a gel in water, lowers cholesterol, and slows the body's absorption of sugar. Fruits, vegetables, whole grains, and legumes contain both types. Adequate consumption of fiber is associated with a lower risk of heart disease and type 2 diabetes.

FLAVONOIDS
A large group of plant-produced compounds (primarily pigments in the yellow and blue to red range), flavonoids may promote antioxidant production and other beneficial responses in the body.

MINERALS
Whereas vitamins are organic (containing carbon) and are produced by plants and animals, minerals are derived from inorganic substances found in the earth and water. Plants absorb these minerals, and the plants are, in turn, eaten by animals. The body needs minerals each day for proper cell growth and overall health. It requires some minerals, such as calcium, in large quantities. Trace minerals, such as chromium, iron, selenium, and zinc, are needed only in small quantities each day.

PHYTONUTRIENTS
Phytonutrients, also called phytochemicals, include a wide range of plant compounds (*phyto* means "plant") that promote health. Some groups of phytonutrients currently under research include carotenoids, phytosterols, and limonoids.

PROTEIN
Along with fats and carbohydrates, protein is a main component for fueling the body. Protein compounds are made up of chains of amino acids. "Complete" dietary proteins, such as quinoa, meat, and cheese, contain all the essential amino acids, while "incomplete" proteins, such as grains, legumes, vegetables, and fruits, contain only some of them. The body breaks down the food's protein into its amino acids and uses them as the building materials for all its cells, as well as for energy.

VITAMINS
Organic compounds made by plants or animals, vitamins are essential for normal growth and they promote a healthy metabolism. There are two varieties of vitamins: fat soluble and water soluble. Fat-soluble vitamins, including A, D, E, and K, are absorbed in fat and can be stored in the body's fatty tissue—for this reason, the body doesn't need a daily supply. Water-soluble vitamins, such as C and the B-complex vitamins, can't be stored: Any excess is carried out of the body, so a fresh supply is needed every day.

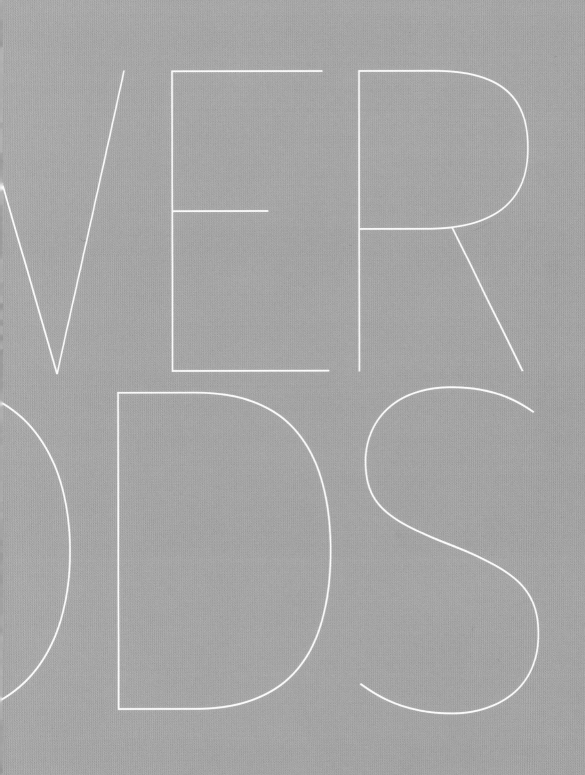

VEGETABLES

Trace the word *vegetable* to its roots and you get "vigorous," "active," "strong," and "lively." So it's a shame that, all too often, vegetables end up overcooked and relegated to the side of the main course, eaten only because they're "good for you." Vegetables deserve more respect—and a bigger piece of the real estate on your plate. For the small amount of calories they contain, they deliver the most nutrients of any class of food. Consider this: If you eat at least five servings of vegetables per day (instead of fewer than three, as most of us do), you cut your risk of developing heart disease by 20 percent. Like fruits, vegetables are excellent low-calorie sources of vitamins, minerals, and fiber. But they also contain nutrients you don't find in fruits: sulforaphane in broccoli and other cruciferous vegetables, for example, and vitamin K in spinach and kale. Moving vegetables from the sidelines to the center of your diet will not only add variety to your meals but could also help you live a healthier, happier life.

ARTICHOKES

Left alone, an unpicked artichoke will blossom into a striking purple flower. But its real beauty lies in what it can do for you. This elegant member of the aster family is one of the best detoxifiers around.

HEALTH BENEFITS

Counting both leaves and heart, one medium artichoke has just 60 calories, more than 6 grams of fiber, and 4 grams of protein. The more significant appeal of artichokes, though, is their ability to promote liver health and soothe digestive ailments (such as nausea, pain, and bloating) owing to the powerful antioxidant silymarin, which boosts liver function by stimulating cell regeneration and scavenging for free radicals. Artichokes also contain cynarin—a caffeoylquinic acid found primarily in the leaves—which promotes the liver's bile production, in turn helping break down fatty foods. According to some studies, cynarin also helps lower cholesterol. Additionally, artichokes are a good source of magnesium, potassium, and folate—nutrients that help improve muscle function and heart health. This versatile vegetable can even stimulate sweet receptors, helping to satiate your sweet tooth. In the 1930s, a scientist found that after consuming artichokes two thirds of his dinner guests thought that even a glass of water tasted sweet (a researcher at Yale University later confirmed this phenomenon).

HOW TO BUY

Look for firm, heavy, medium-size artichokes. To test for freshness, squeeze the artichoke and listen for a squeaky sound.

HOW TO STORE

Refrigerated in a plastic bag, artichokes will keep for up to five days.

PREPARATION TIP

To keep cut artichokes from discoloring, place them in water with the juice of one lemon until you're ready to use them. Steaming is a classic and healthy way to prepare artichokes; see the recipe on page 96.

DID YOU KNOW?

During the Renaissance, physicians considered artichokes an aphrodisiac and prescribed them to men who sought to increase their prowess. Today, we prize the artichoke as much for its flavor as for its intrinsic benefits. But its sex appeal remains: In 1949, Marilyn Monroe was crowned the first California Artichoke Queen.

ASPARAGUS

One of the first vegetables to emerge in spring, asparagus helps fight a range of diseases and may even boost the libido.

HEALTH BENEFITS

This member of the lily family contains the most folate of any vegetable. Folate helps rid the body of the amino acid homocysteine, associated with cardiovascular disease. It also may aid in the production of histamine, which is necessary for achieving orgasm—making asparagus's legendary aphrodisiac powers not quite so far-fetched. Additionally, the stalk is full of vision-promoting vitamin A, kidney-supporting potassium, and selenium. Asparagus is also an excellent source of vitamins C and K. If you're looking for a natural anti-ager, don't skimp on these spears. Asparagus offers high levels of glutathione, which minimizes skin damage from sun exposure, protects and repairs DNA, and promotes healthy cell replication.

HOW TO BUY

Choose firm stalks with tightly closed heads. The base should look well hydrated, not dry. Thin-stalked asparagus tend to be more tender because they are younger.

HOW TO STORE

Refrigerated, asparagus should last several days; either tightly wrap the stalks in plastic wrap or stand them upright in a small amount of water, covering them with a plastic bag.

PREPARATION TIP

Instead of cutting off the fibrous base, hold a stalk loosely and snap off the bottom. The stalk will naturally break where it starts to get tough. To enjoy the vegetable raw, shave it lengthwise with a vegetable peeler or thinly slice it on an angle, then toss into a salad. Most of asparagus's nutrients are left intact, even after it is cooked. To enjoy the vegetable cooked, cover and steam it in a basket or colander over simmering water until bright green and crisp-tender, about 5 minutes.

DID YOU KNOW?

Mild white asparagus lacks green color because, once the plant emerges from the soil in springtime, its shoots are intentionally shielded from light to stave off photosynthesis (which would turn them green). Nutritionally speaking, the white variety pales in comparison to its counterpart.

recipes

AVOCADOS

Rich and filling, avocados are high in fat—the good kind—and relatively calorie-dense (half an avocado contains about 140 calories). The two most common varieties of avocados sold in the United States are Hass, with nubby, very dark green skin, and Fuerte, distinguished by its lighter green, smoother skin.

HEALTH BENEFITS

Monounsaturated fats, the key to the avocado's power-food status, may lower levels of LDL ("bad") cholesterol and increase levels of HDL ("good") cholesterol. Avocados are also unexpectedly high in fiber, providing about 13 grams each, and they offer more potassium per gram than bananas. Bonus: The boron in avocados may help the body absorb calcium.

HOW TO BUY

Choose avocados that feel heavy for their size, and have blemish-free skin. If you need a ripe avocado right away, find one that yields to gentle pressure.

HOW TO STORE

Keep unripe avocados at room temperature (they ripen best between 60 and 75 degrees). To hasten ripening, store in a brown paper bag with a banana, which releases ethylene and speeds up the process. Don't refrigerate an unripe avocado or it will never ripen; once ripe, you can store it in the refrigerator for a few days to keep it from getting too soft.

PREPARATION TIP

Because avocado flesh discolors quickly once removed from the skin, don't cut an avocado until you plan to use it. Add lemon or lime juice to cut avocado pieces (and to dishes such as guacamole) to keep them from turning brown.

BEETS

Beneath the dull, gnarled exterior of these humble root vegetables lie sweet, tender jewels with a buttery flavor and a wealth of nutrients. Cooking the savory greens makes this robust vegetable nutritious from top to bottom.

HEALTH BENEFITS

Renowned for their earthy sweetness, beets have the highest sugar content of any vegetable. Nevertheless, they are low in calories, high in fiber, and rich in iron—plus they're full of cancer-fighting beta-carotene and folic acid, which can help prevent birth defects. (Fresh beets are more nutritious, and have less sugar and sodium than canned.) The leafy greens, which can stand in for their botanical cousin Swiss chard (page 31), are even more nutritious than the roots, with double the potassium, folic acid, calcium, and iron.

HOW TO BUY

At farmers' markets and gourmet grocers you'll likely find golden, white, and striped beets—called Chioggia, or Candy Cane—alongside the red ones. Look for bunches of firm beets with fresh-looking greens. (Wilted beet greens don't necessarily signal bad beets, but better-looking greens mean more vegetable for your money.) Unless you're planning to chop or grate the beets, choose a uniform-sized bunch so they'll cook in the same amount of time. (Small to medium beets are generally more tender.)

HOW TO STORE

Leaving an inch of stem attached to the root, cut away the greens and refrigerate the beets and greens in separate plastic bags. Beets will last at least a month, but you should use the greens within three to four days.

PREPARATION TIP

Preparing beets can be a messy business. Roasting or steaming them with their skins on keeps the color from leaching out; the skins slip off easily once cooked. To roast, trim both ends. Drizzle with olive oil and wrap in parchment-lined foil. Roast at 450°F until tender, 1 to 1½ hours depending on size. Let cool slightly, then rub off skins with paper towels. Prepare beet greens as you would Swiss chard, sautéing the chopped stems and leaves in oil with minced garlic.

recipes

BELL PEPPERS

For a kick of antioxidants and vitamin C, bell peppers deliver. While they come in a rainbow of colors and offer distinctive sweetness and crunch, it's the red, yellow, and orange peppers that triumph nutritionally.

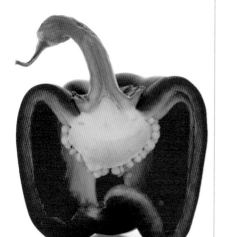

HEALTH BENEFITS

Bell peppers owe their good looks and health effects to carotenoids, pigments that help boost immunity and fight cancer and heart disease. They're valuable for good vision, as well: Orange peppers are a top source of lutein and zeaxanthin, which may guard against cataracts and macular degeneration. In fact, orange peppers contain more zeaxanthin than any fruit or other vegetable (with corn a distant second). Red peppers supply abundant amounts of beta-carotene, which your body converts to vitamin A, a nutrient crucial for night vision. Just one small red, yellow, or orange pepper gives you up to three times your daily requirement of vitamin C. Peppers also provide vitamin B_6, another immune-supporting nutrient.

HOW TO BUY

Look for firm peppers with taut skin free of wrinkles or cracks. Peppers with thick walls are juicier, and feel heavy for their size. Conventionally grown peppers rank high on the list of pesticide-laden vegetables, so buy organic whenever you can.

HOW TO STORE

Refrigerate peppers in a paper bag in the vegetable drawer for up to five days.

PREPARATION TIP

Roasted peppers in your fridge are like money in the bank; they hold promise for endless possibilities and culinary upgrades. Use them in salads, dips, and pasta. To roast, place peppers directly over a gas flame and cook, turning with tongs, until charred all over. Don't rinse to remove the charred skin, or you'll wash away much of the flavor. Instead, transfer to a bowl and cover with plastic wrap until cool enough to handle, then rub off the skins with a paper towel.

DID YOU KNOW?

All red, yellow, and orange peppers start out green. The color (and also the taste) changes depending on how long they're allowed to ripen on the vine. It's this extra time in the sun that makes these brightly hued peppers more expensive than their green counterparts.

BROCCOLI

If broccoli were sold in the drugstore, you'd probably need a prescription: It's that health-changing. Packed with antioxidants, this vegetable protects the heart, helps prevent strokes, and may even fight cancer and ease arthritis pain.

HEALTH BENEFITS

A member of the cabbage family, broccoli is the most nutritious of all its cruciferous cousins, which include brussels sprouts, cauliflower, kale, collards, and bok choy. All these vegetables contain nitrogen compounds called indoles, which are effective in helping to prevent cancerous tumors of the stomach, prostate, and breast. Broccoli, however, goes even further: It contains especially high amounts of enzymes and nutrients, such as carotenoids, that sweep up cancer-promoting free radicals. Beyond that, broccoli's other nutrients make it a produce-aisle panacea. Besides being calcium-rich and high in fiber, broccoli is also a source of vitamin C, folate, riboflavin, potassium, and iron, making it a preventive powerhouse. Ongoing studies suggest that broccoli may help fight cataracts, diabetes, rheumatoid arthritis, osteoporosis, ulcers, high blood pressure, stroke, and heart disease.

HOW TO BUY

Choose young, freshly picked broccoli with tightly closed and uniformly green florets, and stalks that snap crisply. Overly mature broccoli will be tough and woody, and will emit a sulfurous cabbage odor when cooked. Yellowing florets mean that the broccoli is past its prime.

HOW TO STORE

Refrigerate in a perforated plastic bag in the vegetable drawer for up to five days.

PREPARATION TIP

Steaming is the healthiest way to prepare broccoli: Cook in a basket or colander, covered, over simmering water until crisp-tender, about 5 minutes. Boiling, microwaving, or stir-frying will leach away a larger percentage of the nutrients. And go ahead and eat the leaves and stalks: Most people discard them, but they contain a wealth of nutrients. Just be sure to peel the stalks before cooking.

DID YOU KNOW?

Broccoli takes its name from the Latin word *brachium,* or "branch." The flowering stalk has many healthful relatives, including broccoflower, a cross between broccoli and cauliflower, with a milder flavor than either one; broccolini (also called baby broccoli), a cross between Chinese kale and broccoli; and broccoli rabe (also called broccoli raab or rapini), which is more closely related to turnips than to broccoli.

recipes

BRUSSELS SPROUTS

Despite their diminutive size, brussels sprouts are packed with heart-healthy nutrients that detoxify, boost the immune system, and promote healthy, resilient skin.

HEALTH BENEFITS

A cruciferous vegetable, brussels sprouts contain a wealth of phytonutrients called glucosinolates, which are thought to fight cancer and are responsible for the vegetable's pungent smell when cooked. Isothiocyanates, a by-product of these sulfur-containing compounds, trigger the liver to produce detoxifying enzymes, which aid in the elimination of potentially carcinogenic substances. Research has also shown a relationship between the consumption of cruciferous vegetables and a reduced risk of premenopausal breast cancer. These baby cabbages also provide plenty of vitamin A, which promotes a strong immune system and healthy skin. Beyond that, brussels sprouts are high in fiber, vitamin C, and folate.

HOW TO BUY

Look for hard, bright green sprout heads with tightly packed leaves. You can buy the sprouts still on their stalks or, more commonly, loose.

HOW TO STORE

Refrigerate sprouts (separated from stalks, if they came attached) in an airtight plastic bag for up to three days.

PREPARATION TIP

Trim whole sprouts at the base of the head and cut an X into the base so heat can evenly penetrate the sprout. If steaming, cook the sprouts no longer than 10 minutes; overcooking them will yield that unappealing sulfur smell as well as diminish their nutritive value. To roast, spread trimmed and halved sprouts on a rimmed baking sheet and toss with olive oil, salt, and pepper; cook in a 425°F oven until brown and tender, tossing occasionally, 20 to 30 minutes.

recipes

Shredded Brussels Sprouts Salad

Roasted Brussels Sprouts with Pear and Shallots

CARROTS

Carrots provide more health-promoting carotenoids than any other vegetable. Crunch your way to better vision, healthier kidneys, and a stronger liver with this sweet, bright root.

HEALTH BENEFITS

Carotenoids, the antioxidants that give carrots their yellow-orange pigment, may protect against certain types of cancer, heart disease, and cataracts. What's more, beta-carotene is converted by the body into vitamin A, which is essential for healthy skin and for helping the eyes adjust from bright light to darkness. Vitamin A also nourishes the tissues of your respiratory and intestinal tracts, and helps to boost the immune system. Other perks include soluble fiber, vitamin C, and some calcium. Purple carrots also contain anthocyanin, a flavonoid with antioxidant properties that may help prevent heart disease and stroke.

HOW TO BUY

Choose firm, bright orange carrots without splits or cracks. The deeper the orange color, the more beta-carotene is present. The leafy tops should be bright green.

HOW TO STORE

If carrots come with greens, trim them down immediately to one inch; otherwise the carrots will go limp and lose their nutrients more quickly. Compost the greens, discard them, or keep them to integrate into salads. Carrots without their tops will stay fresh for about two weeks stored in a plastic bag in the refrigerator.

PREPARATION TIP

Since beta-carotene is fat-soluble, cook carrots with a bit of healthy fat, such as olive oil, or toss them into a salad with an oil-and-vinegar dressing to help your body absorb the beta-carotene more fully. Steaming carrots until crisp-tender makes their nutrients more available to the body; cook in a basket or colander, covered, over simmering water until tender, 5 to 7 minutes. Watch the mush factor, though—overcooking can diminish the beta-carotene.

DID YOU KNOW?

"Baby carrots" aren't a different breed or shorter versions of regular carrots. Farmers plant these carrots closer together to keep them slim and easier to cut. Once picked, they're peeled, cut to snack size, and packaged for the baby-cut market.

recipes

KALE

Raw or cooked, these showy ruffled greens bundle great taste with a host of key nutrients.

HEALTH BENEFITS

Considered a "nonheading" cabbage (because its central leaves don't form a ball), this vegetable comes in a number of varieties, including the tightly curled Scotch Vates and the red- to purple-veined Red Russian. The latter is sweet enough to eat raw, as is Tuscan or Lacinato kale. Like fellow members of the *Brassica* family, including broccoli, brussels sprouts, and kohlrabi, kale is nutrient dense. The low-calorie green provides an excellent source of vitamins A (as beta-carotene), B_6, and C, along with a decent amount of fiber, iron, and calcium. In fact, our bodies can better absorb the calcium in kale than in spinach, as its leaves contain less oxalic acid, a substance that can disrupt the nutrient's absorption. Kale's vitamin K, essential for proper blood clotting, far surpasses that of broccoli, spinach, and Swiss chard. Perhaps most impressive, this versatile green contains especially high amounts of the carotenoids lutein and zeaxanthin, two powerful phytochemicals that may help safeguard the eyes from macular degeneration and cataracts.

HOW TO BUY

Look for deeply colored, crisp-textured leaves free of blemishes or yellow spots. Avoid bunches that appear wilted or limp.

HOW TO STORE

Kale stored loosely in a plastic bag should last for two to three days in the refrigerator.

PREPARATION TIP

Strip the leaves of extra-thick or woody stems with a paring knife. (Compost or discard the stems.) For easy cutting, stack the leaves, roll them, and cut crosswise into thin ribbons. Braising or sautéing kale works well, but don't boil it; you will lose some vital nutrients.

DID YOU KNOW?

While kale has fans all around the world, the Scottish seem particularly partial to the vegetable. In Scotland, the word *kail* once referred not only to the greens but also to food in general, because it factored into most meals.

MUSHROOMS

Full of flavor, and bursting with compounds that can reduce cholesterol and improve immunity, mushrooms are nutritional—and curative—champions.

HEALTH BENEFITS

Of all the earth's natural substances, mushrooms are among the most medicinal. While researchers are only beginning to understand how the many compounds in mushrooms can fight ailments ranging from infections to cancer, two compounds appear to rise above the rest: terpenoids, potent antiviral, antibiotic, and anti-inflammatory agents, and polyaccharides, chainlike sugars that enhance the immune system and may help the body fight cancerous tumors. All mushrooms are low in fat and are a good source of B vitamins—including folate, which protects against birth defects and may prevent heart disease—as well as fiber and protein. Many mushrooms also provide vitamin D, which helps the body absorb calcium and is present in few other foods. Of course, each type of mushroom has distinct qualities. Shiitakes may boost the immune system, thanks to the carbohydrate lentinan, which has antiviral and antimicrobial properties. Antioxidants thioproline

and ergothioneine may also attack free radicals. In addition, preliminary laboratory research suggests that extracts of shiitake may help inhibit the proliferation of breast and colon cancer cells. Maitake mushrooms (also known as hen-of-the-woods) also have cancer-fighting properties, and have been used to ease the side effects of chemotherapy. They may enhance the immune system, lower blood sugar, and help control high blood pressure. Fan-shaped oyster mushrooms may lower cholesterol by inhibiting an enzyme that's key to cholesterol synthesis. Morels provide seven amino acids, and portobellos (including creminis, also called "baby portobellos") are a prime source of potassium. Even white button mushrooms contain more antioxidants than the more expensive maitakes, and studies have shown that they may also help prevent breast cancer. Dried mushrooms have the same nutritional value as fresh, and a more intense flavor.

HOW TO BUY

When buying fresh, look for mushrooms with a firm texture and gills that are pink or tan. Avoid those that are discolored or slimy, or that have pitted caps. When possible, buy whole mushrooms in bulk rather

recipes

Mushroom and Scallion Frittata p. 86

Grilled Mushroom Burgers with White-Bean Spread p.129

Shiitake Nori Rolls p.137

Mushroom Soup with Poached Eggs and Parmesan Cheese p.156

Soba Noodle Soup with Shiitakes and Spinach p.163

Asparagus with Shiitakes, Shallots, and Peas p.186

Sablefish en Papillote with Shiitake Mushrooms and Orange p.219

Brown Rice with Tofu, Dried Mushrooms, and Baby Spinach p.232

Swiss Chard, Mushroom, and Quinoa Salad p.256

Farro and Mushroom Dressing p.313

(CONTINUED)

MUSHROOMS (CONTINUED)

than presliced and packaged. Dried mushrooms are sold by weight (1 ounce dried equals about 1 cup prepared). Choose packages with large pieces and plenty of caps, which are preferable to stems; avoid mushrooms with lots of holes.

HOW TO STORE

Keep fresh mushrooms in a paper bag in the refrigerator for up to 3 days. Do not store mushrooms in a plastic bag, which will trap moisture and cause them to become soggy. Store dried mushrooms in an airtight container in a cool, dark, and dry place for up to a year (do not refrigerate).

PREPARATION TIP

Use a soft, dry brush or paper towel to remove dirt from fresh mushrooms before using. For stubborn dirt, rinse mushrooms under a thin stream of cool water, then dry thoroughly with paper towels. Do not soak them, as they will absorb water rapidly and turn mushy when you cook them. Trim the spongy tips and any tough stems off white button mushrooms, creminis, portobellos, and oyster mushrooms; the rest is edible. Shiitakes have tough, inedible stems that should

be removed; maitake stems are also tough, and should be sliced thinly if used. Sauté mushrooms in oil over high heat, stirring occasionally, until any liquid has evaporated and they are cooked through, then use in pastas or as a sandwich or pizza topping. Whole Portobello caps can also be grilled (about 4 to 5 minutes on each side) to make meatless burgers. To prepare dried mushrooms, rinse them under cold water to remove grit, then soak them in warm liquid to soften. Drain mushrooms in a sieve lined with a paper towel or coffee filter, and reserve the liquid to use in recipes calling for broth, such as soups or risottos.

DID YOU KNOW?

Mushrooms have been used in China and Japan for centuries, possibly millennia, to boost immunity and fight cancer and other diseases.

SPINACH

When it comes to nutritious foods, spinach ranks highly. This versatile green sports an impressive lineup of vitamins and minerals that promote health from inside out.

HEALTH BENEFITS

Few sources offer more vitamin K than spinach. Vitamin K is essential for blood clotting and bone health. Recent research shows it may also help decrease inflammation, a condition linked to a host of diseases, including Alzheimer's, arthritis, type 2 diabetes, heart disease, and osteoporosis. Carotenoids such as beta-carotene, lutein, and zeaxanthin also rank high in spinach's nutritional roster; they help protect against heart disease and some forms of cancer and may guard eyes from cataracts and macular degeneration. Spinach also contains high doses of vitamins B6 and C, as well as folate and magnesium.

HOW TO BUY

Look for bright green, unwilted leaves without slimy or dark spots. Buy from local growers to decrease the time from farm to table; lengthy, cross-country shipping can expose fresh spinach to warm temperatures, which accelerate folate and carotenoid loss. Spinach tends to be tastiest in spring and fall.

HOW TO STORE

Wrap spinach in paper towels and store in a plastic bag in your refrigerator's vegetable drawer. Whether prebagged or home-bagged, spinach should last for three to four days.

PREPARATION TIP

Right before using, wash off any grit stuck in the leaves and stems (even if the spinach is labeled "prewashed"): Trim off stems, then agitate the leaves in cold water and let the grit sink (repeat until no grit remains on the bottom of the bowl). For crisp salad leaves, shake or spin dry, then wrap in paper towels and refrigerate for an hour or two. To get the most of spinach's fat-soluble nutrients, cook the greens with a healthy fat, such as olive oil: Sauté spinach with oil and minced garlic until just wilted, 2 to 3 minutes.

DID YOU KNOW?

It's not necessarily the iron in spinach that made Popeye strong. While spinach contains plenty of iron, it also has oxalic acid, which limits the body's ability to absorb iron. Even so, the cartoon was credited with boosting spinach sales by 33 percent.

SWEET POTATOES

This satisfying root vegetable comes in a variety of colors, from yellow to dark orange to reddish purple. When cooked, an enzyme in the sweet potato breaks down the tuber's starch and turns it into maltose, creating an appealingly sweet flavor.

HEALTH BENEFITS

Brightly colored sweet potatoes are packed with the antioxidant beta-carotene, which the body converts to retinol, or vitamin A. As a result, sweet potatoes may be good for vision, help to prevent some kinds of cancer, and boost immunity. Low in calories and high in fiber, sweet potatoes are great for weight loss or maintenance; as if all that weren't enough, they deliver folate and vitamins B_6, C, and E.

HOW TO BUY

Look for small or medium-size sweet potatoes that feel firm and heavy, with smooth (not wrinkly), unblemished skin and no sprouts.

HOW TO STORE

In ideal conditions—perfectly dry, about 50 degrees, and dark—sweet potatoes will keep for up to four weeks. Don't refrigerate sweet potatoes; at temperatures below 50 degrees they can develop a condition called hardcore, and their centers will stay solid even after cooking.

DID YOU KNOW?

A sweet potato is not a potato. Nor is it a yam, though many people use the terms interchangeably, and in stores sweet potatoes are often labeled as yams. Sweet potatoes are part of the *Ipomoea* (morning glory) family, while potatoes are in the *Solanum* (nightshade) family. True yams are drier and starchier than sweet potatoes, with thick, scaly skin and very low levels of beta-carotene.

PREPARATION TIP

Besides baking and roasting, try grilling sweet potatoes: Slice them lengthwise about ⅓ inch thick. Brush all over with oil and season with salt and pepper. Grill over medium heat until browned and tender, about 2 minutes per side.

SWISS CHARD

Swiss chard (or just chard) pleases the palate with both taste (earthy, slightly salty) and texture (crisp leaves and crunchy stalks). Don't let its name fool you, though: This green hails from Sicily, not Switzerland, and is a staple of Mediterranean cuisine.

HEALTH BENEFITS
Related to spinach and beets, Swiss chard offers fantastic antioxidant protection in the form of carotenoids such as beta-carotene, lutein, and zeaxanthin, which help maintain eye health and may reduce the risk of cataracts. Further support comes when the body converts beta-carotene to vitamin A, which also helps promote healthy vision, boosts immunity, and may even fight cancer. An additional immunity benefit comes from vitamin C; just one cup of cooked Swiss chard supplies more than a third of your daily recommended amount of the vitamin. Other chard nutrients include vitamin B6, vitamin E, vitamin K, potassium, magnesium, and calcium. The fiber in chard also helps to keep cholesterol levels low and may reduce the risk of heart disease.

HOW TO BUY
You'll typically find three types of chard in stores and at farmers' markets: Rainbow chard has colorful red, pink, yellow, or white stalks; Fordhook Giant is identifiable by crinkly leaves and thick, white, tender stalks; and Ruby Red (or Rhubarb) chard has thin red stalks and a slightly stronger flavor. Regardless of the variety, look for crisp, vibrant green leaves with no small holes or yellow or brown marks.

HOW TO STORE
Rinse the chard lightly, then refrigerate it between moistened paper towels in a plastic bag (with a few pinholes to allow air to circulate) for two or three days.

PREPARATION TIP
The leaves and stalks are both edible. For a quick and delicious side dish, sauté chard (stems first, followed by leaves) with olive oil and minced garlic; season with salt and pepper.

recipes

TOMATOES

Most produce offers greater nutrition when raw. Tomatoes are an exception to that rule. Health studies continue to demonstrate the myriad benefits of lycopene, a phytochemical abundant in tomatoes. And you get more lycopene from a processed or cooked tomato than you do from a freshly picked one.

recipes

HEALTH BENEFITS

Lycopene, responsible for the fruit's bright red and orange colors, is associated with lower risk of both macular degeneration and several types of cancers, including prostate, cervical, skin, breast, and lung. Lycopene may also help lower the risk of coronary artery disease and, along with tomatoes' vitamin C content, stimulate the immune system. Cooked tomatoes contain two to eight times more lycopene than raw because the carotenoid is tightly bound within a tomato's cell walls; heat breaks down those walls, releasing more lycopene for absorption and use by the body. Canned tomatoes, jarred salsa, spaghetti sauce, tomato paste, tomato soup, and even ketchup are all good sources of lycopene, as are sautéed fresh tomatoes. Tomatoes also provide iron, potassium, fiber, a host of B vitamins, and quercetin, a phytochemical that may help protect against cancer as well as heart and degenerative eye diseases.

HOW TO BUY

Look for plump tomatoes with taut skin, dark color, and an earthy scent. Avoid tomatoes with bruises or decay. Heirloom tomatoes are more susceptible to cracking, but as long as the cracks are healed (meaning you can't see the flesh), the blemishes shouldn't affect taste.

HOW TO STORE

Keep fresh tomatoes at room temperature—not in the refrigerator—for a day or two. Unripe tomatoes can be placed in a paper bag to accelerate ripening.

PREPARATION TIP

Since lycopene is fat-soluble, make sure you eat raw or cooked tomatoes with some fat. Olive oil is a traditional choice; also try fresh mozzarella or another favorite cheese.

DID YOU KNOW?

For most of culinary history, the tomato's health benefits were lost on humans. That's because the tomato is part of the nightshade family, some of whose members are deadly, so many people assumed it was poisonous also. (They were on to something: A tomato's leaves and stems *are* toxic.) Only in the last 200 years have people believed tomatoes are safe to eat. Legend has it that Colonel Robert Gibbon Johnson of Salem, New Jersey, shocked his hometown in 1820 by safely consuming a basketful of tomatoes in front of a crowd of spectators.

WINTER SQUASH

These robust, versatile gourds come in a range of quirky shapes, colors, and textures, from the striped carnival squash to the elongated butternut. They're delicious, simple to prepare, and packed with a host of powerful nutrients.

HEALTH BENEFITS

Winter squash get their incredible antioxidant and anti-inflammatory properties from beta-carotene (which your body automatically converts to vitamin A) and high levels of vitamin C. They also provide significant amounts of potassium (good for bone health), vitamin B6 (essential for the immune and nervous systems), and plenty of fiber, making them an especially heart-friendly choice. Folate adds yet another boost to their heart-healthy reputation and, when consumed during pregnancy, helps guard against birth defects of the brain and spinal cord.

HOW TO BUY

Look for squash that are firm, free of mold, and heavy for their size.

HOW TO STORE

Squash can keep for several months in a cool, dry, dark spot.

PREPARATION TIP

Winter squash present the home cook with many culinary possibilities. Place a halved squash, cut side down, on an oiled baking sheet and roast in the oven at 400°F for 30 to 40 minutes, until you can pierce it with a sharp knife. Or you can remove the skin using a vegetable peeler and cut the flesh into chunks for roasting, steaming, or sautéing. Once cooked, mash the squash, puree it for soup, or fold it into a pasta or risotto dish. Butternut and acorn squashes pair particularly well with sage.

DID YOU KNOW?

Native Americans referred to winter squash as "the apple of God" and planted seeds near their homes, believing that this would promote fertility.

FRUITS

Everything about fruit—the bright colors, juicy textures, and especially the sweetness—is aimed at getting us to eat it. What's more, fruit is endowed with nature's own sustainable-design trick, since the seeds humans and animals discard grow into more bushes, vines, or trees. What's good for fruit turns out to be even better for us: Antioxidants give fruit its vibrant hues and shield it from degradation—so when we eat fruit, we reap the benefits of that protection, too. Studies suggest that people with diets high in fruits (and other plants) enjoy a lower risk of heart disease, cancer, and diabetes, plus better memory and eyesight.

Although each kind of fruit brings different nutrients to the table, most offer prodigious amounts of vitamins A and C. Because it is high in water and fiber, and low in calories, fruit makes a perfect snack or dessert.

APRICOTS

The perfect portable snack, apricots offer intense flavor in a relatively small package. Beloved for their fragrant flesh, velvety skin, and sun-drenched color, these delicate stone fruits are packed with vitamins A and C, as well as potassium.

recipes

HEALTH BENEFITS

Apricots' vivid orange color hints at its particularly high levels of carotenoids (including beta-carotene and beta-cryptoxanthin, both precursors to vitamin A), which contribute to healthy eyes, skin, hair, gums, and glands. Additionally, beta-cryptoxanthin is associated with lowered lung-cancer risk. Apricots also contain a healthy supply of vitamin C and potassium. If you can't get fresh apricots, choose dried ones; ounce for ounce, they have more than three times the fiber of fresh and a high dose of potassium. Most varieties of dried apricots are treated with the preservative sulfur dioxide to maintain their sunny color; it's worth seeking out unsulfured fruit.

HOW TO BUY

Choose plump, golden-orange apricots without soft spots. Once home, they shouldn't sit for too long. Because apricots ripen more quickly than other stone fruits, they don't travel well; buy locally grown apricots to ensure the best flavor.

HOW TO STORE

Refrigerated, ripe apricots should last for two days.

PREPARATION TIP

To peel a fresh apricot, first cut an X through the skin on the bottom, then blanch the fruit in boiling water for 20 to 60 seconds. When the skin starts to wrinkle, remove the fruit and plunge it into a bowl of ice water. Once cooled, peel the skin with your fingers or a small paring knife.

DID YOU KNOW?

The Hunza people of northern Pakistan, whose diet is especially apricot-rich, are renowned for their overall excellent health. Their longevity is often attributed to their consumption of the small orange fruit.

BERRIES

Tangy, succulent berries arrive in the spring and summer, dangling from vines and bushes, waiting to be plucked and savored. Blackberries, blueberries, raspberries, and strawberries—all rich in disease-fighting antioxidants—rank among the healthiest fruits and provide some of the tastiest ways to eat well.

HEALTH BENEFITS

In a lovely synthesis of beauty and nutrition, the colors that make berries so distinctive—deep blues, bright reds, rich purples—are part of what makes them so good for you. Flavonoids, a group of phytochemicals, create the pigments and can counter cell damage in the body, potentially reducing the risks of cancer and cardiovascular disease. They may also aid memory and other brain functions that can falter with age. Each berry's color stems from a different collection of flavonoids, so it's best to eat a variety. Blueberries, blackberries, raspberries, and strawberries all contain several anthocyanins, potent antioxidants that help reduce inflammation and may also curb the growth of cancer cells. Blueberries rank among the highest in overall antioxidant power. Just 3.5 ounces provide the equivalent antioxidant capacity of five servings of some other fruits and vegetables. Strawberries also contain ellagitannins, antioxidants that fight cancer, particularly colon and cervical. All berries contain vitamins C and E, and are high in fiber (raspberries contain the most).

HOW TO BUY

The fresher the berries, the better they'll taste, so buy them locally grown or, if you get the chance, pick them yourself. Choose organically grown berries if possible, particularly raspberries and strawberries (both rank high for pesticide residues in commercial samples).

HOW TO STORE

Once you get your berries home, don't wash them—moisture on the surface encourages rot. Instead, discard mushy or moldy berries, pat the others dry, and store them in a clean, dry container. Berries go bad quickly, so eat them within a day or two. Refrigeration will help them last longer, but berries taste best at room temperature. Rinse just before eating.

PREPARATION TIP

If you have extra berries, make them last by freezing them. Wash whole berries, remove any leafy portion on top, and pat dry. Spread the berries in a single layer on a sheet pan and freeze until solid. Transfer to a sealable plastic bag, and freeze for up to 6 months.

recipes

CITRUS

In season during the winter, when other fruits are scarce, refreshingly juicy oranges and grapefruits offer plenty of health-boosting benefits. Both sweet and tart fruits add variety and complexity to a range of dishes and help the body defend against everything from the common cold to heart disease and cancer.

HEALTH BENEFITS

Just one whole orange or grapefruit covers your daily requirement of vitamin C and includes a range of phytonutrients, specifically carotenoid pigments. Blood oranges benefit from anthocyanin, which may help prevent stroke and urinary tract infections, fight inflammation, and reduce the risk of cancer. The lycopene in Cara Cara oranges and red and pink grapefruits is associated with a reduced risk of some cancers and heart disease, and may increase the skin's resistance to sun damage. (Pink and red grapefruits also offer about 35 times more vitamin A than their yellow counterparts.) Oranges and grapefruits provide a robust amount of folate and potassium. When peeling citrus fruits, leave on the white, stringy parts that stick to the fruit; they harbor pectin, a soluble fiber that helps lower cholesterol. Eat a grapefruit just as you would an orange; peel the skin and eat the segments whole to get 50 percent more fiber. And don't toss the peel if it's organic: The zest, used in recipes, offers limonoids, a bitter-tasting lipid that protects citrus fruits from fungi and may lower cholesterol and fight cancers of the skin, breast, lung, stomach, colon, and mouth.

HOW TO BUY

Citrus fruits peak in winter but are available year-round. Choose firm and unblemished fruit that feels heavy for its size. Buy organic when you can, especially if you plan to use the zest. Even with the peel removed, oranges are among the top 25 types of produce most likely to contain pesticide residues.

HOW TO STORE

Citrus fruits keep in the refrigerator for several weeks.

▷ PREPARATION TIP

Since vitamin C helps the body absorb iron from plants, scatter orange or grapefruit segments over spinach salad to get the most out of your greens. Add some nuts or cheese, too; the lycopene in blood oranges and pink or red grapefruit is best absorbed when combined with some fat.

recipes

KIWIFRUITS

This vine-grown fruit with a fuzzy brown peel harbors a juicy interior the color of emeralds or gold, depending on the variety. Regardless of shade, all types offer a creamy texture and an impressive nutritional profile.

HEALTH BENEFITS

Kiwifruit delivers a whopping dose of vitamin C; one variety in particular, the Sanuki Gold, is an especially powerful source of this multitasking antioxidant. The oblong fruit also harbors other antioxidants, including lutein and vitamin E. Studies show that kiwifruits may lower triglycerides (the fats that circulate in the bloodstream and cause high cholesterol levels). They're also rich in dietary fiber and potassium.

HOW TO BUY

Look for firm fruit that gives slightly to gentle pressure. Avoid any kiwifruits that feel soft or look wrinkled—they could be overripe.

HOW TO STORE

To speed ripening, place kiwifruits in a paper bag with other fruit at room temperature. Ripe fruit kept in the refrigerator's crisper should stay fresh for four to five weeks.

DID YOU KNOW?

Contrary to popular belief, the kiwifruit didn't originate in New Zealand but in China during the 14th century. The Chinese gooseberry, as it was then called, eventually made its way to New Zealand. Once the island nation began commercial production, the fruit was renamed after the fuzzy national bird it resembles.

PREPARATION TIP

To peel a kiwifruit, first trim both ends; ease a tablespoon between the flesh and the peel. Turn the kiwi, pressing the back of the spoon against the peel as you go. The fruit should slide right out in one piece —ready for slicing.

recipes

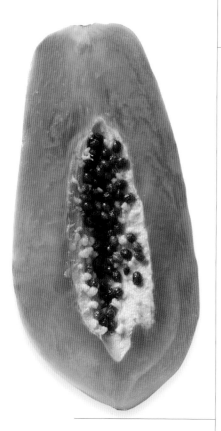

PAPAYAS

Sweet, juicy papaya does more than just stimulate the taste buds. This tropical fruit, sometimes referred to as paw paw, sweetens the nutritional pot with big doses of essential vitamins.

HEALTH BENEFITS

Ripe papayas contain a nearly three-day supply of vitamin C and significant amounts of vitamins A and E, all powerful antioxidants. Papayas may also help improve skin and strengthen nails and hair. Ripe papaya is best known as a potent digestive aid, due to its high fiber content. Unripe, green papaya contains high levels of the digestive enzyme papain, which behaves much like those enzymes produced by the stomach's gastric juices. The fruit also contains a high amount of folate, which aids in cell production and helps prevent anemia.

HOW TO BUY

Choose slightly soft papayas with reddish-orange skin. Yellowish fruit will take several days to ripen. Depending on the variety, a papaya's flesh will appear yellow, orange, or a shade of salmon or red when ripe.

HOW TO STORE

To speed ripening, place the papaya in a paper bag with a banana, which releases the compound ethylene and hastens the process. Ripe papayas will keep for up to a week in the refrigerator.

PREPARATION TIP

To serve, cut a papaya like a melon and remove the seeds, then squeeze lemon or lime juice on top. The acidity of the citrus will enhance the papaya's sweetness. The seeds, which have a slightly peppery taste, are edible as well. Sprinkle a few on a salad or use as a garnish. Unripe green papayas are delicious in Thai- and Vietnamese-style salads.

DID YOU KNOW?

The enzyme papain, found in green papaya, reduces the itch and irritation caused by mosquito bites. Simply rub a bite with a piece of the thinly sliced fruit. (Note: Do not try this remedy if you are allergic to insect venoms.)

recipes

PEARS

Bite into a pear at the perfect moment of ripeness, and you'll understand why Homer, in his epic poem *The Odyssey,* called it a "gift from the gods."

HEALTH BENEFITS

You'd never guess it from the buttery texture, but pears deliver 6 grams of fiber—almost a quarter of the adult daily requirement. The skin contains mostly insoluble fiber, which promotes healthy digestion, while the flesh's soluble fiber, including pectin, helps satiety and blood sugar regulation. Thanks to pectin's well-established ability to lower LDL ("bad") cholesterol, snacking regularly on pears can reduce the risk of cardiovascular disease and diabetes. The pear's other significant nutrients include vitamin C and potassium.

HOW TO BUY

Among the thousands of varieties of pears, just a few, including Bartlett, Bosc, and Anjou, are typically carried in supermarkets. (Seek out other types at farmers' markets and specialty stores.) Most pears ripen best off the tree and are picked while mature but firm. Likewise, choose firm fruit at the store; it will ripen in a few days.

HOW TO STORE

Encourage ripening by storing pears in a paper—not plastic—bag at room temperature for a day or two. Pears are ripe when the flesh near the stem end yields slightly. Because these delicate fruits ripen from the inside out, very soft outer flesh means a pear is past its prime.

PREPARATION TIP

Poached, sautéed, baked, and even grilled, pears complement savory foods such as cheeses, nuts, and meats, particularly chicken and pork. Choose slightly underripe, firm pears for cooking. Anjou and Bosc hold their shape well. To core a pear quickly and easily, use a melon baller.

DID YOU KNOW?

With their globe shape and crunchy texture, Asian pears may resemble apples, but they are true pears—not an apple-pear hybrid, as many believe. Asian varieties boast the same basic nutritional value as their European counterparts. Unlike the Western species, though, they ripen on the tree, so eat them soon after you buy them.

recipes

Roasted Brussels Sprouts with Pear and Shallots p.278

Chocolate-Dipped Pears p.335

Oven-Dried Fruit with Chocolate and Toasted Almonds p.339

GRAINS AND LEGUMES

BROWN RICE
OATS
QUINOA
DRIED BEANS
GREEN PEAS
SOYBEANS (EDAMAME)

In the Middle Ages, when people first planted grains and legumes together, it marked a breakthrough in human nutrition. Each supplies amino acids the other lacks; when combined, the protein they offer is as nutritionally complete as that found in meat. They are among the first foods that humankind learned to preserve by drying. Today, grains and legumes form the foundation of much of the world's diet, accounting for two-thirds of the protein consumed. Cuisines around the globe boast signature dishes based on grain-legume combinations, such as lentils and brown rice, black beans and rice, and hummus with pita bread.

Grains and legumes are amazingly compact storehouses of nutrients. As the individual seeds of plants, grains contain more carbohydrates than any other food on earth. Legumes, on the other hand, are pods filled with individual seeds (when dried, these seeds are called pulses) and are exceptionally high in protein. Grains and legumes also offer fiber, B vitamins, vitamin E, and other antioxidants. With an ample supply of beans and grains in your pantry, a nutritious dinner is always within reach.

BROWN RICE

It would be hard to overestimate the importance of rice: Every day about half of the world's population gets as much as half of its daily calories from this grain. Although much of that rice is sold with the nutritious bran polished away, brown rice's bran and germ are intact, making it a whole grain. Indeed, a growing awareness of the health benefits of whole grains is helping to increase brown rice's popularity. Brown rice takes longer to cook than the white variety, but its nutritional qualities, boosted by a pleasantly chewy texture and hearty flavor, make it worth the wait.

recipes

HEALTH BENEFITS

Brown rice's germ offers the antioxidant vitamin E, as well as cholesterol-lowering phytosterols. Its bran provides plenty of B vitamins, almost a day's worth of manganese, and more than a third of your selenium requirement. Thanks to the bran, a cup of brown rice also contains about 3.5 grams of fiber—more than five times the amount in white rice. And the bran acts as a natural detoxifier, flushing out toxins that accumulate in your body, such as mercury. Because it contains more fiber, brown rice has a gentler effect on blood sugar levels than white rice.

HOW TO BUY

The three basic types of rice—short, medium, and long grain—are all available in their natural brown state. You can also buy brown versions of specialty rices like basmati, jasmine, and Arborio, but the bran will change the flavor and texture somewhat.

HOW TO STORE

Its oil-rich germ makes brown rice more perishable than white rice. Store it in a cool, dry place in an airtight container and use within six months.

PREPARATION TIP

To cook short-grain brown rice, bring 2 cups water, ¼ teaspoon salt, and 1 cup rice to a boil. Reduce heat and simmer, covered, 40 to 50 minutes. Turn off heat and let stand for another 10 minutes for rice to fully absorb all the water (you will have 2½ cups cooked rice). For long-grain rice, follow the same instructions using 1¾ cups water and simmering for 35 to 40 minutes.

DID YOU KNOW?

More than 8,000 varieties of rice are used for food, grown in dozens of countries around the world. In fact, in some Asian languages, the words meaning "to eat" and "to eat rice" are the same.

OATS

There's nothing like a hearty bowl of oatmeal to warm you on a chilly morning. So it's fitting that this grain grows best in the cold, wet climates of northern Europe and North America. Though most Europeans, starting with the ancient Romans, fed oats to their horses, savvy Scots took advantage of oats' nutritious nature and made them a national breakfast dish. Thanks to a mild but rich flavor and heart-protective nutrients, this grain deserves a place at the table.

HEALTH BENEFITS

Oats contain a generous amount of protein—more than you'll find in any other cereal grain. They're also especially rich in soluble fiber, notably a type called beta glucans that lowers cholesterol. Their vitamin and mineral profile impresses, too; just one cup of oatmeal gives you at least a fifth of the thiamine, folate, B5, iron, magnesium, zinc, copper, and manganese that the USDA recommends you consume daily.

HOW TO BUY

The bulk section of a well-stocked natural-foods store offers an overwhelming variety of choices, including whole hulled grains (called groats), as well as oats that have been steel-cut or rolled to different thicknesses. Nutrition-wise, you can't go wrong, no matter which form you choose; they all come from whole grains (although instant, or quick-cooking, oats have less fiber because most of the bran has been removed).

The main differences are in texture and convenience—the smaller or thinner the pieces, the more quickly they cook.

HOW TO STORE

Oats can turn rancid more quickly than other grains. Store them in a cool, dry place—or in the refrigerator—for up two months.

PREPARATION TIP

To make breakfast for two, bring 2 cups water to a boil and stir in ½ cup steel-cut oats. When oatmeal begins to thicken, reduce heat and simmer, stirring occasionally, for 30 minutes. Add mix-ins of your choice, like raisins or maple syrup.

DID YOU KNOW?

Up until a few generations ago, most traditional working-class households in Scotland had a kitchen cabinet with a "porridge drawer." On the weekend, the family cook would make a large batch of oatmeal porridge and pour it into the drawer. Then, during the week, chunks of porridge could be sliced off for meals.

recipes

QUINOA

Surprisingly enough, quinoa (pronounced *KEEN-wah*) isn't a true grain but the seeds of a plant related to chard and spinach. Protein rich and loaded with vitamins and minerals, the sweet, nutty seeds boost energy and can help fight migraines and osteoporosis, as well as improve vision.

HEALTH BENEFITS

Quinoa seeds contain twice the protein of rice, though it's not the quantity but the quality of the protein that stands out. With all nine essential amino acids (nutritional building blocks that help form proteins and muscle), quinoa is considered a complete protein. The tiny seeds also contain vitamin B2 (riboflavin) and magnesium, two nutrients that may help reduce the frequency of migraines. Magnesium may also help prevent hypertension (high blood pressure) and osteoporosis, while riboflavin may ward off cataracts. Quinoa contains vitamins B6 and E, as well as high levels of immunity-boosting iron and zinc. It's also a good source of dietary fiber, packing 5.2 grams per one cup serving. Since it's technically not a grain, quinoa has no gluten, making it tolerable in most cases for those with Celiac disease or grain sensitivities.

HOW TO BUY

You'll find quinoa at most health-food stores in its whole form, and occasionally as flakes or flour. Quinoa comes in a rainbow of colors, including red, brown, pink, orange, and black. Compared with white quinoa, the red variety—the second most common type in the United States—is nuttier and contains more fiber in each serving.

HOW TO STORE

Keep quinoa in an airtight container in a cool, dry cabinet (away from sunlight) for up to two years.

PREPARATION TIP

In its unprocessed state, quinoa is coated with saponin, a bitter substance. Most quinoa has been "desaponized." However, it's still a good idea to rinse it under running water in a fine-mesh strainer before cooking to remove any remaining residue. To cook, combine 1 cup grains with 1½ cups water and ¼ teaspoon salt in a saucepan over medium heat, and bring to a boil. Reduce heat and simmer, covered, 10 to 15 minutes (you will have 2½ cups cooked quinoa).

recipes

DRIED BEANS

Loaded with vitamins, minerals, and fiber, beans are the cornerstone of a healthy diet and a nutritional fountain of youth. Researchers have found that eating these earthy-tasting legumes is one of the most important dietary factors in longevity.

HEALTH BENEFITS

Considered among the most ancient of foods, beans—such as chickpeas, lentils, black-eyed peas, and black, white, navy, and kidney beans—deserve a prominent place in any kitchen. An inexpensive and virtually fat-free source of protein, all beans pack a high dose of folate, B vitamins, and iron. Particularly healthy for the heart, beans may lower blood pressure and cholesterol. Beans contain lignans—phytoestrogens that may reduce the risk of estrogen-related cancers—and recent studies have shown these legumes to be especially effective in curbing pancreatic, colon, and prostate cancers. The plentiful fiber (both soluble and insoluble) in beans helps to lower or normalize blood sugar levels, a boon to those with diabetes, hypoglycemia, or insulin resistance. Besides lentils—which cook quickly and don't need to be presoaked—most dried beans may be used interchangeably in recipes. Canned beans contain comparable nutrients to dried varieties, as long as the can is BPA free.

HOW TO BUY

When purchasing dried beans, look for those that appear largely unbroken, and buy from a source that has a good turnover. When buying canned beans, consider organic brands, especially if you're concerned about sodium.

HOW TO STORE

Don't mix newly purchased dried beans with older ones; the older they are, the longer they take to cook. Beans have a long shelf life; kept in a tightly sealed container in a cool, dry place, beans will stay fresh for up to a year.

PREPARATION TIP

Sort through dried beans before cooking them to remove any small stones or twigs; rinse well. Soak beans overnight (or up to 24 hours) in the refrigerator before cooking. Or, as an alternative, place beans in a saucepan, cover with cold water, and bring to a boil. Turn off heat and soak beans, covered, for 1 hour. To cook, bring beans and soaking liquid to a boil in a large pot; reduce heat and simmer until beans are tender, anywhere from 30 minutes to 3 hours, depending on the type of bean.

recipes

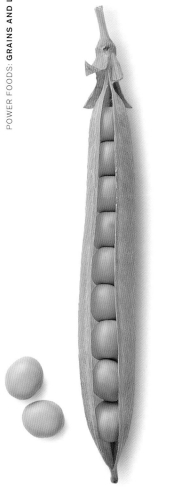

GREEN PEAS

Like beans, common green peas, also known as garden peas or English peas, are a type of legume. In the case of green peas, the pod and seeds are immature and therefore tender enough to eat raw or minimally cooked; the flavor is fresh and sweet.

HEALTH BENEFITS

Like most legumes, peas are a good source of protein, especially for vegetarians, and an excellent source of fiber—a cup of raw green peas packs more than 30 percent of an adult's daily fiber requirements. That same cup of peas is also a surprisingly potent source of vitamin C, offering more than half a day's supply. Peas provide a good dose of vitamin K, folate, and thiamine, too.

HOW TO BUY

If you aren't growing peas yourself, buy the freshest possible from a farm or farmers' market (in season in the spring and again in late summer or early fall); a pea's composition begins to change quickly after it's picked. Look for plump, bright green pods. If fresh peas aren't an option, choose frozen over canned. When peas are frozen quickly after picking, they maintain a decent amount of nutrients, which they lose during the canning process.

HOW TO STORE

Refrigerate fresh peas in their pods inside a plastic bag for up to three days after they're picked.

PREPARATION TIP

To shell fresh peas, remove the stem end of the pod and the stringy fiber along the seam. Pry the pod open with your fingers and push out the peas. Blanch peas in boiling water for 1 to 2 minutes to brighten their color, then toss them into salads, pastas, or risotto and other rice dishes.

DID YOU KNOW?

The same kind of compound—an isobutyl methoxypyrazine—is responsible for the strong, fresh "green" aroma in both green peas and green peppers.

SOYBEANS (EDAMAME)

Embodying the goodness of soy in its least processed form, edamame are simply green soybeans harvested before reaching maturity. They have fuzzy pods, and a mild, buttery flavor that makes them an addictive snack or hors d'oeuvre.

HEALTH BENEFITS

Not only do soybeans provide more protein than other beans, they contain all the essential amino acids in the proportions your body needs. This means soy, minus the saturated fat and cholesterol, is as complete a protein as meat. Soy is also high in folate and potassium. Whenever possible, seek out organic, non-genetically modified soybeans.

HOW TO BUY

In the summer months, look for fresh edamame at farmers' markets; often you'll see them sold in bunches, still attached to the plant. You can also find frozen edamame—both in and out of the pod—year-round in the supermarket.

HOW TO STORE

Fresh edamame in the pod will last for up to a week in the refrigerator. Eat frozen edamame within four to five months (you don't need to thaw before cooking).

PREPARATION TIP

For an easy snack, boil the beans in their pods until bright green and heated through, about 4 minutes. Drain and sprinkle with salt, then eat straight from the pods.

DID YOU KNOW?

Although first domesticated in China, most soybeans now come from the United States (the majority of these soybeans are used for feeding livestock). One of the earliest American proponents of soybeans was Benjamin Franklin. In 1770, he wrote to a friend about the beans, describing how they were made into a sort of "cheese" he called "tau-fu."

recipes

NUTS AND SEEDS

ALMONDS   WALNUTS
PECANS   FLAXSEED
PISTACHIOS   PUMPKIN SEEDS

Perhaps the most remarkable thing about nuts and seeds is their heart-protecting quality. Eating fatty foods to lower your risk of heart disease may sound too good to be true, but that's exactly what happens when you munch on nuts and seeds. They are among the richest sources of phytosterols—components of plant fats that lower cholesterol by blocking your absorption of it.

Nuts and seeds serve as a good protein source, too—most are at least ten percent protein—and are plentiful in other nutrients, like fiber and vitamin E. All in all, this dynamic duo is worth keeping on hand for a quick-energy snack or a crunchy addition to salads and more.

ALMONDS

These nutrition-dense nuts actually grow inside a fuzzy fruit. Once the fruit ripens, it splits apart to expose a shell that hides the almond seed, which we know as the nut. Packed with vitamins, minerals, and unsaturated fats, this sweet nut benefits the heart, supports the immune system, and may reduce cancer risk.

recipes

HEALTH BENEFITS

Eating a handful of almonds a day can protect your heart. The almond's monounsaturated and polyunsaturated fats help lower LDL ("bad") cholesterol. Vitamin E fights inflammation and reduces the blood's ability to clot, decreasing the risk of heart attack and coronary heart disease. For the most nutritional value, choose almonds with the skins on. The skin is where phytonutrients called flavonoids reside; they fight disease by enhancing the body's immunity and helping prevent cell damage caused by environmental pollutants. The flavonoids anthocyanin and quercetin, in particular, may work to prevent stroke and urinary tract infections, fight inflammation, and reduce cancer risk. The almond's hefty dose of protein and fiber contributes to its power-snack status; it keeps blood sugar steady and supports muscles and organs. Additionally, almonds provide bone-strengthening magnesium and calcium, and blood-supporting iron.

HOW TO BUY

Look for almonds sold in airtight containers or sealed bags. If buying from a bulk bin, ask your grocer about the turnover rate; the quicker, the better.

HOW TO STORE

Keep almonds in a tightly closed container in a cool, dry place. Raw whole almonds should stay fresh for two years, while roasted, slivered, sliced, and blanched almonds should keep for about one year (six months if the package is opened). The nuts will last even longer when refrigerated.

PREPARATION TIP

Even though you'll lose some of the nutrients by blanching almonds, some recipes for baked goods call for them. To blanch your own, drop almonds into boiling water for 30 seconds. After draining, pop the skins off with your fingers. Or use regular almonds—the flavor will be the same.

DID YOU KNOW?

Emerging research shows that almonds may be prebiotic, meaning they may fuel the good bacteria in your gut—boosting your overall immune health.

PECANS

A native of North America, now grown mainly in Georgia and Texas, the pecan is the seed of a species of hickory tree. It has long been associated with Southern desserts like pie and pralines, but its rich, satisfying flavor makes it just as perfect for healthier fare such as salads, or as a snack all by itself.

HEALTH BENEFITS

A daily handful of pecans reduces your overall risk of heart disease. Unlike saturated fats, the unsaturated fats in pecans help to *lower* cholesterol levels, especially LDL ("bad") cholesterol. Pecans also contain the amino acid L-arginine, which may improve the flexibility of artery walls and decrease the risk of arterial blood clots. Eating pecans also adds fiber and vitamin E to your diet.

HOW TO BUY

Buy unshelled pecans in the fall, their peak season, and look for shells with no cracks or blemishes. Make sure to buy shelled pecans in an airtight package.

HOW TO STORE

The best place to keep unshelled pecans is in an airtight container in the refrigerator (up to six months) or the freezer (up to one year). Keep shelled pecans well wrapped in a dry, cool spot up to three months (or six months in the freezer).

DID YOU KNOW?

Pecans' high fat content makes them particularly prone to rancidity if bruised or exposed to light, heat, or moisture, so handle with care.

toasting nuts

To toast almonds, pecans, or any other nuts, preheat oven to 350°F. Spread nuts on a rimmed baking sheet. Cook, tossing once or twice, until fragrant, 5 to 10 minutes.

recipes

Pecan Pancakes with Mixed Berry Compote p.89

Sautéed Spinach with Pecans and Goat Cheese p.185

Four-Berry Salad p.327

PISTACHIOS

Grown in the American Southwest today, pistachios originated in central Asia, where the word for the open shell also means "laughing." The vividly colored nuts have a buttery taste that makes them irresistible for snacking; they also add flavor, crunch, and a touch of sophistication to dishes both sweet and savory.

HEALTH BENEFITS

Rich in protein and fiber, pistachios are a great source of energy and are packed with antioxidants. They may even reduce the body's response to stress, making them a wonderful workday treat. The nuts are high in potassium, which helps normalize blood pressure, maintain water balance in the body, and strengthen muscles. Like many other nuts, they contain healthy monounsaturated fats, which can help lower LDL ("bad") cholesterol and prevent heart disease.

HOW TO BUY

Choose nuts with partially opened pale beige shells (avoid dyed pistachios), and purchase them from a store that has frequent turnover. Stick with unsalted pistachios to avoid added sodium, which counteracts the potassium present in the nuts.

HOW TO STORE

Keep nuts in an airtight container in the refrigerator for up to six months, or in the freezer for up to one year.

DID YOU KNOW?

Pistachios get their emerald hue from chlorophyll in the nut, the same compound that gives green leaves their color.

recipes

WALNUTS

Depending on how you split a walnut in its shell, the nut resembles either a heart or a brain—which is so apt, really, since these nuts do wonders for both. Loaded with vitamin E and good-for-you fats, walnuts also help fight inflammation and protect the cardiovascular system.

HEALTH BENEFITS

Most nuts boast healthy oil, but walnuts have an added edge. They are the only nuts—and one of the few foods—that offer appreciable amounts of alpha-linolenic acid, or ALA, an omega-3 fatty acid. ALA, which the body can't manufacture, protects the heart by improving your ratio of HDL ("good") to LDL ("bad") cholesterol and reducing inflammation, while playing a significant role in the development of the brain and cognitive function. Walnuts also provide a concentrated source of disease-fighting antioxidants, including gamma-tocopherol, a type of vitamin E.

HOW TO BUY

Because of their high polyunsaturated fat content, walnuts are more perishable than other nuts. Buy from sources with a high turnover, and choose nuts that are still in the shell if possible. If you do buy shelled walnuts, choose halves rather than pieces, as more cut or broken surfaces encourage oxidation.

HOW TO STORE

Store walnuts in an airtight container in the refrigerator (up to 6 months) or freezer (up to 1 year) to maximize freshness.

DID YOU KNOW?

Artists used to rely on walnut oil as a drying agent for paint because its slow drying time allowed for even application over a broad surface. The oil would form a solid film after long exposure to air, rendering colors rich and luminous with its translucency. In fact, Michelangelo used walnut oil in painting the Sistine Chapel.

recipes

FLAXSEED

Rich in fiber, phytochemicals, and omega-3 fatty acids, flaxseed is extremely nutritious. You can reap its rich rewards by eating only a tablespoon of ground flaxseed a day; add it to your oatmeal or an omelet for breakfast, or slip it into a peanut butter sandwich for lunch.

HEALTH BENEFITS

About the same size as sesame seeds, these shiny brown seeds are one of the richest sources of alpha-linolenic acid (ALA), an essential fatty acid in the omega-3 family, which provides anti-inflammatory benefits and protects against atherosclerosis, heart disease, and stroke. Flaxseed also contains a balance of soluble and insoluble fiber to help with digestion and cardiovascular health, and it's an excellent source of lignans—phytoestrogens associated with lowered risk of hormone-related cancers, including breast cancer. To make the seed's health benefits more available to your body, grind flaxseed before using it. Buy the seed whole and process a few tablespoons at a time using a spice grinder or a specialized flaxseed grinder. The high fat content of flaxseed can make it go rancid quickly once you break the hull, so use it immediately after grinding.

HOW TO BUY

Flaxseed comes in dark brown and golden varieties. To get the highest level of nutrients, buy whole flaxseed and make sure the store has a high turnover to ensure freshness. If purchasing preground flaxmeal, make sure it's been vacuum-packed and kept refrigerated.

HOW TO STORE

To prevent oxidation, refrigerate or freeze whole or ground flaxseed in a tightly sealed container.

PREPARATION TIP

You can integrate more flax into your diet by mixing ground seeds into fruit smoothies, dark sauces, and stews. You can also incorporate flax into many baking recipes without diminishing its health benefits. For every cup of flour, try replacing 1/4 cup with ground flax.

DID YOU KNOW?

Flaxseed comes from the same blue-flowered plant, *Linum usitatissimum,* that brings us linen fabric and the linseed oil used in woodworking.

recipes

PUMPKIN SEEDS

More than just a thrifty snack scooped from a jack-o'-lantern, pumpkin seeds are a true nutritional treasure, rich in protein and minerals. Pumpkins yield large, flat seeds with a slightly chewy texture and a mellow, nutty flavor. Depending on the variety of the pumpkin, some of the olive-green seeds come encased in an edible white shell.

HEALTH BENEFITS

When the ancient Aztecs snacked on pumpkin seeds, they were on to something: Just a handful of these seeds offers a concentrated source of protein and energy-producing magnesium, along with generous amounts of immunity-protecting zinc. Abundant in phytosterols, which help lower cholesterol, pumpkin seeds also provide plenty of fiber when eaten in their shells.

HOW TO BUY

Scoop seeds from an actual pumpkin or buy the seeds raw or roasted, prepackaged or in bulk. "Pepitas" are also pumpkin seeds, typically hulled.

HOW TO STORE

Because of their high oil content, pumpkin seeds turn rancid easily, so refrigerate them in an airtight container and eat within a month or two. You can also freeze them for several months.

PREPARATION TIP

Roasted pumpkin seeds are delicious eaten out of hand or added to granola or trail mix. Toast them in a small skillet over medium, shaking pan occasionally, until just starting to darken, 2 to 3 minutes (be careful not to let them burn). Transfer to a plate to cool.

DID YOU KNOW?

You can roast and eat the seeds of any type of pumpkin, whether it's a culinary pumpkin used to make a sweet pumpkin pie or a field pumpkin carved for Halloween.

recipes

Quinoa and Corn Salad with Toasted Pumpkin Seeds p.173

Arugula with Maple-Roasted Pumpkin p.190

Chicken with Pumpkin-Seed Mole p.263

EGGS, YOGURT,
AND FISH

EGGS
YOGURT
SABLEFISH
RAINBOW TROUT
WILD ALASKAN SALMON

The desire for animal protein is perhaps not universal, but certainly primal. Every cell in your body contains protein; it accounts for half the body's dry weight. Animal foods are one-stop sources for high-quality protein, offering all the essential amino acids needed for good health. Yet not all animal proteins are equal in terms of their nutritional value. Instead of red meat, which is high in saturated fat and therefore raises LDL ("bad") cholesterol, the focus here is on three healthier types of animal protein: eggs, yogurt, and fatty fish. Instead of saturated fat, fatty fish contain mostly polyunsaturated fats, particularly heart-healthy omega-3s. They also pack a wealth of B vitamins and minerals. Yogurt is a rich source of calcium, protein, and beneficial bacteria—and it works wonderfully in all kinds of dishes, including breakfast smoothies, dips, dressings, and desserts. Eggs contain high-quality protein as well. In fact, they are the standard against which all other protein sources are measured. At the same time, they offer valuable vitamins, and you can't beat their versatility in the kitchen.

EGGS

Long known as a foe of the cholesterol-conscious, eggs have garnered a bad rap. However, there is much to redeem this powerful protein source; in moderation, eggs—which were first recorded as food in China around 1400 B.C.—supply a wealth of nutrients in one delicate, affordable package.

recipes

HEALTH BENEFITS

Protein-rich eggs include all the amino acids—the building blocks of protein—the body needs. Not only does this kind of protein preserve lean muscle, it also creates a feeling of fullness, which is integral to weight management. If it's protein you're after, don't rely on the whites alone. While they supply a little more than half an egg's protein—as well as niacin, riboflavin, magnesium, and potassium—the yolks steal the nutritional show. Contributing to eye health and brain function, the bright yellow center contains vitamin A, riboflavin, choline (the egg is nature's best source of this nutrient), folate, and the carotenoids lutein and zeaxanthin, which protect against macular degeneration and cataracts. The yolks do contain all of an egg's cholesterol, but research has shown that only a little makes it into the bloodstream. If you have normal cholesterol levels, an egg a day should not adversely affect your health. For pregnant women, whole eggs can be particularly important for their abundance of B vitamins—nutrients that influence a baby's brain and nervous-system development. Few foods other than eggs contain vitamin D, which increases the body's metabolism of calcium and assists with proper immune function.

HOW TO BUY AND STORE

Egg color is determined by the breed of hen but has no bearing on flavor, quality, or nutrition. The egg's grade—AA, A, or B—indicates its quality in terms of weight and appearance; usually only AA and A are found in stores, with little difference between the two in nutritive value. The weight, age, and breed of a hen determine how the egg is formed and therefore its size: medium, large, or extra-large. Check the carton for the date it was packed: Eggs stored in the coldest part of the refrigerator (not in the door, which is too warm) should last four to five weeks from the packed date. Open the carton to check for cracks before buying.

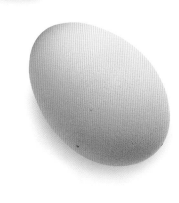

PREPARATION TIP

Medium eggs work well for most uses. The recipes in this book typically call for large eggs. Separate eggs while cold, but bring egg whites to room temperature before beating; this helps them achieve a fuller volume.
To hard cook eggs, place them in a saucepan; add enough water to cover by 1 inch. Bring water to a simmer; remove from heat. Cover, and let stand 12 minutes. Drain and rinse eggs under cold running water. Unpeeled eggs can be refrigerated for up to 1 week.

A BETTER EGG?

Here's how to decipher the labels on the wide range of specialty eggs now available, so you can make an informed buying decision.

OMEGA-3 EGGS are from chickens whose feed includes flaxseed, fish oil, or other foods rich in omega-3 fatty acids, which help reduce the risk of heart disease and stroke. The yolks boast omega-3 levels about three to five times higher than those of regular eggs.

CAGE-FREE EGGS come from hens that live only inside, but roam free in a barn or poultry house.

FREE-RANGE EGGS are produced by hens raised outside or with access to the outdoors (but an open door doesn't mean a hen necessarily stepped outside).

ORGANIC EGGS are laid by hens raised on certified-organic feed and who have access to the outdoors and exercise areas, according to USDA regulations. All antibiotic use is prohibited.

PASTEURIZED EGGS reduce the risk of contamination by salmonella bacteria, the most frequently reported cause of food-borne illness. (Cooking eggs thoroughly kills salmonella, so it's a threat only if you eat your eggs raw.)

LOW-CHOLESTEROL EGGS come from chickens fed an all-vegetarian diet that's also high in canola oil. They contain at least 25 percent less cholesterol than other types of eggs.

YOGURT

Derived from a Turkish word meaning "to thicken," yogurt is a go-to nutritious snack. The very process of yogurt-making increases its health benefits: Milk is first heated, then fermented with bacteria. The result is a creamy, tangy treat alive with friendly microbes that aid digestion.

HEALTH BENEFITS

To boost your calcium intake, reach for yogurt: One cup provides up to 45 percent of an adult's daily requirement. Along with the calcium comes protein, a host of B vitamins, and minerals such as potassium and phosphorus. Yogurt's most unique health attribute, though, is its bacteria; some of these bacteria help ferment the milk, but other strains are probiotic. These live and active cultures include *Lactobacillus bulgaricus* or *L. acidophilus* and *Streptococcus thermophilus* (some yogurt makers add other cultures, too), and may help maintain the health of the digestive tract, boost the immune system, prevent yeast infections, and lower cholesterol.

HOW TO BUY AND STORE

Look for yogurt that contains only milk and live and active cultures—no sugar or artificial sweeteners. (Add your own chopped fruit and natural sweetener, if you want.) Skip yogurt labeled "heat treated," which means it was heated after it was made, a process that destroys live and active cultures. Refrigerate yogurt in an airtight container, and check the sell-by date; it should be safe to eat for a few days after that. Don't freeze it—the freezing process may destroy some of yogurt's healthy bacteria.

DID YOU KNOW?

The lactic acid in yogurt makes its calcium easier to digest, and the cultures in yogurt ease the body's absorption of calcium. So even if a serving of yogurt and a serving of milk contain the same amount of calcium, you get more of it if you choose yogurt.

PREPARATION TIP

If a recipe calls for Greek-style yogurt, and you can't find it, strain regular yogurt to achieve the same creamy texture: Place it in a fine strainer over a bowl; refrigerate for about one hour. Discard liquid accumulated in the bowl.

SABLEFISH

Also known as butterfish or black cod (though it's not related to codfish), this large cold-water fish lives in the north Pacific Ocean. Its flaky white flesh is flavorful and, yes, buttery, with an omega-3 oil content that rivals that of salmon. Sablefish tastes milder than other fatty fish, but, like them, it can be prepared by high-heat cooking methods such as grilling. Limited supplies and high demand in Japan have driven up the price of sablefish, but it's a healthful and flavorful splurge. (And it's an environmentally sound choice.)

HEALTH BENEFITS
Like most fish, sablefish is a great source of protein, B vitamins (especially niacin and B12), and minerals (notably selenium). It shines brightest, however, in fat content: A 5-ounce serving provides about 3 grams of heart-healthy omega-3s, namely the powerful pair of docosahexaenoic acid (DHA) and eicosapentaenoic acid (EPA). Harvested from relatively pure waters, sablefish also has very low levels of mercury, PCBs, and dioxins compared with many other fish.

HOW TO BUY
Choose Alaskan or Canadian sablefish, if possible, which tend to be more sustainably harvested than sablefish from West Coast fisheries. Look for fillets or steaks with firm, moist flesh and little to no fishy smell. Sablefish freezes well, and smoked sablefish has excellent flavor; you can buy both kinds at specialty fish shops and online.

HOW TO STORE
Eat fresh sablefish the same day you buy it; the high oil content makes this fish especially prone to spoilage. Frozen fish should be thawed in the refrigerator, not only for safety but because thawing too quickly can compromise texture.

PREPARATION TIP
To grill, rub fillet all over with oil, and season with salt and pepper. Cook over medium heat until fish flakes with a fork and is opaque throughout, 3 to 4 minutes per side.

DID YOU KNOW?
Sablefish swim at depths as great as 9,800 feet and are among the longest-living species of fish; the oldest documented one was 94 years old.

recipes
Sablefish in Tomato-Saffron Stew p.167

Hoisin-Glazed Sablefish with Bok Choy p.216

Sablefish en Papillote with Shiitake Mushrooms and Orange p.219

RAINBOW TROUT

This native American fish—a relative of Pacific salmon and Arctic char—is prized for its delicate flavor. While fishing is the only way to obtain wild rainbow trout in this country, supermarkets carry stock from U.S. farms. Fortunately, rainbow trout farms are generally well managed and sustainable, with a low risk of pollution.

HEALTH BENEFITS

Compared with other fish, rainbow trout is a relatively inexpensive source of inflammation-fighting omega-3 fatty acids, with 1.6 grams in a 5-ounce serving. Like other fatty fish, trout's omega-3s are mainly the scientifically supported docosahexaenoic acid (DHA) and eicosapentaenoic acid (EPA). Protein-rich trout also harbors plenty of B vitamins; eating one serving gives you 37 percent of the daily requirement of pantothenic acid, 89 percent of niacin, and well over 100 percent of B12. And it provides a healthy dose—89 percent—of the antioxidant selenium.

HOW TO BUY

Relatively small (about a pound per fish), farmed trout are often sold whole; choose a fish with bright red gills and shiny skin. You can also find them butterflied with bones and head removed, or as fillets; look for flesh that's pale pink to white in color and firm to the touch.

HOW TO STORE

Eat trout the same day you buy it; if you need to store it for a day, place the wrapped fish on a bed of crushed ice on the bottom shelf of your refrigerator.

PREPARATION TIP

Brush fillets with oil, and grill or broil until cooked through, 6 to 8 minutes (turn halfway through if grilling).

DID YOU KNOW?

Steelhead trout, another sought-after game fish, are simply rainbow trout that have traveled from freshwater streams to salt water for part of their lives. Their scales lose the characteristic rainbow hue and become silvery gray, a color that improves their chances of survival in the sea.

recipes

Grilled Trout with Oregano p.220

Panfried Trout with Almonds and Parsley p.223

WILD ALASKAN SALMON

Highly regarded for its delicious flavor, salmon has a stellar nutritional reputation, yet lacks the high mercury levels that taint some of its seafood kin. From B vitamins to omega-3s, this power food is a healthy catch in more ways than one.

HEALTH BENEFITS

Celebrated for its omega-3 fatty acids, salmon offers both docosahexaenoic acid (DHA) and eicosapentaenoic acid (EPA), but the amount varies with the type of salmon. Research shows these omega-3s can help lower triglyceride levels and blood pressure and may even alleviate symptoms of rheumatoid arthritis. Wild salmon's pink hue, which comes from a diet of nutrient-rich krill, signals an abundance of carotenoids, mainly astaxanthin, which has anti-inflammatory properties. The mineral selenium, another antioxidant found in salmon, protects healthy cells by fighting off free radicals; it also helps thyroid function. Salmon boasts B vitamins (including niacin, B6, B12) and vitamin D, which is found naturally in few foods. Consider canned wild salmon when fresh is not an option; it yields the same benefits.

HOW TO BUY

Rich-tasting wild salmon is the safest bet. It offers more nutrients than farmed; typically, wild Alaskan salmon makes a better environmental choice, too. The farming process pollutes ocean waters, often requires the use of antibiotics, and results in fish (sold as "Atlantic salmon") with lower levels of vitamin D and omega-3s than wild. Farmed salmon also tend to be high in PCBs (polychlorinated biphenyls), due to their diet of fish meal. And because farmed salmon don't eat wild crustaceans, they either have paler flesh than wild salmon or are fed color-altering dietary supplements. (Ask your fishmonger how the fish was raised or caught.)

HOW TO STORE

Keep fresh salmon in the refrigerator wrapped in paper for up to two days. Frozen salmon may be stored in a resealable plastic bag for up to three months.

PREPARATION TIP

Salmon tastes best when prepared simply, showcasing its nuanced flavor. It pairs well with citrus and fresh herbs. To broil, rub with oil and season with salt and pepper. Cook just until the flesh is opaque, but still moist, 6 to 8 minutes.

DID YOU KNOW?

When wild salmon swim upstream from the ocean into rivers and streams to spawn, they help replenish those freshwater habitats with nutrients such as nitrogen and phosphorus.

recipes

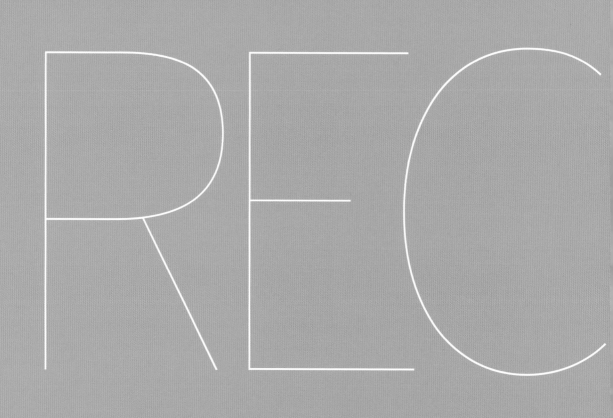

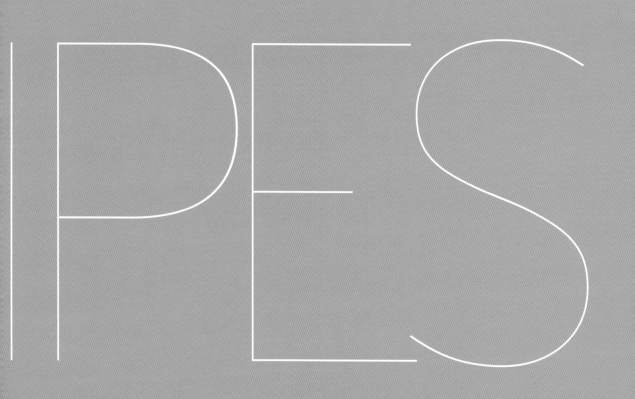

BREAKFAST

INGREDIENTS:
Pasteurized Skim Milk,
Live Active Cultures,
Vegetable Rennet

LIVE CULTURES:
B. Lactis, L. Acidophilus,
L. Delbrueckii Subsp. Bulgaricus,
L. Delbrueckii Subsp. Lactis,
S. Thermophilus

Skyr is the name for thick yogurt
in Icelandic. It is high in protein
and low in fat. We only use milk
from farmers who do not use growth
hormones like rBGH. None of our
products contain any of those
dreadful artificial sweeteners.
I hope you enjoy,

smoothies

POWER PROTEIN SMOOTHIE
SERVES 2

Pomegranate juice offers powerful antioxidants that strengthen the vascular system. Flaxseed adds a boost of fiber and omega-3 fatty acids.

- 2 cups (12 ounces) mixed fresh or frozen berries
- 1 cup (about 8 ounces) drained silken tofu
- ¼ cup unsweetened pomegranate juice
- 2 tablespoons honey, plus more to taste
- 2 tablespoons ground flaxseed
- 1 teaspoon finely grated peeled fresh ginger

Puree all ingredients in a blender until smooth, 15 to 20 seconds, adding up to 1 tablespoon more honey, if desired. Divide between two glasses, and serve.

per serving: 270 calories; .03 g saturated fat; .4 g unsaturated fat; 0 mg cholesterol; 54 g carbohydrates; 8.5 g protein; 6.5 mg sodium; 9.2 g fiber

PAPAYA-GINGER SMOOTHIE
SERVES 4

Papaya supplies hefty doses of vitamin A and enzymes to aid morning digestion.

- 1 large papaya (Mexican or Solo, about 1 pound), peeled, halved lengthwise, seeds removed, cut into ½-inch dice
- 1 cup ice cubes
- ⅔ cup plain low-fat yogurt
- 1 tablespoon finely chopped peeled fresh ginger
- 1 tablespoon honey
  Juice of 2 lemons
- 16 fresh mint leaves, plus 4 sprigs for garnish

Puree first 6 ingredients in a blender. Thin with water as necessary. Blend in mint leaves. Divide among four glasses. Garnish with mint sprigs; serve.

per serving: 92 calories; .5 g saturated fat; .3 g unsaturated fat; 2.4 mg cholesterol; 20.7 g carbohydrates; 3 g protein; 33 mg sodium; 2.2 g fiber

AVOCADO-PEAR SMOOTHIE
SERVES 4

Avocado provides folic acid, fiber, and mono-unsaturated fatty acids; pear adds extra soluble fiber and sweetness.

- 1 ripe, firm Hass avocado
- ½ cup (about 4 ounces) drained silken tofu
- 1 cup unsweetened pear juice
- 2 tablespoons honey
- ½ teaspoon pure vanilla extract
- 2 cups ice cubes

Cut avocado in half lengthwise; remove pit, then score flesh into cubes. With a large spoon, scrape flesh into a blender. Add tofu, pear juice, honey, and vanilla, and puree until smooth. Add ice; blend until smooth. Divide among four glasses, and serve.

per serving: 164 calories; 1.1 g saturated fat; 5.8 g unsaturated fat; 0 mg cholesterol; 23.3 g carbohydrates; 2.3 g protein; 6.5 mg sodium; 3.8 g fiber

CHERRY-BERRY TEA SMOOTHIE
SERVES 4

Cherries help prevent inflammation, and blueberries offer antioxidants, including vitamins C and K. African rooibos is a tea that's high in antioxidants and subtly sweet, but you can also use rose hips, ginger, or hibiscus.

- 1 cup plain Greek-style yogurt (2 percent)
- 2 cups (10 ounces) frozen sweet cherries
- 1 cup (5 ounces) frozen red grapes
- ½ cup (3 ounces) frozen blueberries
- ¾ to 1 cup chilled brewed herbal tea, preferably African rooibos

Puree yogurt, fruit, and ¾ cup tea in a blender until smooth; add more tea as needed. Divide among four glasses, and serve.

per serving: 130 calories; .8 g saturated fat; .1 g unsaturated fat; 3.7 mg cholesterol; 25.3 g carbohydrates; 6.2 g protein; 21.4 mg sodium; 2.4 g fiber

granola MAKES 12 CUPS

Chock-full of grains, nuts, seeds, fruits, and natural sweeteners, granola is easy to prepare, and, when it's homemade, it's much lower in sugar and fat than store-bought varieties. This basic recipe can be easily adapted to create many different versions, including the three variations that follow. You can omit the nuts or the dried fruit, as desired. For a vegan option, simply omit the egg whites; the granola won't be as crunchy but will still be delicious. Freeze granola in an airtight container for up to three months (it thaws quickly), or store at room temperature for up to two weeks.

6 cups old-fashioned rolled oats (not instant)

1¼ cups chopped nuts, such as raw almonds, pistachios, walnuts, pecans, or a combination (optional)

¼ cup raw hulled pumpkin seeds (pepitas) or sunflower seeds

⅓ cup ground flaxseed or toasted wheat germ, or a combination

¾ teaspoon ground cinnamon

3 large egg whites

¾ teaspoon coarse salt

¾ cup sweetener, such as honey, agave, or unsulfured molasses

⅓ cup extra-virgin olive oil

1 cup coarsely chopped dried fruit, such as sour cherries, cranberries, currants, raisins, apricots, figs, or pineapple

1 Preheat oven to 350°F. In a bowl, combine oats, nuts (if using), pumpkin seeds, flaxseed, and cinnamon. In another bowl, whisk together egg whites and salt until frothy. Add honey and oil, and whisk to combine. Stir into oat mixture until combined.

2 Spread mixture in even layers on two rimmed baking sheets. Bake 20 minutes; remove from oven, and use a spatula to gently flip the granola and move it from outer edges to center (to brown evenly). Return to oven, and continue to cook until golden brown, about 10 minutes more. Cool completely on sheets, then transfer to a bowl; stir in dried fruit.

per ½-cup serving: 207 calories; .7 g saturated fat; 5.5 g unsaturated fat; 0 mg cholesterol; 30 g carbohydrates; 6 g protein; 68 mg sodium; 3.8 g fiber

SUGGESTED COMBINATIONS

Pistachios, Sunflower Seeds, Sour Cherries, and Toasted Coconut
Use 1¼ cups chopped pistachios and ¼ cup sunflower seeds in the base. After granola has been baked, stir in 1 cup dried sour cherries and ½ cup toasted unsweetened coconut.

Almonds, Pumpkin Seeds, Currants, and Puffed Brown Rice
Use 1¼ cups sliced almonds and ¼ cup pumpkin seeds in the base. After granola has been baked, stir in 1 cup dried currants and ½ cup puffed brown rice cereal.

Macadamia Nuts with Crystallized Ginger and Pineapple
Use 1¼ cups chopped macadamia nuts, and molasses as the sweetener in the base. Add ¾ teaspoon ground ginger to the oat mixture. After granola has been baked, stir in ¾ cup chopped dried pineapple, ¼ cup chopped crystallized ginger, and ½ cup toasted unsweetened coconut.

quinoa crunch with seasonal fruit and yogurt SERVES 4

High-protein quinoa makes a delicious topping that keeps well. Here, the toasted grain gives crunch to yogurt and fruit. You could also add a few tablespoons to your favorite cereal for added texture.

1 cup quinoa, rinsed and drained

1 tablespoon agave syrup

1 tablespoon neutral-tasting oil, such as canola or safflower

4 cups plain Greek-style yogurt (2 percent)

2 cups mixed fresh fruit, such as berries and cut-up peaches or mango

1 Preheat oven to 375°F. Mix quinoa with syrup and oil; spread in an even layer on a rimmed baking sheet. Bake until crisp, stirring occasionally, 10 to 12 minutes. Transfer to a plate, and let cool before serving. Store quinoa crunch in an airtight container at room temperature for up to 4 weeks.

2 To serve, divide yogurt among four bowls, and top each with fruit and 2 tablespoons quinoa crunch.

per serving: 397 calories; 3.5 g saturated fat; 5 g unsaturated fat; 15 mg cholesterol; 53 g carbohydrates; 25 g protein; 89 mg sodium; 3 g fiber

fresh muesli with apple and almonds SERVES 2

Made from uncooked oats, dried fruits, and nuts, muesli does not contain sweeteners, oil, or other more fattening ingredients found in many store-bought cereals. Nondairy milk, such as hazelnut, almond, or hemp milk, makes an easy substitution for those with lactose intolerance.

¾ cup old-fashioned rolled oats (not instant)

¼ cup sliced almonds

½ cup plain Greek-style yogurt (2 percent)

¼ cup milk

½ apple, diced

2 to 4 tablespoons honey

1 Preheat oven to 350°F. Spread oats and almonds evenly on a rimmed baking sheet. Bake until almonds are golden brown, stirring occasionally, 7 to 8 minutes. Transfer to a plate, and let cool completely. (The cereal can be stored for up to 1 week in an airtight container.)

2 In a small bowl, stir together ¾ cup toasted oat mixture, the yogurt, and milk. Cover and refrigerate until oats are soft, about 1 hour, or up to overnight.

3 To serve, spoon muesli into two bowls. Dividing evenly, top with apple and remaining toasted oat mixture; drizzle with honey.

per serving: 322 calories; 1.4 g saturated fat; 5.4 g unsaturated fat; 5.6 mg cholesterol; 49 g carbohydrates; 13.8 g protein; 36.3 mg sodium; 5.3 g fiber

QUINOA CRUNCH WITH SEASONAL
FRUIT AND YOGURT

FRESH MUESLI WITH APPLE AND ALMONDS

WHOLE-GRAIN TOAST WITH GOAT
CHEESE AND RASPBERRIES

PAPAYA-BERRY YOGURT PARFAITS

whole-grain toast with goat cheese and raspberries SERVES 2

Goat cheese may be a good option for those who can't tolerate cow's milk, and when combined with tart raspberries on toasted bread, it's hard for anyone to resist.

2 slices whole-grain bread, toasted

2 ounces fresh goat cheese

½ cup (3 ounces) fresh raspberries

1 tablespoon honey

Dividing evenly, spread toast with goat cheese and top with berries. Mash the berries slightly with a fork, and drizzle with honey.

per serving: 205 calories; 4.4 g saturated fat; 2.4 g unsaturated fat; 13 mg cholesterol; 28 g carbohydrates; 8.8 g protein; 261 mg sodium; 4 g fiber

papaya-berry yogurt parfaits SERVES 6

Papaya and berries add fiber and antioxidants to these breakfast cups, while mint helps soothe the digestive tract. If you use store-bought granola instead of making your own, be sure to look for varieties that are low in fat and sugar.

1 piece (2 inches) fresh ginger

5 tablespoons honey

1½ teaspoons finely grated lemon zest, plus 1 tablespoon fresh lemon juice

1 large papaya (Mexican or Solo, about 1 pound), peeled, halved lengthwise, seeds removed, cut into ½-inch dice

1 cup (6 ounces) fresh blackberries

1 cup (6 ounces) fresh raspberries

2 cups plain Greek-style yogurt (2 percent)

¼ cup finely chopped fresh mint, plus sprigs for garnish

½ cup Granola (page 73)

1 Using the large holes of a box grater, grate ginger (unpeeled) into a fine sieve set over a bowl; press with a flexible spatula to extract about 1 tablespoon juice (discard solids). Add 2 tablespoons honey and the lemon juice; whisk to combine. Add papaya, blackberries, and raspberries, and toss gently to coat.

2 Mix yogurt, remaining 3 tablespoons honey, and the zest. Spoon half the fruit mixture into six glasses, dividing evenly. Sprinkle with chopped mint. Top with half the yogurt mixture and half the granola, again dividing evenly. Layer with the remaining fruit, yogurt, and granola. Garnish with mint sprigs, and serve.

per serving: 190 calories; 1.2 g saturated fat; 1.1 g unsaturated fat; 5 mg cholesterol; 35 g carbohydrates; 8.5 g protein; 40 mg sodium; 4.7 g fiber

banana bread with walnuts and flaxseed MAKES 1 LOAF; SERVES 8

Banana breads tend to be high in fat and sugar, but this wholesome loaf relies primarily on bananas to keep the bread moist and flavorful. Walnuts and a generous amount of ground flaxseed add texture and plenty of nutrients; substitute toasted pecans for the walnuts if you like, or omit the nuts altogether.

- 2 tablespoons unsalted butter, melted, plus 1 teaspoon, softened, for pan
- ½ cup whole-wheat flour
- ¾ cup all-purpose flour
- ¼ cup ground flaxseed
- ¾ teaspoon coarse salt
- ¾ teaspoon baking powder
- ½ teaspoon baking soda
- 1 large whole egg, plus 1 large egg white
- ½ cup packed light brown sugar
- 1½ teaspoons pure vanilla extract
- ¾ cup mashed very ripe bananas (about 2)
- ½ cup walnuts, toasted (page 53) and coarsely chopped (optional)

1 Preheat oven to 350°F. Brush a 9-by-5-by-3-inch loaf pan with softened butter. In a bowl, whisk together both flours, flaxseed, salt, baking powder, and baking soda.

2 With an electric mixer on medium-low speed, beat whole egg and egg white until thoroughly combined. Add melted butter, the sugar, vanilla, and bananas, and mix until combined. Add the flour mixture, and mix on low speed just until incorporated. Stir in walnuts by hand.

3 Pour batter into prepared pan. Bake until golden brown and a tester inserted into the center comes out clean, about 35 minutes. Let cool slightly in pan on a wire rack before turning out onto rack to cool completely, top side up. The bread can be wrapped tightly in plastic and kept at room temperature for up to 4 days.

per serving: 263 calories; 3 g saturated fat; 7.5 g unsaturated fat; 35 mg cholesterol; 37 g carbohydrates; 6.1 g protein; 231 mg sodium; 4.3 g fiber

oat bran-applesauce mini muffins MAKES 2 DOZEN

Loaded with soluble fiber, the old-fashioned oats in these muffins help reduce cholesterol and regulate blood sugar. Dates and applesauce— both full of fiber, vitamins, and natural sugars—create a complex caramel flavor when combined with the honey.

2 cups unsweetened applesauce

2 ounces dates, pitted and chopped (about ½ cup)

1 cup wheat bran

½ cup low-fat buttermilk

1 large egg

2 tablespoons honey

¾ teaspoon finely grated peeled fresh ginger

½ teaspoon pure vanilla extract

½ cup plus 2 tablespoons all-purpose flour

2 tablespoons ground flaxseed

1¼ teaspoons baking soda

¼ teaspoon salt

¼ teaspoon ground allspice

¼ cup plus 1 tablespoon old-fashioned rolled oats (not instant)

Vegetable oil cooking spray

1 Preheat oven to 375°F. Cook applesauce and dates in a medium saucepan over medium heat, stirring frequently, until mixture is reduced to 1¼ cups, 15 to 20 minutes. Transfer to a large bowl, and let cool completely.

2 Add bran, buttermilk, egg, honey, ginger, and vanilla to applesauce mixture, stirring to combine. Let stand 10 minutes.

3 Whisk together flour, flaxseed, baking soda, salt, allspice, and ¼ cup oats. Stir into applesauce mixture.

4 Coat two mini-muffin tins with cooking spray. Spoon batter into prepared cups, filling each to the brim. Sprinkle the remaining 1 tablespoon oats over muffins, dividing evenly. Bake, rotating tins halfway through, until a tester inserted into the centers comes out clean, 20 to 23 minutes. Let cool completely in tins on wire racks. Muffins can be stored up to 3 days at room temperature in an airtight container.

per serving (1 muffin): 43 calories; .1 g saturated fat; .4 g unsaturated fat; 9 mg cholesterol; 9 g carbohydrates; 1.4 g protein; 86 mg sodium; 1.6 g fiber

egg, kale, and ricotta on toast SERVES 2

Lightly sautéed greens transform a standard egg-and-toast breakfast into a special morning meal that could also serve as a light supper. The kale adds a healthy boost of calcium, folic acid, and carotenoids, as well as vitamin K.

2 tablespoons extra-virgin olive oil

2 garlic cloves, crushed

4 cups chopped trimmed kale (about 1 large bunch), preferably Lacinato

3 tablespoons water

2 tablespoons fresh lemon juice

½ teaspoon coarse salt
Freshly ground pepper

2 slices rustic bread, toasted

3 tablespoons ricotta cheese

2 large eggs

1 Heat 1 tablespoon oil in a medium skillet over medium-high. Cook garlic until barely golden, stirring frequently, about 1 minute. Add kale and the water; cook until tender, stirring occasionally, about 8 minutes. Add lemon juice and salt, and season with pepper; stir to combine.

2 Spread each slice of bread with half of the cheese. Top with kale mixture, dividing evenly.

3 Heat remaining 1 tablespoon oil in another skillet over medium. Crack eggs into skillet, one at a time. Cook until whites are just set, about 2 minutes. With a spatula, carefully place an egg on each bruschetta, and serve.

per serving: 313 calories; 4.2 g saturated fat; 14 g unsaturated fat; 12 mg cholesterol; 27 g carbohydrates; 12.7 g protein; 731 mg sodium; 1.3 g fiber

frittata ranchera with black beans SERVES 4

A frittata is an excellent make-ahead meal, delicious served hot, cold, or at room temperature. Black beans are a great source of fiber, which helps to balance blood sugar.

6 large whole eggs plus 2 large egg whites

¼ cup finely chopped fresh flat-leaf parsley

Coarse salt and freshly ground pepper

1 tablespoon extra-virgin olive oil

1 onion, finely chopped

1½ cups grape or cherry tomatoes, halved

2 jalapeño chiles, finely chopped (ribs and seeds removed for less heat, if desired)

¼ cup crumbled fresh goat cheese

1 can (15 ounces) black beans, drained and rinsed

1 Heat broiler, with rack 4 inches from the heat source. In a large bowl, whisk together whole eggs, egg whites, and parsley; season with ½ teaspoon salt and ¼ teaspoon pepper.

2 Heat oil in a medium ovenproof skillet over medium. Add onion, tomatoes, and jalapeños; cook, stirring occasionally, until onion has softened, about 6 minutes. Add egg mixture. Sprinkle evenly with cheese. Cover, reduce heat to low, and cook until eggs are almost set, 5 to 7 minutes. Meanwhile, heat beans in a small saucepan over medium-low until warmed through (add water if too dry); season with pepper.

3 Uncover skillet, and place frittata under broiler. Cook until the top is set and just beginning to brown, 3 to 4 minutes.

4 Run a flexible spatula around edge of frittata to loosen from pan, then slide onto a plate. Cut frittata into wedges, and serve with black beans.

per serving: 268 calories; 3.3 g saturated fat; 4.1 g unsaturated fat; 3 mg cholesterol; 21 g carbohydrates; 18 g protein; 762 mg sodium; 7 g fiber

mushroom and scallion frittata SERVES 4

Any combination of mushrooms works well in this dish; choose among shiitake, cremini, oyster, or maitake.

3 large whole eggs plus 3 large egg whites

¼ cup cottage cheese

6 mushrooms, trimmed, cleaned, and thinly sliced

4 scallions, trimmed and finely chopped

Coarse salt and freshly ground pepper

1 tablespoon extra-virgin olive oil

1 Heat broiler, with rack 4 inches from heat source. In a large bowl, whisk together whole eggs, egg whites, and cottage cheese. Add mushrooms and scallions; season with ½ teaspoon salt and ¼ teaspoon pepper.

2 Heat oil in a medium ovenproof skillet over medium. Add egg mixture. Cook until eggs are almost set, 3 to 5 minutes.

3 Transfer skillet to broiler. Cook until the top is set and just beginning to brown, 3 to 4 minutes. Run a flexible spatula around edge of frittata to loosen from pan. Cut into wedges, and serve.

per serving: 112 calories; 1.8 g saturated fat; 5 g unsaturated fat; 160 mg cholesterol; 3.5 g carbohydrates; 7.7 g protein; 254 mg sodium; .6 g fiber

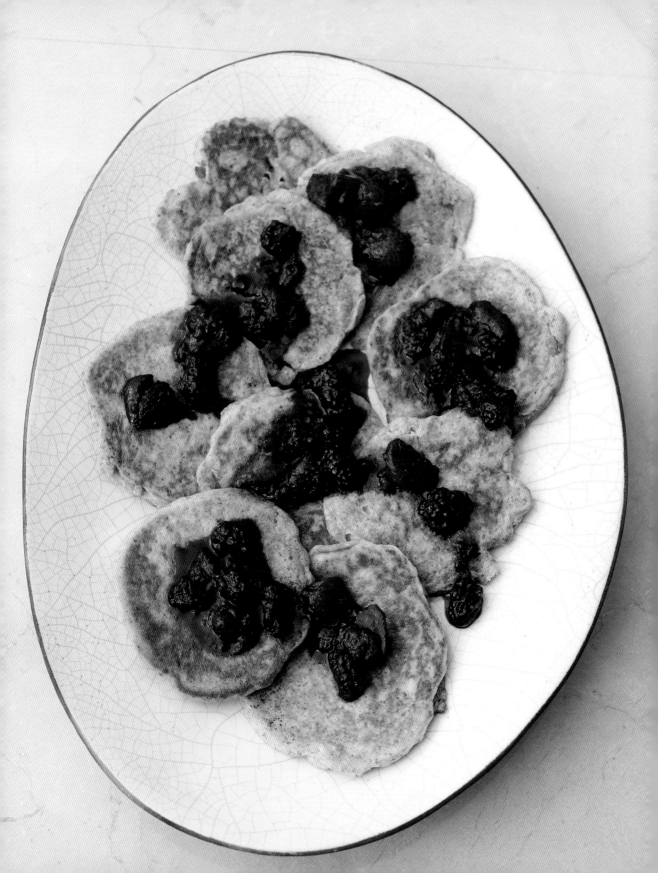

pecan pancakes with mixed berry compote SERVES 4

Combining berries (good sources of vitamin C and anthocyanins) with vitamin E–filled wheat germ and pecans maximizes this breakfast favorite's antioxidant properties.

- 2 cups (12 ounces) mixed fresh or frozen berries (thawed)
- 1 tablespoon honey
- 1 teaspoon finely grated lemon zest
- ½ cup all-purpose flour
- ¼ cup whole-wheat flour
- ¼ cup toasted wheat germ
- 2 teaspoons baking powder
- ½ teaspoon baking soda
- ¼ teaspoon salt
- 1 cup plain low-fat yogurt
- 2 tablespoons unsalted butter, melted, plus more for pan
- 1 large egg
- ½ cup pecans, coarsely chopped

1 In a small saucepan, bring berries, honey, and lemon zest to a boil. Reduce heat to a simmer and cook, stirring occasionally, until thickened, 7 to 8 minutes. Transfer to a bowl.

2 Preheat oven to 200°F. Whisk together flours, wheat germ, baking powder, baking soda, and salt. In another bowl, whisk together yogurt, melted butter, and egg; add flour mixture and pecans and whisk until just moistened (batter should be slightly lumpy; do not overmix).

3 Heat a griddle or large skillet over medium. Lightly coat griddle with butter. Working in batches, add ¼ cup batter per pancake, using the back of a spoon to spread to about 4 inches in diameter. Cook until bubbles appear on surface and start to burst, 1 to 3 minutes. Flip with a thin spatula, and cook until lightly browned on the other side, 1 to 2 minutes more. Transfer to a baking sheet and keep warm in the oven while you make more pancakes with remaining batter. Serve warm, topped with berry mixture.

per serving: 368 calories; 6 g saturated fat; 13 g unsaturated fat; 72 mg cholesterol; 40 g carbohydrates; 12 g protein; 566 mg sodium; 6 g fiber

steamed salmon with avocado SERVES 4

A steamed salmon fillet makes for a healthful—and unexpectedly delicious—morning meal, especially when served with avocado. Both foods are excellent sources of unsaturated fats, which benefit the heart.

2 lemons (1 sliced into thin rounds, 1 cut into wedges)

4 wild salmon fillets (each 1 inch thick and about 4 ounces)

Coarse sea salt, such as fleur de sel

1 ripe, firm Hass avocado

1 Arrange lemon rounds on bottom of a bamboo steamer basket. Season salmon fillets on both sides with ¼ teaspoon sea salt, dividing evenly. Place salmon on top of lemon rounds, and cover with steamer lid.

2 Bring about 1 inch of water to a simmer in a large skillet. Place steamer basket in skillet, and steam until fish is opaque throughout, about 7 minutes.

3 Cut avocado in half lengthwise, and remove pit; peel and thinly slice. Arrange avocado and salmon on plates. Season salmon with more salt, if desired, and serve with lemon wedges.

per serving: 303 calories; 3.2 g saturated fat; 12.3 mg unsaturated fat; 69 mg cholesterol; 7.7 g carbohydrates; 24 g protein; 180 mg sodium; 3.9 g fiber

hard-cooked egg whites with avocado SERVES 4

This breakfast is a good option for anyone monitoring cholesterol intake: Egg whites don't contain any saturated fat, and avocados have monounsaturated fat, which actually helps lower LDL ("bad") cholesterol.

8 large hard-cooked eggs (page 61)

2 ripe, firm Hass avocados

Coarse salt and freshly ground pepper

1 tablespoon extra-virgin olive oil

1 Peel eggs and cut in half. Remove yolks (reserve yolks for another use, if desired). Tear whites into 1-inch pieces; divide among four bowls.

2 Cut avocados in half lengthwise, and remove pits. Using a spoon, scrape out bite-size pieces into bowls, dividing evenly. Season with a pinch of salt and pepper. Drizzle each serving with ¾ teaspoon oil, and serve.

per serving: 211 calories; 2 g saturated fat; 13 g unsaturated fat; 0 mg cholesterol; 9.1 g carbohydrates; 9 g protein; 238 mg sodium; 6 g fiber

STEAMED SALMON WITH AVOCADO

HARD-COOKED EGG WHITES
WITH AVOCADO

STARTERS

AND SNACKS

sweet potato hummus   MAKES 4 CUPS

Sweet potatoes' orange hue is the beautiful result of a wealth of beta-carotene, which helps support eye health and immunity. Chickpeas provide a rich source of soluble fiber and B-vitamins for cardiovascular health. By serving this dip with crisp-tender vegetables such as red peppers and broccoli, you will also get vitamin C, selenium, and sulforaphane, an antioxidant shown to prevent certain types of cancers. Whole-wheat pita bread is another healthful, fiber-rich alternative to crackers.

1 pound sweet potatoes (about 2), peeled and cut into 1-inch pieces

1 can (15 ounces) chickpeas, drained and rinsed

¼ cup fresh lemon juice (from 1 to 2 lemons)

¼ cup tahini (sesame seed paste)

2 tablespoons olive oil

2 teaspoons ground cumin

1 garlic clove, finely chopped

Coarse salt and freshly ground pepper

½ teaspoon hot or smoked paprika, for garnish

1 Fill a large pot with 2 inches of water; set a steamer basket (or colander) inside pot, and bring water to a boil. Add potatoes; reduce heat to a simmer, cover, and cook until potatoes are tender, 10 to 12 minutes.

2 Transfer potatoes to a food processor. Add chickpeas, lemon juice, tahini, oil, cumin, and garlic. Puree until smooth, about 1 minute; thin with up to 2 tablespoons of water if necessary. Add ¼ teaspoon salt and season with pepper. Let cool; refrigerate for up to 1 week in an airtight container. Garnish with paprika before serving.

per ¼-cup serving: 106 calories; .6 g saturated fat; 3.4 g unsaturated fat; 0 mg cholesterol; 14.8 g carbohydrates; 2.9 g protein; 151 mg sodium; 2.7 g fiber

steamed artichokes with two dipping sauces SERVES 4

Steamed artichokes are often served with melted butter and other sauces that are high in fat and have little nutritional value. The dips here use healthier ingredients and integrate spices and herbs for bold flavor.

STEAMED ARTICHOKES

- 1 lemon
- 4 globe artichokes (12 ounces each)

Prepare a bowl of water large enough to hold all of the artichokes. Peel 1 lemon with a vegetable peeler, then cut in half and squeeze the juice into the bowl.

Remove any tough outer leaves from artichokes. Working with one artichoke at a time, use a serrated knife to cut off the top quarter of each. Use kitchen shears to trim sharp tips of the leaves. Remove any small leaves from bottom and trim stem just enough that artichoke can stand upright; place in lemon water to keep it from turning brown while repeating with remaining artichokes.

Fill a large pot with 2 inches of water; set a steamer basket (or colander) inside pot, and bring water to a boil. Place the lemon peel and artichokes, stem ends down, in basket. Cover and steam until bases of artichokes are easily pierced with the tip of a sharp knife, about 20 minutes.

When cool enough to handle, use a small spoon to scoop out center cone; scrape out purple leaves and fuzzy choke. Serve artichokes with dipping sauces, as desired.

per serving (artichoke): 61 calories; .1 g saturated fat; 0 g unsaturated fat; 0 mg cholesterol; 14 g carbohydrates; 4 g protein; 121 mg sodium; 7 g fiber

TARRAGON-YOGURT SAUCE
MAKES 1 CUP

- ¾ cup plain Greek-style yogurt (2 percent)
- 1 teaspoon finely grated lemon zest, and 1 tablespoon plus 1 teaspoon fresh lemon juice

- 1 tablespoon finely minced fresh tarragon
- 1 tablespoon finely minced fresh flat-leaf parsley
  Coarse salt and freshly ground pepper

Mix together yogurt, lemon zest and juice, tarragon, parsley, and 1 teaspoon salt; season with pepper.

per ¼-cup serving: 30 calories; .6 g saturated fat; 0 g unsaturated fat; 2.8 mg cholesterol; 2.3 g carbohydrates; 3.6 g protein; 495 mg sodium; .2 g fiber

SPICY AÏOLI
MAKES 1 CUP

- 2 garlic cloves
- 1 large egg yolk
- 1 tablespoon Dijon mustard
- 2 tablespoons fresh lemon juice
- ¾ cup extra-virgin olive oil
- 1 tablespoon sweet paprika
- ¼ teaspoon cayenne pepper
- ¼ to ½ teaspoon hot sauce, such as Tabasco
  Coarse salt and freshly ground black pepper

Bring 1 inch of water to a boil in a small saucepan. Blanch garlic until tender, 3 to 5 minutes; drain and mash garlic into a paste.

Whisk together garlic, egg yolk, mustard, and lemon juice in a bowl. Slowly whisk in oil until emulsified. Whisk in paprika, cayenne, hot sauce, and 1 teaspoon salt; season with pepper.

per 2-tablespoon serving: 202 calories; 3.2 g saturated fat; 18.5 g unsaturated fat; 25.6 mg cholesterol; 1.5 g carbohydrates; .5 g protein; 287 mg sodium; .3 g fiber

artichoke-spinach dip MAKES ABOUT 2 CUPS

Fiber-rich artichokes are the base of this vegetable-cheese dip — and their tender leaves stand in as "chips." The combination of part-skim ricotta and mozzarella cheeses replaces the sour cream in original recipes for this crowd-pleasing party food, resulting in the same creamy texture but less saturated fat.

2 lemons

5 globe artichokes

2 cups firmly packed baby spinach

2 tablespoons mayonnaise

1 small shallot, finely chopped

1 garlic clove, finely chopped

¾ cup part-skim ricotta cheese

   Coarse salt and freshly ground black pepper

⅛ teaspoon cayenne pepper

⅓ cup plus 2 tablespoons shredded part-skim mozzarella cheese

1 tablespoon shredded parmesan cheese

1 Preheat oven to 350°F. Prepare a large bowl of water. Peel 1 lemon with a vegetable peeler, then cut in half and squeeze the juice into the bowl. Remove any tough outer leaves from artichokes. Working with one artichoke at a time, use a serrated knife to cut off the top quarter of each artichoke. Use kitchen shears to trim sharp tips of the leaves. Remove any small leaves from bottom and trim stem so artichoke can stand upright; keep in lemon water to keep it from turning brown while repeating with remaining artichokes.

2 Fill a large pot with 2 inches of water; set a steamer basket (or colander) inside pot, and bring water to a boil. Place the lemon peel and artichokes, stem ends down, in basket. Cover and steam until bases of artichokes are easily pierced with the tip of a sharp knife, about 20 minutes. Let cool. Pull off leaves, and reserve for serving. Trim inner part of each artichoke to the heart; scrape out fuzzy choke and discard it.

3 While artichokes are cooking, fill another large pot with 2 inches of water; set a steamer basket (or colander) inside pot, and bring water to a boil. Add spinach; cover and cook until wilted, about 2 minutes. Remove basket with spinach; when cool enough to handle, squeeze out as much water as possible, and coarsely chop spinach.

4 Finely grate the zest of remaining lemon, then cut in half and extract juice. In a food processor, combine zest and juice with artichoke hearts, mayonnaise, shallot, garlic, ricotta, ¼ teaspoon salt, and cayenne pepper; season with black pepper. Pulse until combined. Stir in spinach and all but 1 tablespoon mozzarella. Transfer to an ovenproof dish. Sprinkle mixture evenly with parmesan and the remaining 1 tablespoon mozzarella.

5 Bake 10 minutes; remove from oven. Heat broiler. Broil dip until edges are bubbling and top is golden brown, 2 to 3 minutes. Serve immediately with reserved artichoke leaves.

per ¼-cup serving: 226 calories; 2.6 g saturated fat; 1.8 g unsaturated fat; 15 mg cholesterol; 20 g carbohydrates; 9 g protein; 296 mg sodium; 3 g fiber

roasted red pepper and walnut dip MAKES 2¼ CUPS

This robust red-pepper dip is based on *muhammara*, a Middle Eastern specialty whose name describes its brick-red color. For best results, make it a day ahead to let the flavors blend. Serve with toasted pita wedges or crudités.

- 3 red bell peppers (about 1 pound)
- 1 whole-wheat pita (6-inch size), toasted
- 1 cup water
- 1 small garlic clove
- ¾ cup walnut pieces, toasted (page 53), plus more for garnish
- 1½ teaspoons paprika, plus more for garnish (optional)
- ¾ teaspoon ground cumin
- 1 tablespoon balsamic vinegar
- 1 tablespoon fresh lemon juice
- 2 teaspoons extra-virgin olive oil, plus more for drizzling
- Coarse salt and freshly ground pepper

1 Roast peppers directly over flame of a gas-stove burner on high heat, turning with tongs, until blackened all over. (Or place peppers under the broiler, turning often, until skin has charred.) Transfer peppers to a bowl and cover with plastic wrap. Let steam 15 minutes. Using paper towels, rub off skins, then remove stems, seeds, and ribs.

2 Break toasted pita bread into 2-inch pieces; place in a bowl and add the water. Let soak until soft, about 10 minutes. Transfer to a sieve, and drain well, pressing out excess water.

3 Process garlic and walnuts in a food processor until finely ground, about 10 seconds. Add paprika, cumin, the roasted peppers, and the pita bread; process until smooth, about 10 seconds. Add vinegar, lemon juice, oil, and ¼ teaspoon salt (or to taste); season with pepper. Pulse until combined.

4 Transfer dip to a bowl; cover with plastic wrap. Refrigerate at least 1 hour, or up to overnight. Before serving, bring to room temperature; drizzle with oil, and sprinkle with walnuts and paprika, as desired.

per ¼-cup serving: 111 calories; 1 g saturated fat; 7.3 g unsaturated fat; 0 mg cholesterol; 7.6 g carbohydrates; 2.7 g protein; 118 mg sodium; 1.8 g fiber

soy-wasabi spread MAKES 3 CUPS

Edamame are a rich source of fiber and phytochemicals that may help lower cholesterol, protect bones, and balance hormone levels. Serve this spicy spread with rice crackers as an anytime snack or for a party hors d'oeuvre. The dip is also delicious paired with cucumber, celery, and carrot sticks.

1 pound frozen shelled edamame (soybeans)

1 ¼ cups (about 10 ounces) drained silken tofu

1 teaspoon finely grated lemon zest, plus 2 tablespoons fresh lemon juice

1 tablespoon Chinese hot mustard

2 teaspoons wasabi paste

Coarse salt

Black sesame seeds, for garnish

1 Bring a large pot of water to a boil. Add edamame; cook until tender, about 5 minutes. Drain in a colander. Rinse under cold running water to stop the cooking, then drain again.

2 Puree edamame, tofu, lemon zest and juice, mustard, wasabi, and ½ teaspoon salt in a food processor. Spread can be refrigerated in an airtight container for up to 2 days. Garnish with sesame seeds before serving.

per ¼-cup serving: 51 calories; 0 g saturated fat; 0 g unsaturated fat; 0 mg cholesterol; 4 g carbohydrates; 4.7 g protein; 82 mg sodium; 1.9 g fiber

black bean salsa with baked chips

MAKES 2 CUPS SALSA AND 48 CHIPS

This zesty salsa is high in protein and fiber and low in fat, and it makes a great accompaniment to grilled meat, chicken, or fish. It's quick work to make your own baked tortilla chips, and they are so much more healthful than anything you can buy from the store.

1 can (19 ounces) black beans, drained and rinsed

1 small tomato, seeded and cut into ½-inch dice

2 scallions, trimmed and finely chopped

1 jalapeño chile, minced (ribs and seeds removed for less heat, if desired)

½ cup coarsely chopped cilantro

2 tablespoons fresh lime juice (from 2 limes)

Coarse salt

6 flour tortillas (8-inch size), preferably whole-wheat

2 teaspoons extra-virgin olive oil

1 Heat broiler. Pulse ¼ cup black beans in a food processor until coarsely chopped; transfer to a bowl. Add remaining beans to bowl along with the tomato, scallions, jalapeño, cilantro, lime juice, and ½ teaspoon salt. Stir to combine.

2 Cut each tortilla into 8 wedges. Arrange in a single layer on a baking sheet; brush with oil, dividing evenly. Broil until crisp and golden brown, 1 to 2 minutes per side. Transfer chips to a wire rack to cool. Serve with salsa.

per ¼-cup dip and 6 chip serving: 179 calories; .2 g saturated fat; .6 g unsaturated fat; 0 mg cholesterol; 26.8 g carbohydrates; 7 g protein; 349 mg sodium; 5.5 g fiber

classic guacamole MAKES 1½ CUPS

Good guacamole relies on soft, ripe avocados. The Hass variety has a buttery flesh with delicate herbal flavor. If you don't have a mortar and pestle, crush the first four ingredients in a bowl with a wooden spoon, then use a fork to mash the guacamole.

2 tablespoons finely chopped white onion

2 tablespoons finely chopped cilantro

1¼ teaspoons finely chopped jalapeño chile (ribs and seeds removed for less heat, if desired)

Coarse salt

1 ripe Hass avocado

Juice of 1 lime

3 tablespoons finely chopped, seeded tomato (optional)

1 With a large mortar and pestle, mash onion, 1 tablespoon cilantro, jalapeño, and ¼ teaspoon coarse salt until smooth and juicy.

2 Cut avocado in half lengthwise, and remove pit. Score into cubes, then use a spoon to scoop out flesh into mortar. Mash slightly (avocado should remain somewhat chunky). Stir in lime juice, tomato (if using), and remaining tablespoon cilantro. Season with more salt, as desired. Serve immediately.

per ¼-cup serving: 56 calories; .7 g saturated fat; 3.9 g unsaturated fat; 0 mg cholesterol; 3.4 g carbohydrates; .8 g protein; 88 mg sodium; 2.4 g fiber

BLACK BEAN SALSA WITH BAKED CHIPS

CLASSIC GUACAMOLE

crisp tofu with vegetables and sesame-ginger dipping sauce SERVES 4

Low in calories and saturated fat, tofu provides a healthful source of protein and makes an energizing snack. Pressing the tofu extracts some of the liquid so it will crisp in the oven.

21 ounces (1½ packages) firm tofu, drained and halved crosswise

1 tablespoon sesame seeds, toasted (page 57)

1½ teaspoons toasted sesame oil

Coarse salt

5 teaspoons coarsely chopped peeled fresh ginger

¼ cup tahini (sesame seed paste)

5 teaspoons low-sodium tamari soy sauce

1½ teaspoons honey

1 teaspoon rice vinegar

3 tablespoons cool water

8 ounces green beans, trimmed

½ head green cabbage, cut into ½-inch-thick wedges

1 red bell pepper, ribs and seeds removed, cut lengthwise into ½-inch-thick strips

1 Preheat oven to 400°F. Place tofu on a rimmed baking sheet lined with a double layer of paper towels; cover with another double layer of paper towels. Place a baking sheet on top, and weight with canned goods or a heavy skillet. Let drain 30 minutes, then transfer to a cutting board and pat dry with more paper towels.

2 Cut tofu into 24 pieces and place in a bowl. Add sesame seeds, ½ teaspoon sesame oil, and ¼ teaspoon salt; toss to combine. Arrange tofu in a single layer on a rimmed baking sheet. Bake until golden brown and lightly crisp on bottom, 12 to 15 minutes. Use a spatula to flip tofu, and bake until other side is crisp, about 10 minutes more. Transfer to a plate and let cool completely.

3 Pulse ginger in a food processor until finely chopped. Add tahini, tamari, honey, remaining 1 teaspoon sesame oil, and the vinegar; process until combined. With machine running, add the water. Process until smooth.

4 Prepare an ice-water bath. Bring a pot of water to a boil. Blanch green beans until crisp-tender and bright green, 1 to 2 minutes. Use a slotted spoon to transfer beans to the ice bath to stop the cooking. Let cool, stirring frequently, then drain and pat dry with paper towels.

5 Divide green beans, cabbage, bell pepper, and tofu into four servings. Divide sauce among four small cups for dipping, and serve within 2 hours, or refrigerate, covered, for up to 1 day.

per serving: 314 calories; 2.3 g saturated fat; 8 g unsaturated fat; 0 mg cholesterol; 21.3 g carbohydrates; 19.4 g protein; 412 mg sodium; 6.7 g fiber

two dips for crudités

Vegetables, of course, make healthy snacks, and are especially appetizing when served with flavorful dips. Yellow split peas are the protein-rich basis of one spread; tarama—cured carp or cod roe, used in Greek and Turkish cooking—flavors the other. The roe is soaked in water to remove much of its saltiness, then squeezed of excess moisture. Look for tarama at specialty food stores. Serve dips with crudités and toasted baguette or whole-grain bread slices.

YELLOW SPLIT PEA DIP
MAKES 2 CUPS

- 2 carrots, coarsely chopped
- 2 celery stalks, coarsely chopped
- ½ white onion
- 4 sprigs thyme
- 4 sprigs flat-leaf parsley
- 1 tablespoon whole black peppercorns
- 1 cup (8 ounces) yellow split peas
- 4 cups water
  Coarse salt and freshly ground pepper
- 1 tablespoon fresh lemon juice
  Extra-virgin olive oil, for drizzling
- 1 small red onion, thinly sliced
- 1 tablespoon plus 1 teaspoon capers, rinsed and drained

Wrap carrots, celery, white onion, herbs, and peppercorns into a bundle; tie with kitchen twine.

Combine split peas with the water, ½ teaspoon salt, and herb bundle in a saucepan. Bring to a boil. Reduce to a simmer; cook until split peas are tender, about 45 minutes. Discard bundle. Reserve ½ cup cooking liquid. Drain split peas; let cool slightly.

Puree split peas, lemon juice, 1 teaspoon salt, and ¼ cup reserved cooking liquid in a food processor until smooth, adding more liquid as needed. To serve, drizzle spread with oil, top with red onion and capers, and season with pepper.

per ¼-cup serving: 124 calories; .5 g saturated fat; 3 g unsaturated fat; 0 mg cholesterol; 17 g carbohydrates; 6.54 g protein; 408 mg sodium; .2 g fiber

TARAMASALATA
MAKES 1 CUP

- ½ cup tarama (from one 8-ounce jar)
- ½ russet potato, peeled and cut into 1-inch chunks
  Coarse salt and freshly ground pepper
- 1 tablespoon plus 1 teaspoon fresh lemon juice
- 2 tablespoons extra-virgin olive oil

Place roe in a bowl and cover with cold water; soak 10 minutes. Drain in a fine sieve lined with cheesecloth. Rinse; drain again. Gather cheesecloth around roe, and squeeze out as much liquid as possible.

Meanwhile, cover potato in a saucepan with 2 inches cold water and add ½ teaspoon salt. Bring to a boil, and cook until tender, about 5 minutes. Drain, and let cool.

Puree roe, potato, and lemon juice in a food processor. With machine running, add oil and process until smooth. Season with pepper.

per ¼-cup serving: 101 calories; 1 g saturated fat; 4.6 g unsaturated fat; 136 mg cholesterol; 3.3 g carbohydrates; 8.4 g protein; 104 mg sodium; .2 g fiber

CRUDITÉS
The dips here are accompanied by spring produce, but nearly any vegetable can be used in a platter of crudités. Serve tender vegetables, such as celery, snap peas, and baby carrots, raw; broccoli, green beans, and cauliflower are better (and lose little nutritional value) when blanched for 2 to 3 minutes in boiling water and then shocked in an ice-water bath.

quinoa, apricot, and nut clusters MAKES 20

In this version of a granola bar, clusters of quinoa, apricots, pistachios, and sunflower seeds make a sweet and delightfully chewy snack. White quinoa is used in this recipe, but you can substitute any variety; all share the same nutritional qualities, flavor, and texture.

1 ½ cups water

¾ cup white quinoa, rinsed and drained

1 ½ cups old-fashioned rolled oats (not instant)

½ cup raw shelled sunflower seeds

½ cup raw shelled pistachios, coarsely chopped

1 cup dried apricots, preferably unsulfured, thinly sliced

¼ cup sugar

½ teaspoon coarse salt

¼ cup honey

2 tablespoons neutral-tasting oil, such as canola or safflower

1 ½ teaspoons pure vanilla extract

2 large eggs plus 1 large egg white, lightly beaten

Vegetable oil cooking spray

1 Preheat oven to 350°F. Bring the water to a boil in a small saucepan. Add quinoa; return to a boil. Stir once; cover, and reduce heat to a simmer. Cook until quinoa is slightly underdone (it will finish cooking in the oven) and has absorbed most of the liquid, about 12 minutes. Using a slotted spoon, transfer quinoa to a rimmed baking sheet. Bake, fluffing with a fork occasionally, until pale golden, 30 to 35 minutes. Transfer to a large bowl, and let cool.

2 Spread oats evenly on the baking sheet; bake, stirring occasionally, until lightly browned, about 15 minutes. Add oats to bowl with quinoa. Spread seeds on baking sheet; bake, stirring occasionally, until lightly toasted, about 7 minutes. Add to quinoa mixture; let cool. Reduce oven temperature to 300°F.

3 Toss nuts, apricots, sugar, and salt with quinoa mixture. Mix honey, oil, and vanilla into eggs; stir into quinoa mixture.

4 Line an unrimmed baking sheet with parchment paper; lightly coat with cooking spray. Place ¼ cup mixture onto sheet for each cluster, spacing them 3 inches apart. Flatten to ¼ inch thick. Bake, rotating sheet halfway through, until crisp, about 25 minutes. Let cool completely on a wire rack. Store loosely covered with aluminum foil, for up to 2 days, at room temperature.

per serving (2 clusters): 329 calories; 3.4 g saturated fat; 7.2 g unsaturated fat; 42.3 mg cholesterol; 49 g carbohydrates; 10 g protein; 139 mg sodium; 5 g fiber

beet chips SERVES 4

A mandoline makes easy work of slicing beets paper thin; if you don't have one, you can use a very sharp knife, but the slices will take longer to dry out in the oven and won't be as crisp once cooled. You'll need four rimmed baking sheets to make the chips, or you can bake them in batches.

2 beets

1 teaspoon extra-virgin olive oil

1 Preheat oven to 350°F, with racks in upper and lower thirds. Peel beets and slice into 1⁄16-inch-thick rounds with a mandoline. In a large bowl, toss beets with the oil. Divide beets among two rimmed baking sheets, arranging them in single layers. Stack another rimmed baking sheet on top of each.

2 Bake until edges of beets begin to dry out, about 20 minutes. Remove top sheets and rotate bottom sheets from upper to lower racks and from front to back. Continue baking, uncovered, 10 to 20 minutes more, removing chips as they dry out completely (they will lighten in color). Transfer to a wire rack; chips will crisp as they cool. Store in an airtight container for up to 5 days at room temperature.

per serving: 28 calories; .2 g saturated fat; .3 g unsaturated fat; 0 mg cholesterol; 3.9 g carbohydrates; .7 g protein; 32 mg sodium; 1.1 g fiber

roasted red peppers with anchovies SERVES 4

Anchovies are among the best sources of omega-3 fatty acids. Here, the tiny fish top strips of roasted red peppers and are served over crusty bread—but the mixture can also be added to sandwiches or salads. Look for anchovy fillets packed in salt, which can be rinsed off for a less salty flavor than the oil-packed kind.

2 red bell peppers

1 garlic clove, very thinly sliced

1 tablespoon plus 1 teaspoon extra-virgin olive oil

4 anchovy fillets, quartered

Crushed red pepper flakes (optional)

1 Roast bell peppers directly over the flame of a gas burner, turning with tongs, until blackened all over. (Alternately, roast peppers under the broiler, turning, until skin has charred.) Transfer peppers to a large bowl, and cover with plastic wrap. Let steam about 15 minutes. Using paper towels, rub off skins; remove stems, ribs, and seeds. Cut each pepper lengthwise into 8 strips. Transfer to a small nonreactive (glass or ceramic) bowl.

2 Add garlic and 1 tablespoon oil to peppers; let marinate at least 1 hour (or up to 2 days in the refrigerator, covered tightly).

3 To serve, arrange peppers on a platter, and top each strip with an anchovy quarter. Sprinkle with crushed red pepper flakes, if desired, and drizzle with remaining teaspoon oil, dividing evenly.

per serving: 67 calories; 1 g saturated fat; 4 g unsaturated fat; 3 mg cholesterol; 4 g carbohydrates; 2 g protein; 149 mg sodium; 1 g fiber

chickpea nibbles and crunchy split pea bites

Loaded with folate, iron, and B vitamins, chickpeas and split peas are also high in protein and fiber. Here they combine to make a satisfying mid-afternoon snack; you can also serve either of them as an easy hors d'oeuvre, alongside a bowl of olives.

CHICKPEA NIBBLES
MAKES 1 CUP

- 1 can (15 ounces) chickpeas, drained and rinsed
- 2 tablespoons olive oil
  Coarse salt
- 1 teaspoon chili powder

Preheat oven to 375°F. Pat chickpeas dry, then toss in a bowl with oil, ½ teaspoon salt (or to taste), and the chili powder. Spread in an even layer on a rimmed baking sheet, and bake until crunchy, stirring occasionally, 40 to 45 minutes. Let cool before serving. Peas may be kept in an airtight container for 3 days at room temperature.

per ¼-cup serving: 239 calories; 1.3 g saturated fat; 7.9 g unsaturated fat; 0 mg cholesterol; 29.5 g carbohydrates; 9.5 g protein; 84 mg sodium; 5.1 g fiber

CRUNCHY SPLIT PEA BITES
MAKES 1½ CUPS

- 1 cup dried green or yellow split peas
- 3 cups water
- 4 teaspoons sesame oil
- 4 teaspoons neutral-tasting oil, such as canola or safflower
  Coarse salt

Place split peas in a large bowl; add the water and cover bowl with plastic wrap. Let soak at room temperature until softened, 4 to 5 hours.

Drain split peas and thoroughly pat dry with paper towels. Heat a large skillet over medium-high and add 2 teaspoons of each type of oil. Add half the peas and cook, stirring frequently, until they begin to turn golden brown in spots and become crunchy, 6 to 8 minutes. Transfer to a paper towel–lined baking sheet. Season with ¼ teaspoon salt (or to taste). Repeat with the remaining oil and peas. Let cool before serving. Peas may be kept for 3 days in an airtight container at room temperature.

per ¼-cup serving: 166 calories; .7 g saturated fat; 5.4 g unsaturated fat; 0 mg cholesterol; 20 g carbohydrates; 8.1 g protein; 52 mg sodium; 8.4 g fiber

spiced nuts and seeds MAKES 4 CUPS

Store-bought snack nuts tend to contain high amounts of salt and sugar, and can sit on the shelf for months. This healthier mixture relies on spices and honey for flavor, and it tastes much fresher than the prepackaged varieties.

- 3 cups raw nuts, such as walnuts and almonds
- ¼ cup flaxseed
- ¼ cup raw hulled sunflower seeds
- ¼ cup quinoa
- 2 large egg whites
  Coarse salt
- ¼ teaspoon cayenne pepper
- ¼ teaspoon ground cumin
- ¼ teaspoon ground cinnamon
- 2 tablespoons honey

1 Preheat oven to 325°F. Mix nuts, flaxseed, sunflower seeds, and quinoa in a bowl. In another bowl, whisk together egg whites and 1½ teaspoons salt with the cayenne, cumin, cinnamon, and honey. Pour over nut mixture, and toss to combine.

2 Spread evenly on a parchment-lined baking sheet, and bake until dry and darkened, stirring occasionally, about 30 minutes. Season with more salt, if desired. Remove mixture from parchment while cooling so it does not stick. Nuts can be stored for up to 2 weeks in an airtight container at room temperature.

per ¼-cup serving; 169 calories; 1.2 g saturated fat; 11.3 g unsaturated fat; 0 mg cholesterol; 8.4 g carbohydrates; 5.5 g protein; 113 mg sodium; 2.6 g fiber

SANDWICHES

AND WRAPS

open-faced tomato sandwiches with herbs and creamy tofu spread MAKES 2

These open-faced sandwiches are a delicious way to showcase the season's best tomatoes. Try the tofu spread as a low-fat and nutritious alternative to cream cheese; the recipe makes about three-quarters of a cup, enough for four additional sandwiches.

FOR THE SPREAD

- 7 ounces (½ package) firm or extra-firm tofu, drained
- 3 tablespoons neutral-tasting oil, such as canola or safflower
- 1 tablespoon extra-virgin olive oil
- 2 tablespoons fresh lemon juice

  Coarse salt

FOR THE SANDWICHES

- 4 slices whole-grain bread
- 2 tomatoes, cut into 8 slices
- ⅓ cup mixed fresh herb leaves, such as parsley, basil, chives, and cilantro, chopped (or left whole if small)

  Coarse salt

Pat dry tofu with a clean kitchen towel. Transfer to blender and puree with both oils and the lemon juice until smooth; season with ½ teaspoon salt (or to taste). Spread onto bread and top with tomato slices. Sprinkle with herbs and salt, and serve immediately.

per serving: 540 calories; 3 g saturated fat; 26.3 unsaturated fat; 0 mg cholesterol; 39.2 g carbohydrates; 18 g protein; 599 mg sodium; 7.5 g fiber

GREEK-YOGURT AND VEGETABLE
SANDWICHES

EGG SALAD SANDWICHES

greek-yogurt and vegetable sandwiches MAKES 2

A nutrition-rich combination of yogurt, carrots, walnuts, and avocado is made even more healthful with the addition of sprouts, an excellent source of phytonutrients.

2 carrots, peeled

1 ripe, firm avocado

4 slices whole-wheat bread

½ cup plain Greek-style yogurt (2 percent)

⅓ cup walnut pieces, toasted (page 53) and chopped

1 cup sunflower sprouts

1 teaspoon extra-virgin olive oil

Coarse salt and freshly ground pepper

1 Grate carrots on the large holes of a box grater. Cut avocado in half lengthwise, and remove pit. Peel and thinly slice.

2 Spread 2 slices of bread with the yogurt, dividing evenly. Top each with carrots, avocado, walnuts, and sunflower sprouts. Drizzle with oil, sprinkle with a pinch each of salt and pepper, and top with remaining slices of bread; serve.

per serving: 543 calories; 5 g saturated fat; 26.5 g unsaturated fat; 3.7 mg cholesterol; 50.5 g carbohydrates; 17.5 g protein; 529 mg sodium; 14.5 g fiber

egg salad sandwiches MAKES 4

Egg salad sandwiches are often loaded with mayonnaise, but this version relies instead on ricotta and yogurt for creaminess. Watercress and whole-grain bread are other healthful updates. Eggs, of course, provide high-quality protein in addition to a variety of other nutrients, such as choline.

8 large hard-cooked eggs (page 61)

3 tablespoons part-skim ricotta cheese

3 tablespoons plain Greek-style yogurt (2 percent)

2 teaspoons Dijon mustard

2 teaspoons finely chopped fresh chives

Coarse salt and freshly ground pepper

2 cups watercress, thick stems removed

8 thin slices whole-grain bread

1 Peel eggs; cut in half, and remove yolks. Crumble yolks into a bowl. Finely chop egg whites, and add to bowl.

2 Whisk together ricotta, yogurt, mustard, chives, and ½ teaspoon salt in a small bowl; season with pepper. Add to egg mixture, and gently stir to combine.

3 Arrange egg salad, then watercress, over 4 slices of bread, dividing evenly. Top with remaining slices of bread, and serve.

per serving: 308 calories; 4.9 g saturated fat; 6.7 g unsaturated fat; 429 mg cholesterol; 26.6 g carbohydrates; 20.2 g protein; 718 mg sodium; 3.4 g fiber

salmon salad and curried egg on multigrain bread SERVES 4

Wild salmon is widely available in cans. To ensure that you're getting the most sustainable option, look for the blue Marine Stewardship Council logo on the label. The warming spices that make up curry powder—typically a combination of turmeric, coriander, cinnamon, and cumin, among others—also offer a wealth of health benefits, including boosting metabolism and decreasing inflammation.

1 can (7.5 ounces) wild red Alaskan or sockeye salmon (about 1 cup), drained

1 tablespoon plus 1 teaspoon extra-virgin olive oil

2 teaspoons finely grated lemon zest, plus 1 tablespoon fresh lemon juice

2 teaspoons minced shallot

Coarse salt and freshly ground pepper

4 slices multigrain bread

4 hard-cooked eggs (page 61)

½ teaspoon curry powder

1 pint pea shoots or sprouts, such as alfalfa, radish, or broccoli

1 Mix salmon and oil in a bowl, using a fork to flake the salmon. Stir in 1 teaspoon lemon zest along with the lemon juice and shallot. Season with pepper. Spread onto bread slices, dividing evenly.

2 Peel and slice eggs, and place 2 slices on each piece of bread. Mix 1½ teaspoons salt with the curry powder in a small bowl; sprinkle on top of each egg slice. Dividing evenly, sprinkle each with remaining lemon zest and top with sprouts; serve.

per serving: 318 calories; 3.1 g saturated fat; 9.3 g unsaturated fat; 235 mg cholesterol; 23.3 g carbohydrates; 21.3 g protein; 620 mg sodium; 2.2 g fiber

grilled mushroom burgers with white bean spread MAKES 4

Portobello mushrooms are a nutritious and satisfying alternative to burgers made with beef or turkey. Here they are accompanied by a spread of pureed cannellini beans for added protein — and flavor. To clean the mushroom caps, wipe them with a damp paper towel; do not rinse or soak, or they will remain soggy even after cooking.

2 large garlic cloves, minced

2 tablespoons chopped fresh thyme

1 cup canned cannellini beans, drained and rinsed

2 tablespoons plus 2 teaspoons extra-virgin olive oil

Freshly ground pepper

8 large portobello mushroom caps (about 1 pound), cleaned

1 tablespoon plus 1 teaspoon balsamic vinegar

2 large red onions (about 1 pound), sliced ¼ inch thick

4 whole-grain hamburger buns

4 thin slices cheddar cheese (2 ounces)

½ small bunch arugula (about 2½ ounces), washed and dried

1 Heat a grill or grill pan to medium (if using a charcoal grill, coals are ready when you can hold your hand 5 inches above grill for just 6 to 8 seconds). In a food processor, puree one-quarter of the garlic (about ½ teaspoon), 1 tablespoon thyme, the cannellini beans, and 1 teaspoon oil until smooth. If mixture is too thick to spread, add a bit of water. Season with pepper, and pulse to combine.

2 Combine the remaining garlic and remaining 1 tablespoon thyme with 1 tablespoon plus 2 teaspoons oil in a shallow dish. Place the mushroom caps in the garlic mixture, and turn to coat. Season with pepper; drizzle with vinegar.

3 Place onion slices on a plate, and lightly coat each side with remaining 2 teaspoons oil. Grill the onions until lightly charred on the first side, about 3 minutes. Flip the onions, and continue grilling until tender and charred on the other side, about 3 minutes more. Transfer onions to a clean plate; cover to keep warm.

4 Working in batches if necessary, place mushrooms on the grill, stem side up. Grill until browned on the first side and juices have begun to collect in the centers, about 5 minutes. Flip mushrooms, and continue cooking until stem side of each cap is browned and center is tender, about 4 minutes more.

5 Split hamburger buns, and place cut side down on the grill; cook just until warm and toasted. Spread ¼ cup bean puree on the bottom half of each bun, and top with 2 grilled mushroom caps. Layer each with sliced cheese, grilled onions, and a small handful of arugula. Top with remaining roll halves, and serve.

per serving: 382 calories; 4.2 g saturated fat; 9.8 g unsaturated fat; 15 mg cholesterol; 46.7 g carbohydrates; 14 g protein; 447 mg sodium; 9.2 g fiber

kiwifruit summer rolls SERVES 4

This refreshing roll packs a lot of health within its wrapper: Kiwifruit provides vitamin C; savory peanuts are rich with B vitamins, vitamin E, and healthy monounsaturated fat; fresh mint leaves soothe the digestive tract. Look for the noodles and wrappers in the Asian foods section of your grocery store.

2 ounces thin rice noodles

¼ cup packed fresh mint leaves

¼ cup honey

1 tablespoon fresh lime juice

⅛ teaspoon chili powder

8 round spring roll wrappers (8-inch)

4 kiwifruit, sliced in half lengthwise, peeled (page 39), and thinly sliced crosswise

⅓ cup peanuts, coarsely chopped

1 Cook noodles in a pot of boiling water until tender, according to package directions. Drain and rinse under cool water; pat dry with paper towels. In a bowl, toss noodles with mint and 1 tablespoon honey.

2 For the dipping sauce, whisk remaining 3 tablespoons honey with 1 tablespoon water, the lime juice, and chili powder.

3 Forming one roll at a time, soak wrapper in a bowl of warm water until softened, about 30 seconds. Lift out and transfer to work surface. Dividing evenly, layer kiwi, noodles, and peanuts at one end of wrapper. Fold over ends and roll tightly to enclose filling. Cover rolls with a damp kitchen cloth while you work.

4 To serve, slice rolls in half on the diagonal, and pass dipping sauce alongside.

per serving: 275 calories; .9 g saturated fat; 5.2 g unsaturated fat; 0 mg cholesterol; 52 g carbohydrates; 5.8 g protein; 111 mg sodium; 4.1 g fiber

pita sandwiches with spinach-chickpea spread SERVES 4

Iron- and folate-rich chickpeas and spinach combine in a delicious sandwich spread that can also be served atop halved cherry tomatoes for a snack.

1 tablespoon extra-virgin olive oil

2 garlic cloves, minced

1 can (15 ounces) chickpeas, drained and rinsed

1 tablespoon plus 1 teaspoon fresh lemon juice

10 ounces spinach, trimmed, washed well, and drained

Coarse salt

½ teaspoon crushed red pepper flakes

2 teaspoons tahini (sesame seed paste)

2 whole-wheat pitas (6-inch), halved

1 tomato, thinly sliced

1 Heat oil in a large saucepan over medium. Cook garlic, stirring, until fragrant, about 1 minute. Add chickpeas and 1 tablespoon lemon juice. Cook, stirring, 1 minute. Add spinach, ¼ teaspoon salt, and the crushed red pepper flakes. Cover; raise heat to medium-high. Cook, stirring once, until spinach has wilted, about 4 minutes. Uncover; raise heat to high. Cook, stirring, until most of the liquid has evaporated, about 2 minutes. Let cool.

2 Pulse chickpea mixture with tahini, remaining 1 teaspoon lemon juice, and ¼ teaspoon salt in a food processor until slightly chunky. (Spread can be refrigerated for up to 2 days in an airtight container.)

3 To serve, fill each pita half with ¼ cup spread, and layer with tomato slices.

per serving: 265 calories; .9 g saturated fat; 4.7 g unsaturated fat; 0 mg cholesterol; 42 g carbohydrates; 11.8 g protein; 494 mg sodium; 8.7 g fiber

quinoa-and-turkey patties in pita with tahini sauce SERVES 6

These patties are inspired by the Middle Eastern dish *kibbe,* most often made of ground lamb and bulgur wheat. The combination of turkey and quinoa is particularly rich in protein, with a chewy texture that contrasts nicely with the crisp cucumber and red-onion slices, and the creamy tahini dressing served alongside.

2¼ cups water, or more as needed

1 cup quinoa, rinsed and drained

1 garlic clove

¼ cup tahini (sesame seed paste)

¼ cup fresh lemon juice

12 ounces ground turkey, preferably at least 7% fat

¼ teaspoon plus 1 pinch ground allspice

½ teaspoon plus 1 pinch ground cumin

Pinch of crushed red pepper flakes (optional)

2 tablespoons finely chopped fresh mint

2 scallions, trimmed and finely chopped

Coarse salt

2 teaspoons neutral-tasting oil, such as canola or safflower, plus more if needed

6 lettuce leaves, torn into large pieces

1 English cucumber, thinly sliced

1 small red onion, halved and thinly sliced

6 pitas (6-inch)

1 Bring 2 cups water to a boil in a medium saucepan. Add quinoa; return to a boil. Stir once, cover, and reduce heat to a simmer. Cook until quinoa is tender but still chewy and has absorbed all the liquid, about 15 minutes. Fluff quinoa with a fork; let cool.

2 Meanwhile, process garlic, tahini, lemon juice, and remaining ¼ cup water in a food processor until smooth. If mixture is too thick to pour, thin with more water. Transfer dressing to a small bowl; cover and refrigerate.

3 In a clean food processor, pulse turkey, allspice, cumin, crushed red pepper flakes (if using), mint, scallions, and ¾ teaspoon salt until a smooth paste forms. Add quinoa; process until mixture comes together around the blade, about 2 minutes. Transfer to a bowl. With dampened hands, roll about 2 tablespoons quinoa mixture into a ball; flatten slightly, and place on a plate. Repeat with remaining mixture to make 24 patties.

4 Heat the oil in a large cast-iron skillet or grill pan over medium, until hot but not smoking. Working in batches, fry patties until cooked through, about 8 minutes per side. Transfer patties to a clean plate, and cover loosely with foil to keep warm. Add more oil to skillet between batches as necessary.

5 Divide lettuce, cucumber, and red onion evenly among pita breads. Top each with 4 quinoa patties, then drizzle each sandwich with about 1 tablespoon tahini dressing. Fold pitas over filling, and serve.

per serving: 434 calories; 2.1 g saturated fat; 6.9 g unsaturated fat; 32.5 mg cholesterol; 60 g carbohydrates; 23 g protein; 380 mg sodium; 5.1 g fiber

shiitake nori rolls SERVES 6

In these vegetarian rolls, shredded cabbage adds cancer-fighting beta-carotene; nori—sheets of dried seaweed—supplies calcium, magnesium, and iron; and shiitakes boost the immune system, thanks to the active compound lentinan. Look for soba noodles and nori in the Asian foods section of your grocery store.

12 dried shiitake mushrooms (1 to 2 ounces)

1½ cups hot water

2 teaspoons fresh lime juice

2 tablespoons low-sodium tamari soy sauce

2 tablespoons plus 1 teaspoon finely chopped cilantro

Coarse salt

4 ounces soba noodles (preferably 100 percent buckwheat)

½ teaspoon toasted sesame oil

1 tablespoon neutral-tasting oil, such as canola or safflower

2 large shallots, thinly sliced

4 garlic cloves, minced

2 tablespoons minced peeled fresh ginger

5 cups finely shredded savoy cabbage (from about ½ head)

4 scallions, trimmed (3 thinly sliced crosswise on the diagonal; 1 julienned for sauce)

6 nori sheets

1 Place dried mushrooms in a bowl and add the hot water. Set a small bowl or plate on top of mushrooms to keep them submerged. Let stand until mushrooms are soft, about 20 minutes. Remove mushrooms with a slotted spoon, and cut into ¼-inch strips. Pass soaking liquid through a sieve into another bowl; reserve liquid.

2 To make the dipping sauce, stir together 1 cup reserved liquid, the lime juice, 1 teaspoon each tamari and cilantro, and a pinch of salt.

3 Bring a medium pot of water to a boil. Cook noodles according to package instructions. Drain in a colander. Rinse with cold water; drain again. Transfer to a bowl; toss with sesame oil and remaining 2 tablespoons cilantro.

4 Heat the canola oil in a large skillet over medium-high. Stir in shallots, garlic, and ginger. Cook, stirring occasionally, until shallots begin to brown, about 2 minutes (if the shallots begin to stick to pan, stir in 1 tablespoon reserved liquid). Add cabbage, and toss to combine. Reduce heat to medium. Cook, stirring occasionally, until cabbage wilts slightly, about 2 minutes. Stir in mushrooms, ¼ cup reserved soaking liquid, and remaining 1 tablespoon plus 2 teaspoons tamari. Cover, and cook, stirring occasionally, until cabbage is tender, about 7 minutes. Stir in sliced scallions. Remove from heat.

5 Using tongs, pass each nori sheet over the medium-hot flame of a gas burner, turning, until fragrant and crisp, about three times on each side. (Alternatively, toast sheets directly over a medium-hot electric burner for 30 seconds to 1 minute each, flipping once.)

6 Forming one roll at a time, and dividing filling evenly, place noodles along one edge of the nori, leaving a 1-inch border; top with cabbage mixture. Starting at the side with the filling, roll up sheet, enclosing filling. Slice rolls in half on the diagonal. Garnish dipping sauce with julienned scallion, and serve.

per serving: 151 calories; .3 g saturated fat; 2.5 g unsaturated fat; 0 mg cholesterol; 28 g carbohydrates; 6.4 g protein; 461 mg sodium; 3.6 g fiber

SOUPS AND

STEWS

carrot soup SERVES 6

Made with both carrots and carrot juice, this brightly colored soup is loaded with beta-carotene. If you don't have a vegetable juicer, look for bottled carrot juice at your grocery store or health-food market, or better yet, buy it fresh from a juice bar.

1 tablespoon unsalted butter

1 onion, coarsely chopped

1 pound carrots, chopped

2 cups (16 ounces) carrot juice

2 cups homemade or reduced-sodium store-bought chicken or vegetable broth

½ teaspoon ground cumin

1 tablespoon honey

Coarse salt and freshly ground white pepper

2 tablespoons half-and-half (optional)

Snipped fresh chives, for garnish

Cayenne pepper, for garnish

1 Heat butter in a large saucepan over medium-low. Cook onion, stirring occasionally, until translucent, about 5 minutes. Add carrots; cook until very tender, stirring occasionally, about 15 minutes. Add carrot juice, broth, cumin, honey, 1 teaspoon salt, and ¼ teaspoon white pepper. Bring to a simmer; cook until vegetables are very soft, about 30 minutes.

2 Let soup cool slightly. Working in batches, puree soup in a blender or food processor, filling no more than halfway each time. (Alternately, use an immersion blender.) Return to pan; warm over low heat, thinning with a little water if necessary. Stir in half-and-half, if using. Serve immediately, garnished with chives and cayenne.

per serving: 105 calories; 1.2 g saturated fat; .7 g unsaturated fat; 5 mg cholesterol; 20.2 g carbohydrates; 1.9 g protein; 535 mg sodium; .9 g fiber

autumn greens soup SERVES 4

Verdant, leafy greens lend this soup a wealth of vitamins and minerals. If using chard, kale, or other hearty greens, remove the thickest center ribs; finely chop the ribs and add to the pot with the other ingredients. Packages of "stir-fry" greens are a quick alternative.

1 quart homemade or reduced-sodium store-bought chicken or vegetable broth

1 russet potato, peeled and cut into ½-inch dice

2 garlic cloves

2 scallions, trimmed and sliced

3 cups mixed leafy greens, such as spinach, chard, and kale, trimmed, washed, drained, and chopped

Coarse salt and freshly ground pepper

Shaved parmesan cheese

1 Bring broth to a boil in a medium saucepan; add potato, garlic, scallions, mixed greens, and ½ teaspoon salt. Simmer until potato is tender, 5 to 10 minutes.

2 Let soup cool slightly. Working in batches, puree soup in a blender or food processor, filling no more than halfway each time. (Alternately, use an immersion blender.) Season with pepper and more salt, if desired. Serve immediately, garnished with parmesan shavings.

per serving: 75 calories; .4 g saturated fat; 1 g unsaturated fat; 0 mg cholesterol; 11.8 g carbohydrates; 6.6 g protein; 492 mg sodium; 1.5 g fiber

CARROT SOUP

AUTUMN GREENS SOUP

chilled asparagus soup with spinach and avocado SERVES 4

Serve this no-cook soup straight from the blender when it is still frothy, or well chilled during warmer months. Bright, lemony sorrel makes a nice garnish. If you are unable to find pencil-thin asparagus, trim thicker stalks with a vegetable peeler or paring knife.

- 1 Kirby cucumber, peeled
- 8 ounces asparagus, preferably pencil thin, tough ends trimmed and spears cut into 2-inch pieces
- 2 cups cold water
- 4 ounces spinach, trimmed, washed well, and drained
- 4 scallions, trimmed and cut into 2-inch lengths
- 1 ripe, firm avocado, halved lengthwise, pitted, and peeled
- ¼ cup packed fresh mint, plus more for garnish
- 2 tablespoons fresh lemon juice

  Coarse salt and freshly ground pepper
- 4 to 6 fresh sorrel leaves, cut into fine strips, for garnish (optional)

1 Halve cucumber lengthwise; cut one half into eighths and the other into ¼-inch dice. Puree asparagus in a blender with ½ cup cold water until smooth.

2 Add spinach, scallions, cucumber eighths, and another ½ cup water. Blend until completely smooth. Add avocado, mint, and lemon juice; puree until smooth, adding remaining 1 cup water a little at a time until soup reaches desired consistency. Add ¾ teaspoon salt, and season with pepper. Scrape down sides of blender with a flexible spatula, and puree 5 seconds more. If you would like the soup chilled, refrigerate at least 30 minutes (and up to 1 day, covered).

3 Divide soup among four bowls, and garnish each with diced cucumber, sorrel (if using), and a mint sprig. Serve immediately.

per serving: 119 calories; 1.1 g saturated fat; 6 g unsaturated fat; 0 mg cholesterol; 11 g carbohydrates; 3.9 g protein; 277 mg sodium; 6.4 g fiber

golden pepper soup SERVES 6

Sweet yellow peppers are exceptionally rich in vitamin C. Serve the soup either hot for a comforting wintertime meal, or chilled in the warm-weather months.

- 3 cups homemade or reduced-sodium store-bought chicken or vegetable broth
- Generous pinch of saffron threads
- 1 tablespoon unsalted butter
- 1 large onion, diced
- 3 garlic cloves, minced
- 2 celery stalks, diced
- 4 large yellow bell peppers (about 2 pounds), ribs and seeds removed, diced
- ¼ cup dry white wine
- Coarse salt
- ½ teaspoon ground cumin
- 2 tablespoons half-and-half or milk
- Pinch of cayenne pepper, or to taste
- Plain low-fat yogurt, for garnish

1 Bring broth to a boil in a small saucepan. Add saffron; stir to dissolve. Turn off heat; cover and let steep.

2 Heat butter in a large saucepan over medium-low. Cook onion and garlic, stirring frequently, until they begin to soften, about 4 minutes. Add celery and bell peppers, cover, and cook, stirring occasionally, until softened, 18 to 20 minutes.

3 Add wine and cook, stirring occasionally, until evaporated. Add broth, 1 teaspoon salt, and the cumin. Bring to a simmer, and cook until vegetables are very tender, about 10 minutes.

4 Remove from heat; let soup cool slightly. Working in batches, puree soup in a blender or food processor, filling no more than halfway each time. (Alternately, use an immersion blender.) Return to clean saucepan; stir in half-and-half or milk, and reheat gently (do not boil, as mixture will curdle). Season with cayenne pepper. Serve immediately, or let cool completely and refrigerate at least 2 hours (and up to 2 days). Garnish with yogurt before serving.

per serving: 96 calories; 1.6 saturated fat; 1.1 g unsaturated fat; 5.5 mg cholesterol; 13 g carbohydrates; 4.3 g protein; 373 mg sodium; 1.8 g fiber

sweet red pepper and beet soup SERVES 8

Bell peppers offer B vitamins and beta-carotene; beets bring even more beta-carotene, plus folic acid. If the beets come with their greens attached, reserve them to sauté as you would other leafy greens.

1 tablespoon extra-virgin olive oil

2 shallots, coarsely chopped

3 red bell peppers (about 1½ pounds), ribs and seeds removed, cut into ½-inch pieces

2 red beets (about 1 pound), trimmed, peeled, and cut into ½-inch pieces

1 cup water

3½ cups homemade or reduced-sodium store-bought chicken or vegetable broth

2 tablespoons fresh lemon juice

Coarse salt and freshly ground pepper

4 ounces fresh goat cheese, crumbled (about 1 cup)

Lemon wedges, for serving

1 Heat oil in a medium saucepan over medium. Cook shallots, stirring occasionally, until translucent and tender, about 4 minutes. Add bell peppers and beets, and stir to coat. Add the water and broth, and bring to a boil. Cover partially, and reduce heat to a simmer. Cook until beets are very tender when pierced with the tip of a sharp knife, about 1 hour.

2 Let cool slightly. Stir in lemon juice; add 1 teaspoon salt, and season with pepper. Working in batches, puree soup in a blender or food processor, filling no more than halfway each time. (Alternately, use an immersion blender.) Transfer to a large bowl, and refrigerate until chilled, up to overnight (covered).

3 Divide soup among bowls. Sprinkle evenly with goat cheese, season with pepper and more salt, if desired, and serve with lemon wedges.

per serving: 125 calories; 2.6 g saturated fat; 2 g unsaturated fat; 6.5 mg cholesterol; 13.9 g carbohydrates; 6.7 g protein; 374 mg sodium; 3.4 g fiber

hearty spinach and chickpea soup SERVES 6

Woodsy shiitake mushrooms, protein-rich chickpeas, and brown rice make this a substantial, satisfying soup.

1⅓ cups water

½ cup short-grain brown rice

1 tablespoon olive oil, plus more for drizzling

1 onion, finely chopped (1½ cups)

2 garlic cloves, minced

8 ounces fresh shiitake mushrooms, stems removed, caps cleaned and thinly sliced (about 4 cups)

6 cups homemade or reduced-sodium store-bought chicken or vegetable broth

½ teaspoon dried rosemary, crumbled

1 can (15 ounces) chickpeas, drained and rinsed

10 ounces baby spinach

Coarse salt and freshly ground pepper

2 ounces grated parmesan cheese (½ cup)

1 In a large saucepan, bring the water to a rapid boil. Stir in brown rice and return to a boil; reduce heat to a simmer. Cover and cook until rice is tender and has absorbed all the liquid, 30 to 40 minutes.

2 Meanwhile, in a large saucepan or Dutch oven, heat oil over medium. Cook onion, stirring occasionally, until tender, about 5 minutes. Add garlic and mushrooms; cook, stirring occasionally, until mushrooms are tender, about 5 minutes. Add broth and rosemary; bring to a boil. Cover and remove from heat.

3 Stir rice and chickpeas into broth mixture; return to a boil. Reduce to a simmer, cover, and continue cooking 5 minutes more to allow flavors to blend.

4 Stir in spinach and cook, uncovered, until just wilted, about 1 minute. Add ½ teaspoon salt, or to taste, and season with pepper. Serve immediately, sprinkled with grated parmesan and drizzled with more oil.

per serving: 244 calories; 2 g saturated fat; 4.1 g unsaturated fat; 5.9 mg cholesterol; 32.8 g carbohydrates; 14.9 g protein; 395 mg sodium; 5.2 g fiber

spicy sweet potato soup SERVES 4

The toasted turmeric, coriander, and cumin in this Indian-influenced soup have soothing, anti-inflammatory benefits, and add so much flavor, there's little need for salt. With only one tablespoon of oil in the whole pot, the soup is also low in fat.

1 tablespoon neutral-tasting oil, such as canola or safflower

¼ teaspoon cumin seeds

½ teaspoon coriander seeds, crushed

½ teaspoon yellow mustard seeds

¼ teaspoon turmeric

1 piece (2 inches) fresh ginger, peeled and cut into fine strips

2 garlic cloves, minced

1 small hot chile (such as Thai bird chile), finely chopped (ribs and seeds removed for less heat, if desired)

3 canned whole plum tomatoes, coarsely chopped

3½ cups homemade or reduced-sodium store-bought chicken or vegetable broth

Coarse salt

1 sweet potato (about 8 ounces), peeled, quartered lengthwise, and cut crosswise into ¼-inch-thick pieces

Lime wedges, for serving

Cilantro sprigs, for serving (optional)

1 Heat oil in a medium saucepan over medium-high. Add cumin, coriander, and mustard seeds. Cook, shaking pan often, until seeds are fragrant and begin to pop, about 30 seconds. Add turmeric, ginger, garlic, and chile; cook, stirring, 1 minute.

2 Stir in tomatoes, broth, and ½ teaspoon salt; bring to a boil. Add sweet potato; return to a boil. Reduce heat; simmer until sweet potato is tender, about 10 minutes. Serve immediately, with lime wedges and cilantro, as desired.

per serving: 131 calories; .7 g saturated fat; 4.1 g unsaturated fat; 0 mg cholesterol; 17.6 g carbohydrates; 6 g protein; 382 mg sodium; 2.6 g fiber

lentil, carrot, and lemon soup with fresh dill SERVES 4

The fiber in lentils helps to lower cholesterol and regulate blood sugar. French green lentils cook more quickly and retain a firmer texture than the more common brown ones.

1½ cups French green lentils

4 carrots, peeled and sliced
½ inch thick on the diagonal
(1½ cups)

4 garlic cloves, thinly sliced

Coarse salt and freshly
ground pepper

3 tablespoons fresh lemon
juice (from 1 to 2 lemons)

½ cup coarsely chopped fresh
dill, for garnish

Combine lentils with carrots, garlic, and 1 teaspoon salt in a medium saucepan. Add enough water to cover by 2 inches (about 6 cups), and bring to a boil. Reduce heat to a simmer, and cook (uncovered), stirring occasionally, until carrots are tender, 20 to 25 minutes. Stir in lemon juice and season with pepper and more salt, as desired. Add about 2 tablespoons chopped dill to each bowl just before serving.

per serving: 261 calories; 0 g saturated fat; .1 g unsaturated fat; 0 mg cholesterol; 49.2 g carbohydrates; 15.9 g protein; 538 mg sodium; 12.6 g fiber

chilled tomato-dill soup SERVES 8

Heating tomatoes helps make the cancer-fighting carotenoid lycopene more available to the body. Because lycopene is fat soluble, cooking tomatoes in a little oil helps the body absorb even more of this potent antioxidant.

TOMATO-DILL SOUP

- 12 ripe tomatoes (about 5 pounds), halved lengthwise
- Coarse salt and freshly ground pepper
- 15 large sprigs dill
- 1 navel orange
- 1 tablespoon olive oil
- 1 large garlic clove, minced
- 1 small onion, finely chopped
- 2 cups homemade or reduced-sodium store-bought chicken or vegetable broth
- 2 cups water
- 2 tablespoons balsamic vinegar
- ½ cup plain low-fat yogurt
- Spicy Croutons (see right)

Preheat oven to 450°F. Arrange tomatoes on a rimmed baking sheet, cut side up, and sprinkle with ½ teaspoon salt. Roast until softened, about 30 minutes. Let cool and peel off skin.

Tie 13 dill sprigs into a bundle with kitchen twine. With a vegetable peeler, remove a 2-inch strip of orange zest. Squeeze juice from orange.

Heat oil in a medium pot over low. Cook garlic and onion, stirring occasionally, until translucent, about 7 minutes. Add tomatoes, broth, dill bundle, reserved orange zest and juice, 1¼ teaspoons salt, and the water; season with pepper. Bring to a boil. Reduce heat to medium low; simmer 20 minutes. Let cool slightly. Discard dill and zest.

Working in batches, puree soup in a blender or food processor, filling no more than halfway each

time. (Alternately, use an immersion blender.) Stir in vinegar, then let cool completely. Cover and refrigerate at least 2 hours, or up to overnight.

Divide soup among eight bowls; garnish each with 1 tablespoon yogurt. Snip remaining dill over soup; serve with croutons.

per serving: 100 calories; .5 g saturated fat; 1.9 g unsaturated fat; .9 mg cholesterol; 17.3 g carbohydrates; 3.9 g protein; 442 mg sodium; 4.2 g fiber

SPICY CROUTONS
MAKES 8 LARGE CROUTONS

Any combination of fennel, dill, caraway, or celery seed works well here; their flavors complement the paprika on the croutons as well as the dill and tomato in the soup.

- 8 slices (¼ inch thick) country-style bread
- 2 teaspoons extra-virgin olive oil
- 2 tablespoons spice seeds, such as fennel, dill, caraway, or celery seed, toasted (page 107)
- ¼ teaspoon paprika (sweet or hot)
- Coarse salt

Preheat oven to 400°F. Brush bread with olive oil, dividing evenly; place on a baking sheet.

In a spice grinder or clean coffee mill, finely grind seeds to a powder. Transfer to a small bowl; stir in paprika and ¼ teaspoon salt. Place spice combination in a fine sieve; sift over bread. Brush again with olive oil; toast until crisp, about 15 minutes.

per serving (slice): 126 calories; 1 g saturated fat; .2 g unsaturated fat; 3 mg cholesterol; 23 g carbohydrates; 3.3 g protein; 282 mg sodium; 1.4 g fiber

mushroom soup with poached eggs and parmesan cheese SERVES 4

This refined mushroom soup, made with dried and fresh varieties and topped with a poached egg, is beautiful *and* nutritious. Look for porcini mushrooms near the produce section of your grocery store.

3½ cups water

½ ounce (about ½ cup) dried mushrooms, such as porcini

1½ tablespoons extra-virgin olive oil

1 onion, halved and thinly sliced

3 garlic cloves, minced

1 celery stalk, finely chopped

1 pound cremini or white button mushrooms, caps and stems thinly sliced lengthwise (about 6 cups)

Coarse salt and freshly ground pepper

½ cup dry white wine

2 cups homemade or reduced-sodium store-bought chicken or vegetable broth

1 to 2 tablespoons finely chopped fresh tarragon, plus 4 sprigs for garnish

4 large eggs, poached (see below)

1 ounce parmesan cheese, shaved (½ cup)

1 Bring 2 cups water to a boil. Place dried mushrooms in a bowl, then pour in the boiling water; cover, and let soak until soft, about 20 minutes. Lift out mushrooms; squeeze out excess liquid into bowl. Finely chop mushrooms. Pass soaking liquid through a fine sieve into another bowl; reserve.

2 Heat oil in a medium saucepan over medium. Add onion, garlic, and celery; cook, stirring occasionally, until soft, about 8 minutes. Add fresh mushrooms and ½ teaspoon salt; cook, stirring occasionally, until most of the liquid has evaporated and mushrooms are soft, about 12 minutes. Raise heat to high. Add wine, reserved dried mushrooms and soaking liquid, broth, and remaining 1½ cups water; bring to a simmer. Reduce heat to medium low; cook 30 minutes. Add chopped tarragon.

3 Divide soup among four bowls. Transfer a poached egg to each bowl; top with cheese, dividing evenly. Season with pepper, and garnish each serving with a tarragon sprig.

per serving: 252 calories; 3.8 g saturated fat; 8.6 g unsaturated fat; 218 mg cholesterol; 12.8 g carbohydrates; 15.9 g protein; 477 mg sodium; 1.5 g fiber

POACHING EGGS
Bring a large skillet filled with 2 inches of water to a simmer over medium heat. Add 1 tablespoon vinegar. Break 1 egg into a cup, and then gently slide egg out of cup into skillet. Repeat with remaining eggs. Simmer until whites are set and yolks are slightly set but still soft, about 3 minutes. With a slotted spatula, transfer 1 egg at a time to paper towels to drain. If desired, trim edges with a paring knife or kitchen shears.

miso soup with tofu, spinach, and carrots SERVES 4

Be sure to purchase firm or extra-firm tofu for this soup, as it will hold up better in hot liquid than softer varieties. Miso should be added only at the end of cooking because its flavor and healthful qualities are affected when it's boiled or exposed to prolonged high temperatures. Whisk it with a bit of liquid first so that it is quickly and evenly distributed.

3 cups homemade or reduced-sodium store-bought vegetable or chicken broth

2 cups water

2 carrots, peeled and cut into matchsticks

6 ounces spinach, tough stems removed, washed well and drained, cut into 1-inch strips

7 ounces (½ package) firm or extra-firm tofu, drained and cut into ¾-inch cubes

2 tablespoons white miso

1 scallion, trimmed and cut into 1-inch lengths

1 In a medium saucepan, bring broth and the water to a boil over high heat. Reduce heat to medium-low, and add carrots. Cook until carrots are crisp-tender, about 2 minutes.

2 Add spinach and tofu, and stir to combine. Continue cooking just until spinach is wilted and tofu is heated through, about 1 minute more.

3 Place miso in a small bowl, and add ¼ cup cooking liquid, stirring until miso is dissolved. Add mixture to saucepan, and stir to combine; do not let soup boil. Remove from heat. Serve immediately, garnished with scallion.

per serving: 102 calories; 0 g saturated fat; .3 g unsaturated fat; 0 mg cholesterol; 13 g carbohydrates; 6.7 g protein; 640 mg sodium; 3.4 g fiber

polenta and spinach soup SERVES 4

In this simple dish that originated in the northeast of Italy, olive oil serves as both a key ingredient and a garnish.

½ cup plus 4 teaspoons extra-virgin olive oil

3 garlic cloves, minced

6 cups water

½ cup yellow stone-ground cornmeal

2 ounces finely grated parmesan cheese (½ cup)

3 cups coarsely chopped baby spinach (about 2 ounces)

Coarse salt and freshly ground pepper

1 lemon, cut into wedges

1 Heat ¼ cup oil and the garlic in a medium saucepan over medium until garlic is fragrant, stirring frequently, about 1 minute.

2 Add the water; bring to a boil. Whisking constantly, add cornmeal in a slow, steady stream. Reduce heat to medium; cook, stirring occasionally, until soup has thickened slightly, about 8 minutes. Add cheese and ¼ cup oil; cook, stirring, until oil is incorporated, about 1 minute. Stir in spinach and 1 teaspoon salt; cook, stirring, until spinach is bright green and wilted, about 1 minute more.

3 Divide soup among four bowls; drizzle each with 1 teaspoon oil. Season soup with pepper and more salt, as desired, and serve with lemon wedges.

per serving: 409 calories; 6.4 g saturated fat; 29.5 g unsaturated fat; 8.8 mg cholesterol; 16.8 g carbohydrates; 5.9 g protein; 668 mg sodium; 2.6 g fiber

soba noodle soup with shiitakes and spinach SERVES 4

Traditional Japanese soba noodles can be made of wheat or buckwheat, a fruit seed related to rhubarb that's loaded with manganese and the antioxidants quercetin and kaempferol. Because the seed is also gluten free, buckwheat noodles are a good choice for those with gluten sensitivities.

2 tablespoons neutral-tasting oil, such as canola or safflower

12 ounces shiitake mushrooms, stems removed, caps cleaned and thinly sliced

4 scallions, trimmed, white and green parts separated and thinly sliced

1 garlic clove, minced

1 tablespoon minced peeled fresh ginger

Coarse salt

4 cups homemade or reduced-sodium store-bought chicken or vegetable broth

3 cups water

4 ounces soba noodles (preferably 100 percent buckwheat)

1 bunch flat-leaf spinach, trimmed, washed well, and drained, and torn into bite-size pieces

2 tablespoons fresh lime juice (from 1 to 2 limes)

1 tablespoon low-sodium tamari soy sauce

1 In a large saucepan, heat oil over medium. Add mushrooms, scallion whites, garlic, ginger, and ¼ teaspoon salt. Cook, stirring occasionally, until mushrooms are tender, about 6 minutes.

2 Add broth and the water; bring to a boil. Add soba; reduce heat to a simmer, and cook 5 minutes. Add spinach; cook just until wilted, about 1 minute. Add lime juice and tamari. Serve immediately, garnished with scallion greens.

per serving: 249 calories; 1 g saturated fat; 7.2 g unsaturated fat; 0 mg cholesterol; 34.6 g carbohydrates; 14.3 g protein; 647 mg sodium; 3.2 g fiber

chili with chicken and beans SERVES 6

For milder chili, reduce the green chiles by half. You can also replace the canned beans with 4 cups cooked dried beans (page 202); replace half the chicken broth with bean cooking liquid.

1 tablespoon plus 1 teaspoon olive oil

1 tablespoon cumin seeds

2 onions, finely chopped (about 3 cups)

5 garlic cloves, coarsely chopped

1 green bell pepper, ribs and seeds removed, finely chopped

1¾ pounds boneless, skinless chicken breast halves (about 4), cut into 1-inch pieces

2 teaspoons chili powder

1 teaspoon dried oregano

1 dried bay leaf

1 can (28 ounces) chopped tomatoes

1 can (4 ounces) green chiles, drained and finely chopped

2½ cups homemade or reduced-sodium store-bought chicken broth

Coarse salt and freshly ground pepper

2 cans (15 ounces each) kidney beans, drained and rinsed

¼ cup plain low-fat yogurt or sour cream, for garnish (optional)

Cilantro leaves, for garnish (optional)

1 In a Dutch oven or large, heavy-bottomed pot, heat 1 tablespoon oil and the cumin seeds over medium, stirring, until the cumin is lightly toasted and aromatic, about 1 minute. Add onions, garlic, and bell pepper; cook, stirring occasionally, until vegetables are soft and lightly golden, about 15 minutes.

2 Push the onion mixture to the edges of the pot, add remaining 1 teaspoon oil, and increase heat to medium-high. Add the chicken, cooking on one side until seared, 3 to 5 minutes. Turn chicken pieces and cook an additional 2 to 3 minutes. With a slotted spoon, transfer the chicken to a plate.

3 Add chili powder, oregano, and bay leaf to the pot, and cook 30 seconds. Add tomatoes and their juice and green chiles, and stir to combine. Bring to a simmer. Add broth, ½ teaspoon salt, and the beans; season with pepper, and stir to combine.

4 Bring to a simmer. Stir contents, reduce heat to medium-low, and gently simmer. Cook, uncovered, until bean mixture thickens, about 45 minutes. Return chicken pieces, along with any accumulated juices from plate, to the pot and cook until chicken is tender, stirring occasionally, about 15 minutes.

5 Serve immediately, garnished with a dollop of yogurt and cilantro leaves, as desired.

per serving: 372 calories; 1.3 g saturated fat; 4.9 g unsaturated fat; 76.7 mg cholesterol; 35.8 g carbohydrates; 42.7 g protein; 924 mg sodium; 9.4 g fiber

sablefish in tomato-saffron stew SERVES 4

This aromatic stew can be made with other types of fish, including haddock or regular cod, but sablefish delivers higher amounts of omega-3 fatty acids. A whole-wheat baguette is good for sopping up the broth.

¼ cup sliced almonds

3 tablespoons extra-virgin olive oil

2 garlic cloves, thinly sliced

¼ teaspoon crushed red pepper flakes

½ teaspoon fennel seeds

⅛ teaspoon saffron threads

1 can (28 ounces) whole peeled tomatoes

Coarse salt and freshly ground pepper

1½ pounds skinless sablefish, cut into 1- to 2-inch pieces

¼ cup dried currants

3 scallions, trimmed and thinly sliced

1 Preheat oven to 350°F. Spread almonds in an even layer on a rimmed baking sheet; toast in oven just until turning golden and fragrant, tossing occasionally, 5 to 7 minutes. Transfer to a plate to cool.

2 Heat oil in a heavy pot over medium. Cook garlic, stirring, 1 minute. Add red pepper flakes, fennel seeds, and saffron. Cook, stirring, until fragrant, about 1 minute. Add tomatoes, and crush with a wooden spoon; season with ½ teaspoon salt. Bring to a simmer; cook, stirring occasionally, until mixture has thickened, about 15 minutes.

3 Season fish on both sides with ½ teaspoon salt, dividing evenly, and pepper. Add to pot along with the currants. Cover and cook 5 minutes. Gently stir to combine; cover, and continue to cook until fish is opaque throughout, about 5 minutes more.

4 To serve, divide among four bowls. Sprinkle with almonds and sliced scallions.

per serving: 529 calories; 7.2 g saturated fat; 29 g unsaturated fat; 83.3 mg cholesterol; 17.9 g carbohydrates; 26.4 g protein; 1103 mg sodium; 3.8 g fiber

SALADS

shredded brussels sprouts salad SERVES 4

Although more commonly cooked, brussels sprouts, Swiss chard, and kale also make delicious raw salads, as long as they're thinly sliced. This salad— which combines two of the vegetables—serves as a particularly nice fall or winter first course, when it's hard to find flavorful leaf lettuces.

1 tablespoon whole-grain mustard

3 tablespoons fresh lemon juice (from 1 to 2 lemons)

Coarse salt

1 tablespoon plus 1 teaspoon pure maple syrup

2 tablespoons sunflower oil, preferably cold-pressed

8 ounces brussels sprouts, very thinly sliced (about 3 cups)

4 to 6 leaves Swiss chard or kale (preferably Lacinato), or a combination, stemmed and thinly sliced (3 cups)

1/3 cup raw hulled sunflower seeds, toasted (page 57)

1 Stir together mustard, lemon juice, ¾ teaspoon salt, and the maple syrup; whisk in oil until emulsified.

2 In a salad bowl, toss together brussels sprouts and chard. Add sunflower seeds and dressing; toss to coat. Serve immediately.

per serving: 178 calories; 1.4 g saturated fat; 11 g unsaturated fat; 0 mg cholesterol; 13.8 g carbohydrates; 5.2 g protein; 433 mg sodium; 3.9 g fiber

quinoa and corn salad with toasted pumpkin seeds SERVES 4

This salad's simple appearance belies its delicious combination of Mexican-inspired flavors. Studded with corn, pumpkin seeds, and red peppers, it makes a substantial lunch on its own, or a side dish for dinner.

¼ cup fresh lime juice (from 2 or 3 limes), plus 1 lime cut into wedges

1 teaspoon ground cumin

1 teaspoon chili powder

1 garlic clove, minced or pressed

½ cup extra-virgin olive oil

Coarse salt

2¾ cups water

1½ cups quinoa, rinsed and drained

2 ears corn, kernels cut from cob

1 red bell pepper, ribs and seeds removed, diced

3 scallions, trimmed and thinly sliced

1 large jalapeño chile, diced (ribs and seeds removed for less heat, if desired)

¼ cup coarsely chopped cilantro

1 ripe, firm avocado

1 head red-leaf lettuce, leaves separated (inner leaves reserved for another use)

¼ cup raw hulled pumpkin seeds (pepitas), toasted (page 57)

1 Whisk together lime juice, cumin, chili powder, garlic, oil, and ¼ teaspoon salt.

2 Bring the water to a boil in a small saucepan. Add quinoa; return to a boil. Stir once, cover, and reduce heat to a simmer. Cook until quinoa is tender but still chewy and has absorbed all liquid, about 15 minutes. Turn off heat. Fluff quinoa with a fork. Place corn kernels on top of quinoa, cover pan, and let stand 5 minutes. Stir corn into quinoa, and transfer to a large bowl to cool.

3 Add red pepper, scallions, jalapeño, and cilantro to quinoa mixture, along with ½ cup dressing (or to taste); toss until combined. Season with salt, if desired.

4 Cut avocado in half lengthwise; remove pit. Peel avocado and thinly slice.

5 Line a large serving platter with lettuce leaves. Mound quinoa salad in center. Arrange avocado and lime on the side. Sprinkle pumpkin seeds over salad. Serve immediately.

per serving: 504 calories; 5.4 g saturated fat; 31.8 g unsaturated fat; 0 mg cholesterol; 39.9 g carbohydrates; 7.7 g protein; 398 mg sodium; 9.4 g fiber

oranges with olives and parsley SERVES 4

Oranges are the standout in this supremely easy salad, providing hefty amounts of vitamin C and fiber. Olives (and olive oil) add healthful monounsaturated fat.

4 navel oranges

¼ cup Niçoise olives, pitted and halved

½ teaspoon paprika

2 tablespoons fresh lemon juice

1 tablespoon extra-virgin olive oil

2 tablespoons finely chopped fresh flat-leaf parsley, plus whole leaves for garnish

1   Using a sharp knife, slice off both ends of each orange. Carefully slice downward following the curve of the fruit to remove rind and bitter white pith. Slice each orange crosswise into about six rounds, then arrange them in overlapping rows on a serving platter. Sprinkle evenly with olives.

2   In a small bowl, combine paprika and lemon juice; whisk in oil until emulsified. Add chopped parsley, and whisk to combine. Drizzle dressing over oranges and olives; garnish with parsley leaves, and serve.

per serving: 113 calories; .6 g saturated fat; 3.9 g unsaturated fat; 0 mg cholesterol; 19 g carbohydrates; 1.4 g protein; 76 mg sodium; 3.5 g fiber

papaya, endive, and crabmeat salad SERVES 4

Papaya is packed with vitamin C and beta-carotene; endive is an excellent source of fiber and vitamins A and C.

1 teaspoon finely grated peeled fresh ginger

3 tablespoons fresh lime juice (from 2 to 3 limes)

2 tablespoons grapeseed oil

Coarse salt

½ large papaya (Mexican or Solo; about 1 pound), peeled, halved lengthwise, seeds removed, and cut into 1-inch pieces

2 large Belgian endive, halved lengthwise, cored, and cut into matchsticks (about 3 cups)

½ English cucumber, very thinly sliced

¾ cup jumbo lump crabmeat, picked over and rinsed

Whisk together ginger, lime juice, grapeseed oil, and ¼ teaspoon salt in a large bowl. Add diced papaya, endive, cucumber, and crabmeat; gently toss to combine. Serve immediately.

per serving: 219 calories; 2.1 g saturated fat; 12 g unsaturated fat; .5 mg cholesterol; 8.1 g carbohydrates; 2.5 g protein; 71.4 mg sodium; 1 g fiber

ORANGES WITH OLIVES AND PARSLEY

PAPAYA, ENDIVE, AND CRABMEAT SALAD

fattoush SERVES 4

Like Italian panzanella, this salad—a specialty of the eastern Mediterranean—pairs fresh vegetables and bread. The combination of vegetables, beans, and herbs is excellent for reducing high cholesterol.

1   whole-wheat pita
    (8-inch), split

12 cherry or small tomatoes,
    halved or quartered

1   red or yellow bell pepper
    (or half of each), ribs and
    seeds removed, cut into
    1-inch strips

½   English cucumber, cut into
    ½-inch dice

¼   red onion, cut into thin
    wedges, or 2 scallions,
    trimmed and thinly sliced
    lengthwise

1   cup canned chickpeas,
    drained and rinsed

¼   cup torn fresh mint leaves

¼   cup torn fresh flat-leaf
    parsley leaves

3   tablespoons red-wine
    vinegar

2   tablespoons extra-virgin
    olive oil

    Coarse salt and freshly
    ground pepper

1 Preheat oven to 375°F. Place pita on a baking sheet and toast until crisp, about 10 minutes. Let cool completely, then break into 1-inch pieces.

2 In a bowl, combine tomatoes, pepper, cucumber, red onion, chickpeas, mint, and parsley; toss to combine. Add vinegar, oil, and ½ teaspoon salt (or to taste); season with pepper, and toss to combine. Add pita pieces, toss, and serve.

per serving: 220 calories; 1.1 g saturated fat; 6.5 g unsaturated fat; 0 mg cholesterol; 30.4 g carbohydrates; 7.2 g protein; 390 mg sodium; 6.2 g fiber

cannellini-bean niçoise salad SERVES 4

This vegetarian version of the classic dish omits the anchovies and replaces the tuna with cannellini beans; navy beans or chickpeas are other options.

FOR THE DRESSING

- ¼ cup plus 2 tablespoons fresh lemon juice (from 2 to 3 lemons)
- 1 teaspoon Dijon mustard
- 1 large shallot, minced
- ¾ cup extra-virgin olive oil
- ¼ cup finely chopped fresh flat-leaf parsley
- ¼ cup torn fresh basil

  Coarse salt and freshly ground pepper

FOR THE SALAD

- 1 pound small red potatoes, scrubbed
- 1 pound haricots verts or green beans, trimmed and cut into 1-inch pieces
- 5 ounces baby spinach
- 1½ cans (15 ounces each) cannellini beans, rinsed and drained
- 1 celery stalk, diced
- 3 tablespoons capers, rinsed and drained
- 2 teaspoons finely grated lemon zest

  Coarse salt and freshly ground pepper

- 2 ripe tomatoes, cored and cut into wedges
- 2 hard-cooked eggs (page 61), peeled and halved lengthwise
- ½ cup Niçoise olives

1 Make the dressing: In a small bowl, whisk together lemon juice, mustard, shallot, oil, parsley, basil, and ½ teaspoon salt; season with pepper.

2 Prepare the salad: Place potatoes in a medium saucepan and add enough cool water to cover by 1 inch. Bring to a boil; reduce to a simmer. Cook until tender when pierced with the tip of a sharp knife, about 15 minutes. Drain and set aside to cool.

3 Bring a pot of water to a boil and prepare an ice-water bath. Blanch haricots verts until crisp-tender and color brightens, 45 to 60 seconds. With a slotted spoon, immediately transfer beans to ice-water bath to stop the cooking; once cool, drain and pat dry with paper towels.

4 In a large bowl, toss spinach with 2 tablespoons dressing. Transfer spinach to platter. Place cannellini beans in empty bowl and mash about half of them slightly. Add celery, capers, lemon zest, 3 to 4 tablespoons dressing, and ¼ teaspoon salt (or to taste); season with pepper. Stir to combine; then spoon mixture onto spinach. Arrange potatoes on one side of the bean mixture and tomato wedges on the other.

5 Arrange haricots verts, eggs, and olives on the plate. Drizzle with remaining dressing, and serve immediately.

per serving: 790 calories; 7.1 g saturated fat; 39.8 g unsaturated fat; 106 mg cholesterol; 73 g carbohydrates; 20.7 g protein; 984 mg sodium; 23.2 g fiber

green bean, corn, and tomato salad SERVES 6

For convenience, you can cook the corn and beans early in the day, toss them with olive oil and smashed garlic, and keep them (covered) in the refrigerator. To remove corn kernels from the cob, stand the ear upright on its flat end; with a sharp knife, cut along the length of the cob, turning as you go.

3 ears corn, husked

1½ pounds green beans, trimmed

3 garlic cloves, smashed

¼ cup extra-virgin olive oil

3 tablespoons red-wine vinegar

½ small red onion, thinly sliced

1 yellow tomato, sliced ½ inch thick

2 cups mixed small tomatoes, preferably heirloom, halved

Coarse salt

1 Bring a large pot of water to a boil. Cook the corn until kernels are crisp-tender, 5 to 7 minutes. Remove corn with tongs and let cool. Using a small sieve, remove any corn silk remaining in the pot.

2 Add green beans to pot, return water to a boil, and cook until very tender, 5 to 8 minutes (depending on the size). Meanwhile, slice the corn kernels from the cobs into a large bowl. Drain the green beans in a colander, shake to remove excess water, and add to corn. Add garlic and 3 tablespoons oil. Toss well and let stand 30 minutes to allow flavors to blend. (Bean mixture can be refrigerated, covered with plastic wrap, up to 8 hours; bring to room temperature before proceeding.)

3 Just before serving, remove the garlic and add the remaining tablespoon of oil along with vinegar, onion, and tomatoes. Season with ½ teaspoon salt (or to taste), and serve.

per serving: 201 calories; 1.5 g saturated fat; 8.9 g unsaturated fat; 0 mg cholesterol; 25.7 g carbohydrates; 5.3 g protein; 189 mg sodium; 6.8 g fiber

endive, avocado, and red grapefruit salad SERVES 4

The eye-popping combination of hues in this salad is sure to perk up the appetite, which in turn stimulates digestive enzymes. Pairing grapefruit and avocado also delivers nutritionally: Red grapefruit contains lycopene— which may help lower risk of heart disease and pancreatic, lung, and prostate cancers—and the antioxidant is best absorbed when eaten with healthy fat, such as that contained in avocado.

2 red grapefruits

¾ teaspoon white-wine vinegar

1 tablespoon honey

2 tablespoons plain low-fat yogurt or sour cream

Coarse salt and freshly ground pepper

2 tablespoons extra-virgin olive oil

4 Belgian endive

1 ripe, firm Hass avocado

1 Using a sharp knife, slice off both ends of each grapefruit. Carefully slice downward following the curve of the fruit to remove rind and bitter white pith. Working over a bowl to catch the juices, cut segments from membranes, letting them fall into bowl. Squeeze the remaining juice from membranes into bowl.

2 In a small bowl, whisk together vinegar, honey, yogurt, ⅛ teaspoon salt, and 3 tablespoons grapefruit juice. Season with pepper. Whisk in oil until emulsified.

3 Halve endive lengthwise, and cut out core; cut leaves into 1-inch pieces. Toss with three-quarters of the dressing.

4 Cut avocado in half lengthwise, and remove pit. Peel and slice avocado into ¼-inch wedges. Divide endive and avocado among four plates. Drizzle servings with remaining dressing, dividing evenly. Divide grapefruit segments among plates, and serve immediately.

per serving: 202 calories; 1.9 g saturated fat; 10.4 g unsaturated fat; .3 mg cholesterol; 23 g carbohydrates; 2.4 g protein; 70 mg sodium; 6.6 g fiber

SAUTÉED SPINACH WITH PECANS
AND GOAT CHEESE

LEMONY LENTIL SALAD

sautéed spinach with pecans and goat cheese SERVES 6

In this heart-healthy wilted salad, the spinach contributes folate, and pecans help lower LDL ("bad") cholesterol.

- 2 tablespoons extra-virgin olive oil
- 1 red onion, halved and thinly sliced
- 1¼ pounds baby spinach
- 2 tablespoons sherry vinegar
- ¾ cup pecans, toasted (page 53) and coarsely chopped
- ¼ cup crumbled fresh goat cheese (about 2 ounces)

1 Heat oil in a large skillet over medium. Cook onion, stirring occasionally, until softened, about 5 minutes. Add spinach; cook, tossing, until spinach has started to wilt, about 2 minutes. Transfer to a serving platter.

2 Add vinegar to skillet, and heat for 5 seconds. Drizzle over spinach and onion. Sprinkle with pecans and goat cheese, and gently toss to combine. Serve immediately.

per serving: 175 calories; 2.6 g saturated fat; 10 g unsaturated fat; 4.3 mg cholesterol; 13 g carbohydrates; 5 g protein; 186 mg sodium; 5.6 g fiber

lemony lentil salad SERVES 6

Lentils are a particularly robust source of protein, folate, and iron. Red, orange, and yellow bell peppers provide more vitamin C and carotenoids than green ones; these powerful antioxidants support eye health, boost immunity, and fight heart disease. This nutritious make-ahead salad is perfect for a packable lunch, picnic, or barbecue.

- Coarse salt and freshly ground pepper
- 1½ cups brown or French green lentils
- ¾ teaspoon finely grated lemon zest, plus 2 tablespoons fresh lemon juice
- 3 tablespoons extra-virgin olive oil
- 1½ teaspoons Dijon mustard
- 1½ teaspoons fresh tarragon leaves, finely chopped
- 2 orange, red, or yellow bell peppers (or a mix), cut into ½-inch dice (about 2 cups)
- 4 scallions, trimmed and thinly sliced (1 cup)

1 Bring a medium saucepan of water to a boil; add 1 teaspoon salt. Cook lentils until tender but not at all mushy, 15 to 20 minutes. Drain in a fine sieve, rinse under cold water to stop the cooking, and drain again.

2 Meanwhile, whisk together lemon zest and juice, oil, mustard, and tarragon in a serving bowl. Add lentils, bell peppers, scallions, and ½ teaspoon salt (or to taste); season with pepper. Salad can be refrigerated, covered, up to 1 day. Serve chilled or at room temperature.

per serving: 257 calories; 1 g saturated fat; 7.1 g unsaturated fat; 0 mg cholesterol; 36 g carbohydrates; 15 g protein; 34 mg sodium; 7.7 g fiber

asparagus with shiitakes, shallots, and peas SERVES 6

If you'd like to use fresh peas (you'll need about a pound for one cup shelled), add them along with the mushrooms.

2 tablespoons olive oil

5 shallots, halved and thinly sliced lengthwise

8 ounces fresh shiitake mushrooms, stems removed, caps cleaned

Coarse salt and freshly ground pepper

1½ teaspoons finely grated lemon zest, plus 2 teaspoons fresh lemon juice

2 bunches medium-thick asparagus (about 2 pounds), tough ends trimmed, cut on the diagonal into 2-inch lengths

1 cup frozen peas (do not thaw)

1 In a large skillet, heat oil over medium. Cook shallots, stirring frequently, until they begin to turn golden, about 3 minutes. Add mushrooms and ¼ teaspoon salt; season with pepper. Cook, tossing occasionally, until mushrooms are tender, 3 to 5 minutes. Transfer to a bowl. Add lemon zest, and toss to combine.

2 In the same skillet, bring 2 inches of water to a boil. Add asparagus and ½ teaspoon salt; cover, and cook until asparagus is bright green and crisp-tender, 3 to 4 minutes. Stir in peas, then remove from heat. Drain and transfer to bowl with mushrooms. Add lemon juice; toss to combine. Serve warm or at room temperature.

per serving: 127 calories; .7 g saturated fat; 3.9 g unsaturated fat; 0 mg cholesterol; 15.6 g carbohydrates; 6.6 g protein; 268 mg sodium; 5.2 g fiber

marinated beet salad SERVES 4

You can vary this recipe by using half olive oil and half walnut oil and topping the beets with toasted walnuts. For the most visually appealing presentation, use a mixture of beets such as Chioggia, golden, and red.

5 beets (about 1 pound without greens), trimmed and halved

1 garlic clove, smashed

1 tablespoon sherry vinegar

2 tablespoons extra-virgin olive oil

Coarse salt and freshly ground pepper

¼ cup fresh mint leaves, coarsely chopped

¼ cup crumbled goat cheese (about 2 ounces)

1 Fill a large saucepan with 2 inches of water; set a steamer basket (or colander) inside pan, and bring to a boil. Place beets in basket, cover pot, and reduce heat to a gentle simmer. Steam until beets are tender when pierced with the tip of a sharp knife, 30 to 35 minutes. Remove beets. When cool enough to handle, rub with paper towels to remove skins. Cut the beets into thin slices.

2 Combine beets, garlic, vinegar, oil, and 1 teaspoon salt; season with pepper. Toss to combine. Cover and refrigerate at least 3 hours, or up to overnight.

3 When ready to serve, remove and discard garlic. Top beets with mint and goat cheese.

per serving: 145 calories; 3 g saturated fat; 6.5 g unsaturated fat; 6.5 mg cholesterol; 10.4 g carbohydrates; 4.4 g protein; 613 mg sodium; 3 g fiber

arugula with maple-roasted pumpkin SERVES 4

Roasted garlic serves as the base of the salad dressing. The allium not only adds depth of flavor but can also help lower cholesterol. Pumpkin is rich in potassium, fiber, and vitamin C.

1 sugar pumpkin (3½ to 4 pounds), peeled, seeded, and cut into 1½-inch pieces

¼ cup plus 1 tablespoon olive oil

6 garlic cloves (unpeeled)

¼ to ½ teaspoon crushed red pepper flakes

Coarse salt and freshly ground black pepper

2 tablespoons plus 1 teaspoon pure maple syrup

3 tablespoons fresh lime juice (from 2 limes)

1 tablespoon Dijon mustard

1½ pounds arugula (2 to 3 bunches, thick stems removed), washed well and dried

¼ cup raw hulled pumpkin seeds (pepitas), toasted (page 57)

6 ounces feta cheese, crumbled

1 Preheat oven to 450°F. On a rimmed baking sheet, combine pumpkin pieces with 2 tablespoons oil, the garlic, crushed red pepper flakes, and ½ teaspoon salt; season with black pepper. Toss to combine, then spread in an even layer. Roast, tossing occasionally, until pumpkin is tender, 25 to 30 minutes.

2 Remove garlic from sheet and reserve. Drizzle pumpkin with 2 tablespoons maple syrup; toss to coat. Return to oven and continue roasting, tossing occasionally, until pumpkin is glazed, 10 to 15 minutes more; let cool.

3 Meanwhile, cut off root ends of garlic cloves; squeeze out garlic and mash to a paste with the side of a large knife. Transfer to a large bowl. Add lime juice, mustard, remaining 1 teaspoon maple syrup, and ½ teaspoon salt; season with pepper. Whisk in remaining 3 tablespoons oil until emulsified.

4 Add arugula and pumpkin to dressing, and toss to combine. Sprinkle salad with toasted pumpkin seeds and crumbled feta cheese, and serve immediately.

per serving: 515 calories; 10 g saturated fat; 17 g unsaturated fat; 38 mg cholesterol; 46 g carbohydrates; 17.4 g protein; 979 mg sodium; 5.2 g fiber

chicken and mango salad SERVES 4

This salad features Madras curry powder—a blend of spices that includes turmeric, coriander, cumin, and cinnamon, all of which are antioxidants, anti-inflammatories, and detoxifiers. Watercress is also a potent detoxifier.

FOR THE CHICKEN

- ¼ cup olive oil, plus more for brushing grill
- ¼ cup white-wine vinegar
- 1 tablespoon Dijon mustard
- 4 skinless, boneless chicken breast halves (about 6 ounces each)
- Coarse salt

FOR MANGO DRESSING

- 1 mango, peeled and pitted (see below), then diced
- ¼ cup packed cilantro
- ¼ cup fresh mint leaves
- 1 tablespoon curry powder, preferably Madras
- Coarse salt and freshly ground pepper
- 1 tablespoon white-wine vinegar
- ¼ cup extra-virgin olive oil

FOR THE SALAD

- 1 ripe, firm avocado, halved lengthwise, pitted, peeled, and cut into ½-inch wedges
- 1 large bunch watercress, tough stems removed (about 3 cups)
- ½ small red onion, thinly sliced

1 In a shallow pan large enough to hold chicken in a single layer, whisk together oil, vinegar, and mustard; add chicken, turning to coat. Cover and refrigerate for at least 2 hours, or up to overnight.

2 Heat grill to medium-high (if using a charcoal grill, coals are ready when you can hold your hand 5 inches above grill for just 4 to 5 seconds). Lightly oil the grates. Lift chicken from marinade and discard any remaining marinade. Sprinkle chicken on both sides with 1 teaspoon salt, dividing evenly. Grill chicken until cooked through and opaque throughout, 6 to 8 minutes per side.

3 For the dressing: In a blender, combine mango, cilantro, mint, curry powder, ¼ teaspoon salt, and the vinegar; season with pepper. Puree until smooth. With the motor running, add oil in a slow, steady stream until emulsified.

4 Slice chicken crosswise. Arrange on a platter or four serving plates (dividing evenly), along with avocado, watercress, and onion; serve the dressing on the side.

per serving: 440 calories; 5.2 g saturated fat; 29.2 g unsaturated fat; 34.2 mg cholesterol; 17 g carbohydrates; 16.6 g protein; 509 mg sodium; 5.5 g fiber

PREPARING MANGO

Holding mango on a cutting board with a paper towel, use a vegetable peeler to remove skin. With a sharp knife, slice off wide, flat part of fruit on both sides of pit, cutting lengthwise. Discard peel and pit.

roasted asparagus salad with poached eggs SERVES 4

Roasting offers an easy, no-fuss way to quickly prepare asparagus. Reducing the balsamic vinegar before drizzling it over the vegetables concentrates its flavor to mimic aged varieties. Serve the dish for lunch or along with a green salad for a light dinner.

1 bunch medium-thick asparagus (about 1 pound), tough ends trimmed

2 tablespoons olive oil

Coarse salt

½ cup balsamic vinegar

1 teaspoon light brown sugar

1 tablespoon apple-cider vinegar

4 large eggs, poached (page 156)

2 ounces parmesan cheese, shaved (¾ cup)

1 Preheat oven to 400°F. On a rimmed baking sheet, drizzle asparagus with oil and sprinkle with ½ teaspoon salt; toss to combine, then spread in an even layer. Roast until asparagus is lightly browned and tender, 15 to 18 minutes.

2 Meanwhile, in a small saucepan, heat balsamic vinegar and brown sugar over medium-high until syrupy and reduced to 3 tablespoons, stirring frequently, about 6 minutes.

3 To serve, divide asparagus evenly among four plates; drizzle with balsamic mixture. Top each portion with a poached egg and shaved parmesan.

per serving: 253 calories; 5 g saturated fat; 9.6 g unsaturated fat; 224 mg cholesterol; 12 g carbohydrates; 14.4 g protein; 778 mg sodium; 2.3 g fiber

crisp mackerel salad with grainy mustard vinaigrette SERVES 4

Fatty cold-water fish, such as Atlantic mackerel (also called Boston mackerel), deliver the most important forms of omega-3 fatty acids, helping to reduce cholesterol and even stave off type 2 diabetes and some cancers. Avoid king mackerel, however, as it has high mercury levels. Here the fish is marinated in lemon juice, then broiled so the skin crisps.

4 skin-on fresh Atlantic mackerel fillets (about 4 ounces each)

Juice of 1 lemon

2 tablespoons white-wine vinegar

1 tablespoon finely chopped shallot

1 tablespoon whole-grain mustard

1 small garlic clove, minced

Coarse salt and freshly ground pepper

3 tablespoons extra-virgin olive oil, plus more for broiler pan

1 tablespoon finely chopped fresh tarragon

1 tablespoon snipped fresh chives

1 to 2 bunches watercress, thick stems removed (4 cups)

1 Heat broiler with rack 4 inches from heat source. Place mackerel in a nonreactive (glass or ceramic) baking dish. Pour lemon juice over fish, and let stand 10 minutes, turning once or twice.

2 Meanwhile, whisk together vinegar, shallot, mustard, garlic, and ¼ teaspoon salt; season with pepper. Let stand 10 minutes. Gradually add oil, whisking until emulsified. Whisk in tarragon and chives.

3 Remove mackerel from lemon juice (discard juice), and pat dry with paper towels. Score skin a few times with a sharp knife. Sprinkle with ¼ teaspoon salt and season with pepper.

4 Lightly brush a broiler pan or rimmed baking sheet with oil. Arrange mackerel, skin side up, on pan. Broil until fish is cooked through and skin is crisp and browned, 3 to 4 minutes.

5 Toss watercress with 1 tablespoon vinaigrette. Divide watercress among four plates; top each with a fish fillet, and drizzle with remaining vinaigrette, dividing evenly.

per serving: 338 calories; 5.2 g saturated fat; 19 g unsaturated fat; 79.4 mg cholesterol; 2.2 g carbohydrates; 22 g protein; 405 mg sodium; .3 g fiber

asian chicken salad with bok choy SERVES 4

Cooking the chicken with the skin and bones intact ultimately makes the dish more flavorful (and economical), but feel free to substitute two boneless, skinless breast halves for the whole breast in this salad if you prefer (reduce the cooking time to 15 minutes). Bok choy, abundant with cancer-fighting compounds, makes a nutritious accompaniment.

- 1 whole bone-in chicken breast (about 1 pound)
- 4 heads baby bok choy, trimmed and halved lengthwise
- 3 tablespoons fresh lime juice (from 2 to 3 limes)
- 2 teaspoons low-sodium tamari soy sauce
- 1 teaspoon sugar
- ⅛ teaspoon cayenne pepper
- 3 ounces snow peas, strings removed, thinly sliced lengthwise (about 1 cup)
- 3 small shallots, thinly sliced
- ¼ cup packed fresh mint leaves, coarsely chopped

1 Place chicken in a large pot, and add enough water to just cover. Bring to a boil; reduce heat, and simmer, partially covered, until chicken is cooked through, about 35 minutes, skimming off foam as needed. Transfer chicken to a plate. When cool enough to handle, remove skin and pull meat from bone (keep it in one piece), then thinly slice meat. (At this point, chicken can be refrigerated in an airtight container for up to 2 days.)

2 In a small pot, bring 1 inch of water to a boil; add bok choy. Cover, and simmer until tender, 3 to 5 minutes; drain, and let cool.

3 In a bowl, whisk together lime juice, tamari, sugar, and cayenne pepper. Add chicken, peas, and shallots; toss to combine. Transfer chicken mixture to a serving platter, top with mint, and serve bok choy alongside.

per serving: 204 calories; .5 g saturated fat; 1.3 g unsaturated fat; 53 mg cholesterol; 18.8 g carbohydrates; 32 g protein; 571 mg sodium; 7 g fiber

parsley-leaf salad with pine nuts, olives, and orange dressing SERVES 6

In addition to vitamins A, C, and K, parsley contains the phytochemical polyacetylene, which helps reduce cancer risk.

1 navel orange

½ teaspoon sherry vinegar or red-wine vinegar

¼ red onion, halved and very thinly sliced

Coarse salt and freshly ground pepper

1 tablespoon capers, rinsed and drained

¼ cup brine-cured black olives, such as Kalamata or Gaeta, pitted and halved

3 cups loosely packed fresh flat-leaf parsley leaves (from about 2 bunches)

¼ cup pine nuts, toasted (page 53)

1 tablespoon extra-virgin olive oil

1 With a vegetable peeler, remove 8 long pieces of zest from orange (leave bitter white pith behind); cut lengthwise into very thin strips. Halve orange; squeeze 2 tablespoons juice into a bowl (reserve remaining portion for another use). Add vinegar, onion, and a pinch of salt; let soak 10 minutes (or up to 24 hours; the longer it soaks, the milder its flavor will become).

2 To orange juice mixture, add capers, olives, parsley, pine nuts, and zest. Season with pepper; toss thoroughly with oil. Divide among plates and serve immediately.

per serving: 109 calories; .9 g saturated fat; 7.3 g unsaturated fat; 0 mg cholesterol; 6.8 g carbohydrates; 2.1 g protein; 270 mg sodium; 1.8 g fiber

wilted kale with cranberry beans and delicata squash SERVES 4

This nutrient-dense salad capitalizes on fall and winter's best produce, while delivering ample health benefits. The squash and cranberry beans (also called borlotti or Roman beans) provide fiber, which helps lower cholesterol; the kale prompts the liver to release enzymes that may fight cancer. Other types of winter squash, such as butternut or acorn, would also work in this recipe, as would cannellini or navy beans.

- 2 delicata squash (about 2 pounds), halved lengthwise and seeded
- 1 tablespoon plus 1 teaspoon extra-virgin olive oil
- 2 tablespoons honey
- 2 tablespoons balsamic vinegar
- 1 large shallot, finely chopped
- 1 garlic clove, minced
- 1 tablespoon red-wine vinegar
- 5 ounces kale (½ bunch), large stems removed, leaves cut into 1-inch pieces
  Coarse salt and freshly ground pepper
- 2 cups cooked cranberry beans (see right), drained and rinsed

1 Preheat oven to 400°F. Cut squash into ½-inch-thick half-moons. Toss with 1 teaspoon oil, and spread evenly on a parchment-lined baking sheet. Roast until just tender, 15 to 18 minutes. Mix honey and balsamic vinegar. Brush some of the mixture onto squash slices (reserve remaining mixture). Roast 5 minutes more.

2 Heat remaining 1 tablespoon oil in a large skillet over medium. Add shallot and garlic; cook, stirring frequently, until slightly softened, about 4 minutes. Add red-wine vinegar and remaining honey mixture to pan, and bring to a boil. Add kale to pan and sprinkle with 1 teaspoon salt; season with pepper. Add squash and beans. Cover skillet, and let stand 5 minutes, then toss until kale wilts slightly. Serve warm or at room temperature.

per serving: 279 calories; 1 g saturated fat; 4 g unsaturated fat; 0 mg cholesterol; 57 g carbohydrates; 6 g protein; 642 mg sodium; 8 g fiber

COOKING DRIED BEANS

Dried beans tend to be much more flavorful and have a firmer texture than canned. Soaking the beans first will shorten their cooking time. Dried beans double in volume once cooked; 1 cup dried beans yields 2 cups cooked. Cooked beans will keep for up to one year in an airtight container in the freezer. They can be incorporated into salsas, dips, soups, salads, and any other dishes that call for canned beans.

To soak beans: Sort the beans, discarding any debris, and rinse. Place in a large bowl, and cover with double the amount of water. Cover bowl, and let beans soak overnight. (Alternately, use the quick-soak method: Combine beans in a large pot with double the amount of water. Bring to a boil, and cook 3 minutes. Cover, and let soak 1 hour.)

To cook beans: Transfer beans and soaking liquid to a heavy pot. Bring to a boil; reduce heat. Simmer, partially covered, until tender, 1 to 2 hours (3 to 4 hours for unsoaked beans). Drain and let cool before storing.

MAIN DISHES

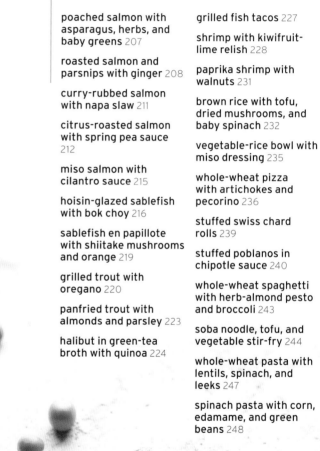

poached salmon with asparagus, herbs, and baby greens SERVES 4

This basic poaching recipe yields salmon that can be served warm, at room temperature, or chilled. Here, salmon and a few hard-cooked eggs provide protein to a colorful salad composed of fresh vegetables and mixed herbs from the farmers' market.

1 skin-on wild Alaskan salmon fillet (about 1½ pounds and 1 inch thick)

½ teaspoon finely grated lemon zest, plus ⅓ cup plus 2 tablespoons fresh lemon juice (from about 4 lemons)

Coarse salt

1 bunch medium-thick asparagus (about 1 pound), tough ends trimmed

1 shallot, thinly sliced into half moons

½ teaspoon finely grated orange zest plus 1 tablespoon fresh orange juice

2 teaspoons champagne vinegar

¼ cup extra-virgin olive oil

4 cups mixed baby greens, such as spinach and tatsoi

¼ cup mixed fresh herb leaves, such as mint, basil, and tarragon

12 radishes, trimmed and halved

4 hard-cooked eggs (page 61), peeled and halved lengthwise

1 Fill a saucepan wide enough to hold salmon with 2 to 3 inches cold water. Stir in ⅓ cup lemon juice and 2 teaspoons salt. Bring to a boil; reduce heat to a simmer and gently place salmon in pan, skin side down. Reduce heat and cook at a bare simmer until salmon is just opaque throughout, 10 to 12 minutes. Transfer to a plate. Cover loosely with a piece of parchment paper to prevent surface from drying, and let cool 20 to 30 minutes. Once cool, salmon can be refrigerated, covered tightly with plastic wrap, for up to 2 days.

2 Bring a pot of water to a boil and prepare an ice-water bath. Blanch asparagus until crisp-tender and color brightens, 45 to 60 seconds. With a slotted spoon, immediately transfer asparagus to ice-water bath to stop the cooking; once cool, drain and pat dry with paper towels.

3 Combine shallot, lemon and orange zests, 2 tablespoons lemon juice, the orange juice, vinegar, and ¼ teaspoon salt in a small bowl. Gradually whisk in the olive oil until emulsified.

4 Assemble asparagus, greens, herbs, radishes, and eggs on a platter. Break salmon into large pieces, arrange on top, and drizzle with vinaigrette. Serve immediately.

per serving: 480 calories; 5.3 g saturated fat; 22.7 g unsaturated fat; 306 mg cholesterol; 7.9 g carbohydrates; 42.2 g protein; 303 mg sodium; 3 g fiber

roasted salmon and parsnips with ginger SERVES 4

The flavorful ginger dressing that coats the parsnips calls for tamari, a sauce made from soybeans that's darker and richer than conventional soy sauce (it's also gluten free). Serve the fish with a wedge of orange along with peppery greens, such as watercress or arugula.

- 1 pound parsnips (about 5), peeled and sliced ¾ inch thick
- 3 tablespoons neutral-tasting oil, such as canola or safflower
- 2 teaspoons finely grated peeled fresh ginger
- 2 teaspoons finely chopped fresh rosemary
- 2 tablespoons low-sodium tamari soy sauce
- ¼ cup plus 2 tablespoons fresh orange juice (from 1 to 2 oranges)
- 4 skinless wild Alaskan salmon fillets (about 6 ounces each)

1 Preheat oven to 425°F. Place parsnips on a rimmed baking sheet and drizzle with 2 tablespoons oil; toss to coat, then spread in a single layer. Roast until beginning to brown around the edges, about 15 minutes. Meanwhile, combine ginger, rosemary, tamari, orange juice, and remaining 1 tablespoon oil.

2 Flip parsnips and push to edges of baking sheet. Place fillets in the middle. Cook, flipping halfway through, until fillets are opaque around the edges and flake slightly in center when pressed, 12 to 15 minutes. Remove from oven.

3 Transfer a fillet to each of four plates. Pour ginger mixture over parsnips and gently toss to coat. Divide parsnips among plates. Spoon extra sauce from baking sheet over fish and parsnips, and serve.

per serving: 458 calories; 1 g saturated fat; 13 g unsaturated fat; 107 mg cholesterol; 21 g carbohydrates; 41 g protein; 598 mg sodium; 5 g fiber

curry-rubbed salmon
with napa slaw SERVES 4

Broiling is a good way to brown the salmon without adding fat. For a golden color and crisp finish, don't turn the fish while it is under the broiler; it will still cook all the way through without this extra step.

2 cups water

1 cup brown basmati rice

Coarse salt and freshly ground pepper

½ head napa cabbage (1 pound), thinly sliced crosswise

1 pound carrots, peeled and coarsely grated

½ cup loosely packed fresh mint leaves

¼ cup fresh lime juice (from 2 to 3 limes), plus lime wedges for serving

2 tablespoons grapeseed oil

4 skinless wild Alaskan salmon fillets (about 6 ounces each)

2 teaspoons curry powder

1 In a large saucepan, bring the water to a boil; add the rice and ½ teaspoon salt. Cover and reduce heat to medium-low. Cook until rice is tender and has absorbed all liquid, 30 to 35 minutes. Remove from heat; let stand, covered, 10 minutes.

2 Meanwhile, in a large bowl, combine cabbage, carrots, mint, lime juice, oil, and ½ teaspoon salt; season with pepper. Toss to combine.

3 Heat broiler, with rack set 4 inches from heat source. While rice is standing, place salmon on a broiler pan or rimmed baking sheet. Rub fillets with curry powder and ½ teaspoon salt, dividing evenly; season with pepper. Broil until just cooked through, 6 to 8 minutes.

4 Divide salmon and cabbage mixture among four plates. Fluff rice with a fork and serve alongside.

per serving: 583 calories; 6 g saturated fat; 18.3 g unsaturated fat; 85 mg cholesterol; 47.2 g carbohydrates; 39.8 g protein; 1140 mg sodium; 7.3 g fiber

citrus-roasted salmon with spring pea sauce SERVES 8

Salmon seasoned with orange, lemon, and lime contrasts beautifully with a fresh-pea puree. Green peas—actually legumes, not vegetables—are high in protein and vitamin K, which boosts bone health.

CITRUS-ROASTED SALMON

- 3 oranges
- 3 lemons
  Freshly grated zest of 1 lime
- 2 teaspoons sugar
  Coarse salt and freshly ground white pepper
- 1 teaspoon coriander seeds, crushed
- 1 side of wild Alaskan salmon (about 3 pounds), trimmed of fat and excess skin, small pin bones removed with tweezers
- 2 tablespoons extra-virgin olive oil
  Spring Pea Sauce (see right)
  Pea shoots or watercress, for garnish

Finely grate the zest of 2 oranges and 2 lemons. Cut the remaining orange and lemon into ¼-inch-thick rounds. Stir together citrus zests (including lime), sugar, 2 teaspoons salt, 1½ teaspoons pepper, and the coriander in a small bowl.

Place salmon, skin side down, in a nonreactive (glass or ceramic) baking dish large enough for it to lay flat. Rub spice blend all over salmon. Cover with plastic wrap. Refrigerate 2 hours.

Remove salmon from refrigerator. Wipe off spice blend with paper towels. Let fish stand at room temperature 20 minutes. Meanwhile, preheat oven to 400°F.

Arrange half the orange and lemon rounds in a single layer in a large roasting pan; place salmon, skin side down, on top. Rub the oil all over salmon. Roast until opaque throughout, about 17 minutes. Remove from oven; cut salmon crosswise into 8 pieces.

To serve, divide sauce among eight serving plates, and top each with a piece of salmon. Garnish with pea shoots and remaining orange and lemon rounds.

per serving: 432 calories; 4.9 g saturated fat; 13.4 g unsaturated fat; 109 mg cholesterol; 16.2 g carbohydrates; 36.8 g protein; 686 mg sodium; 3.6 g fiber

SPRING PEA SAUCE
MAKES ¾ CUP

You can make this sauce with thawed frozen peas instead of fresh, in which case they don't need to be blanched.

- 1⅓ cups shelled fresh peas
- 1½ cup loosely packed trimmed watercress (½ bunch)
- 1½ tablespoons cold unsalted butter, cut into small pieces
  Coarse salt

Prepare an ice-water bath. Bring a pot of water to a boil. Blanch peas and watercress until bright green, about 45 seconds. Immediately transfer with a slotted spoon to the ice bath to stop the cooking.

Drain peas and watercress, then puree in a blender until smooth, adding 4 to 5 tablespoons water to thin (mixture should be just thick enough to coat the back of a spoon). Pass puree through a fine sieve into a small saucepan. Place over low heat, and whisk in butter, 1 piece at a time; whisk until emulsified, then remove from heat. Season sauce with ½ teaspoon salt (or to taste). Serve warm.

per serving: 37 calories; 1.2 g saturated fat; .6 g unsaturated fat; 5 mg cholesterol; 3.5 g carbohydrates; 1.4 g protein; 123 mg sodium; 1.2 g fiber

miso salmon with cilantro sauce SERVES 4

Miso, a combination of fermented soybeans and rice or barley, is a great source of zinc, a natural immunity booster. White miso has less sodium than other types; here, it's combined with rice vinegar, brown sugar, and water to make a marinade for salmon. Cilantro, ginger, and chile (along with a few other ingredients) are quickly pureed into a sauce for the broiled fish. Serve with brown rice or soba (buckwheat) noodles.

- 1 cup white miso
- ⅓ cup rice vinegar (unseasoned)
- ¼ cup packed dark brown sugar plus 1 teaspoon
- ⅓ cup water
- 4 skinless wild Alaskan salmon fillets (about 6 ounces each)
- 1 cup packed cilantro leaves, coarsely chopped
- ¼ cup fresh lime juice (from 2 to 3 limes)
- 1 shallot, coarsely chopped
- 1 small fresh red chile, such as Thai bird or jalapeño, coarsely chopped (ribs and seeds removed for less heat, if desired)
- 1 garlic clove
- 1 piece (2 inches) fresh ginger, peeled and finely grated (1 tablespoon)
- 2 tablespoons neutral-tasting oil, such as canola or safflower

1 In a medium saucepan, combine miso, vinegar, ¼ cup brown sugar, and the water. Cook over medium heat, stirring occasionally, just until miso and sugar have dissolved (do not boil); remove from heat, and let cool to room temperature.

2 Place salmon in a shallow dish or a resealable plastic bag, and add miso mixture, turning to coat. Cover (or seal) and marinate in the refrigerator 1 hour (place bag on a plate in case of leaks).

3 Meanwhile, puree cilantro, lime juice, shallot, chile, garlic, ginger, oil, and remaining teaspoon brown sugar in a blender until sauce is smooth.

4 Heat broiler with rack 6 to 8 inches from heat source. Lift fillets from marinade and wipe off excess (discard marinade); broil until fillets are opaque around edges and flake slightly in center when pressed, 4 to 6 minutes. Transfer salmon to each of four plates, and serve with cilantro sauce.

per serving: 500 calories; 2.2 g saturated fat; 16.2 g unsaturated fat; 94 mg cholesterol; 40.6 g carbohydrates; 39.5 protein; 1964 mg sodium; 0 g fiber

hoisin-glazed sablefish with bok choy SERVES 4

Sablefish, also known as black cod, is among the best sources of heart-friendly omega-3 fatty acids. Here, the fish is combined with bok choy, which contains antioxidants and fiber. The hoisin mixture, brushed on top of the fish before broiling, is essentially a quick barbecue sauce.

2 tablespoons neutral-tasting oil, such as canola or safflower

1 piece (3 inches) fresh ginger, peeled, thinly sliced, and cut into very thin matchsticks

3 garlic cloves, thinly sliced

1 head bok choy (1½ pounds), trimmed and sliced crosswise into 1-inch-wide pieces, greens and stalks separated

2 celery stalks, quartered lengthwise and cut crosswise into 2-inch lengths

Coarse salt and freshly ground pepper

1 bunch scallions, trimmed and cut into 2-inch lengths

3 tablespoons hoisin sauce

1 tablespoon ketchup

1½ teaspoons Dijon mustard

1 teaspoon fresh lemon juice

4 skinless sablefish fillets (about 5 ounces each)

1 In a large saucepan, heat the oil over medium. Add ginger and garlic; cook, stirring, until fragrant, about 1 minute. Add bok choy stalks, celery, and ½ teaspoon salt; season with pepper. Cook, stirring frequently, until crisp-tender, 5 to 7 minutes. Add scallions, and cook, stirring, until wilted, about 3 minutes.

2 Heat broiler with rack 4 inches from heat source. Stir together hoisin, ketchup, mustard, and ½ teaspoon lemon juice. Place fish on a broiler pan or rimmed baking sheet. Season on both sides with ½ teaspoon salt, dividing evenly, and pepper. Brush tops with hoisin mixture. Broil until fish is glazed and opaque throughout, 5 to 7 minutes.

3 Add remaining ½ teaspoon lemon juice to bok choy greens; spoon onto four plates and top each with a fish fillet. Serve immediately.

per serving: 400 calories; 5.2 g saturated fat; 20.8 g unsaturated fat; 70 mg cholesterol; 12.3 g carbohydrates; 22.4 g protein; 968 mg sodium; 2.6 g fiber

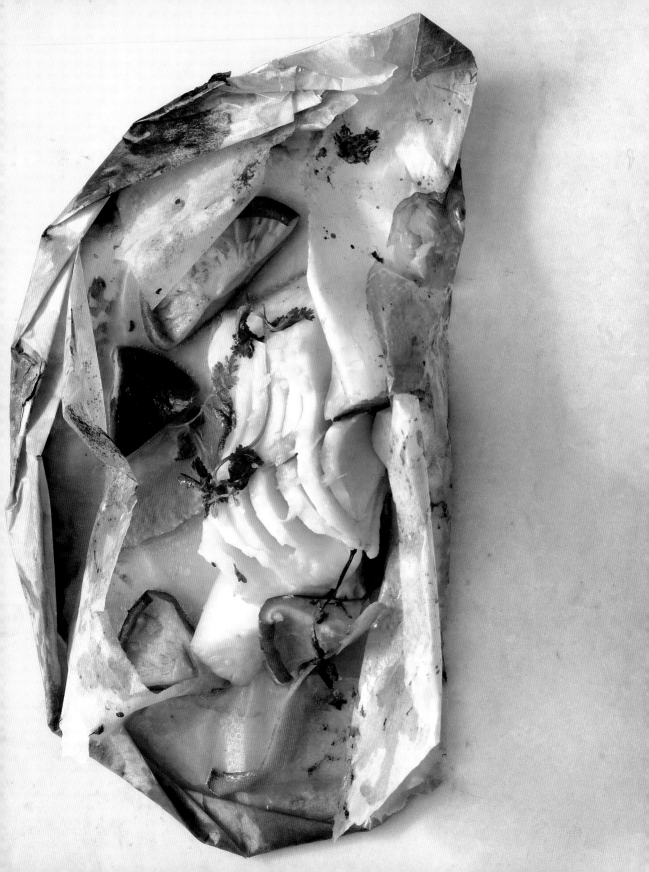

sablefish en papillote with shiitake mushrooms and orange SERVES 4

Sablefish's succulent texture and high oil content make it an exceptional choice for steaming. In this recipe, the fish is steamed in parchment-paper packets (*en papillote*), which seal in moisture and flavor.

1 navel orange

4 skinless sablefish fillets (about 5 ounces each)

Coarse salt and freshly ground pepper

2 teaspoons minced peeled fresh ginger

1 tablespoon plus 1 teaspoon extra-virgin olive oil

12 fresh shiitake mushrooms, stems removed, caps cleaned and halved

24 cilantro sprigs

1 Preheat oven to 425°F. Use a vegetable peeler to remove 8 strips of orange zest, leaving bitter white pith behind. Halve the orange and extract the juice. Cut out four 15-inch squares of parchment paper; fold each in half to make a crease, then open again. Place a fillet on one half of each parchment. Season all fish on both sides with 1 teaspoon salt, dividing evenly, and pepper; sprinkle with ginger, and drizzle with oil and juice. Arrange 2 zest strips, 6 shiitake pieces, and 6 cilantro sprigs on top of each fillet.

2 Fold parchment over fish, and crimp the edges to form a half-moon shape, pleating repeatedly all the way around to seal. Place packets on a baking sheet and cook until paper puffs up, about 10 minutes. Remove from oven; place packets on plates, and serve immediately, cutting them open at the table.

per serving: 352 calories; 5.2 g saturated fat; 18.4 g unsaturated fat; 69.5 mg cholesterol; 6.9 g carbohydrates; 20.9 g protein; 564 mg sodium; 1.2 g fiber

grilled trout with oregano SERVES 4

Fresh herbs are a healthy way to season fish and other lean proteins. Here, pungent oregano and bright lemon juice balance the richness of the trout. The whole trout are grilled in this recipe, but you can use the broiler instead; lightly coat the broiler pan or a rimmed baking sheet with oil before heating, and cook the fish for the same amount of time.

2 tablespoons neutral-tasting oil, such as canola or safflower, plus more for grill

4 whole trout (about 12 ounces each), preferably U.S. farmed, cleaned and scaled

Coarse salt and freshly ground pepper

2 lemons, 1 sliced into 8 rounds, 1 cut into wedges for garnish

1 large bunch oregano

1 Heat a grill to medium-high (if using a charcoal grill, coals are ready when you can hold your hand 5 inches above grate for just 4 to 5 seconds); brush grates with oil. Sprinkle exterior and cavity of each fish with ¼ teaspoon salt, and season with pepper. Tuck 2 lemon rounds and a few oregano sprigs in cavity of each fish.

2 Rub each fish with ½ teaspoon oil, and place on grill. Cook until golden and firm, about 4 minutes per side. Transfer to a serving platter; drizzle each fish with 1 teaspoon oil. Garnish with lemon wedges and remaining oregano, and serve.

per serving: 382 calories; 1.3 g saturated fat; 6.7 g unsaturated fat; 0 mg cholesterol; 12.4 g carbohydrates; 54 g protein; 123 mg sodium; 5.4 g fiber

panfried trout with almonds and parsley SERVES 4

Chopped almonds contribute substantial fiber, calcium, potassium, and zinc to simply prepared trout fillets. For a light supper, serve the fish with baby lettuce leaves and lemon wedges for squeezing over the dish.

1 tablespoon plus 2 teaspoons neutral-tasting oil, such as canola or safflower

4 skin-on trout fillets (preferably U.S. farmed)

Coarse salt and freshly ground pepper

3 ounces raw whole almonds, coarsely chopped

1 cup loosely packed fresh flat-leaf parsley leaves, coarsely chopped

Finely grated zest plus freshly squeezed juice of 2 lemons

1 Heat 1 teaspoon oil in a large skillet over medium-high. Season fillets with ¾ teaspoon salt, dividing evenly, and pepper. Gently place 2 fillets in skillet, skin side up. Reduce heat to medium, and cook until golden brown on one side, 4 to 5 minutes. Carefully flip fish, using two spatulas if necessary. Cook until slightly flaky in the center when pierced with a fork, about 2 minutes more. Transfer fish to a serving platter; keep in a warm spot. Wipe out skillet, and repeat with 1 teaspoon oil and remaining 2 fillets.

2 Wipe out skillet again; add remaining 1 tablespoon oil and the almonds. Cook over medium heat, stirring, until almonds start to turn golden, about 1 minute. Remove from heat, and immediately add parsley and lemon zest; stir to combine. Stir in lemon juice; as soon as it starts to bubble, pour sauce over fish. Serve immediately.

per serving: 315 calories; 2.7 g saturated fat; 19.3 g unsaturated fat; 45.8 mg cholesterol; 7.4 g carbohydrates; 21.8 g protein; 410 mg sodium; 3.3 g fiber

halibut in green-tea
broth with quinoa SERVES 4

In addition to the beneficial omega-3s provided by halibut, the green tea in this dish contains epigallocatechin gallate, or EGCG — a powerful antioxidant shown to help prevent cancer. Quinoa is high in protein and fiber.

- 4 wild Pacific halibut fillets (about 6 ounces each)

  Coarse salt and freshly ground pepper

- 2 cups water

- 1 cup quinoa, rinsed and drained

- 2 tablespoons neutral-tasting oil, such as canola or safflower

- 1 piece (2 inches) fresh ginger, peeled and finely chopped

- 1 head baby bok choy, trimmed and thinly sliced lengthwise

- 1 cup frozen shelled edamame, thawed

- 4 ounces fresh shiitake mushrooms, stems removed, caps cleaned and thinly sliced

- ½ cup snow peas, strings removed, thinly sliced lengthwise

- 1 cup brewed green tea

- 1 tablespoon low-sodium tamari soy sauce

- 1 teaspoon honey

- 3 scallions, trimmed and thinly sliced on the diagonal

  Basil leaves, for garnish

1 Preheat oven to 400°F. Season each halibut fillet on both sides with ½ teaspoon salt, dividing evenly, and pepper.

2 In a medium saucepan, bring the water to a boil. Add quinoa and ½ teaspoon salt; reduce heat to a simmer. Cover and cook until quinoa is tender and has absorbed all liquid, about 15 minutes. Remove from heat.

3 Meanwhile, in a large skillet, heat the oil over medium-high. Cook fillets until golden, 2 to 3 minutes per side. Using a slotted spatula, transfer fish to an ovenproof dish and bake until just opaque throughout, 8 to 10 minutes.

4 Add ginger, bok choy, edamame, shiitakes, and snow peas to skillet; reduce heat to medium and cook, stirring constantly, until shiitakes begin to soften, about 3 minutes. Add green tea, soy sauce, and honey. Cook, stirring, until edamame are tender, about 3 minutes more. Stir in scallions and remove from heat.

5 Divide broth and vegetables among four shallow bowls. Top each with a fish fillet and garnish with basil leaves. Serve quinoa in separate bowls.

per serving: 470 calories; 2.3 g saturated fat; 9.8 g unsaturated fat; 54.4 mg cholesterol; 38.2 g carbohydrates; 46.2 g protein; 771 mg sodium; 5.5 g fiber

grilled fish tacos MAKES 1 DOZEN

Fresh, clean flavors define these grilled fish tacos. The cabbage is also a potent cancer fighter. Set out the fish and toppings (use a melon baller to scoop avocado into neat balls), and let guests assemble their own tacos.

1 teaspoon ground cumin

1 tablespoon dried oregano

1 tablespoon chili powder

Coarse salt

¼ cup extra-virgin olive oil

¼ cup finely chopped cilantro, plus sprigs for garnish

2 pounds skin-on striped bass or red snapper fillets

5 cups shredded green cabbage (½ head)

Neutral-tasting oil, such as canola or safflower, for grill

12 corn tortillas

Lime wedges, avocado, Mexican crema (or sour cream), and hot sauce, for serving

Quick Pickled Vegetables, for serving (optional; see right)

Stir together cumin, oregano, chili powder, and 2 teaspoons salt. Mix in the olive oil and cilantro. Use a sharp knife to make shallow slits about 1½ inches apart into the fish skin; transfer to a large dish and rub both sides with spice mixture. Refrigerate, covered, for 30 minutes to 2 hours.

Toss together cabbage and 1½ teaspoons salt in a medium bowl. Let sit 30 minutes.

Heat grill (or grill pan) to high (if using a charcoal grill, coals are ready when you can hold your hand 5 inches above grill for just 2 to 3 seconds); lightly oil grates. Place fish, skin side up, on grill. Cook, without moving fish, until opaque throughout, 3 to 5 minutes. Carefully flip, using two spatulas if necessary. Cook until fish flakes slightly when pressed in the center, 5 to 7 minutes more.

Transfer fish to a serving platter; let cool slightly, then shred with a fork into bite-size pieces. Garnish platter with lime wedges and cilantro sprigs. Serve warm or at room temperature (within 1 hour). Allow guests to assemble their own tacos, layering fish with cabbage, avocado, crema, hot sauce, pickled vegetables, and other toppings, as desired.

per serving (1 taco): 184 calories; 1 g saturated fat; 6 g unsaturated fat; 60 mg cholesterol; 14 g carbohydrates; 15 g protein; 404 mg sodium; 3 g fiber

QUICK PICKLED VEGETABLES
MAKES 1 QUART

2½ cups apple-cider vinegar

⅓ cup sugar

2 teaspoons coarse salt

3 cups cold water

4 carrots, peeled and sliced diagonally ¼ inch thick

2 small red onions, halved and sliced into ¾-inch wedges

4 jalapeño chiles, quartered lengthwise; ribs and seeds removed

Combine vinegar, sugar, and salt in a saucepan with the water; bring to a boil over high heat and stir to dissolve sugar. Add carrots, onions, and jalapeños, and reduce heat to medium-high. Simmer until carrots are just tender, 10 to 12 minutes. Pour into a bowl; let cool completely before covering and refrigerating. (Pickles will keep up to 2 weeks.)

per serving: 39.7 calories; 0 g saturated fat; 0 g unsaturated fat; 0 mg cholesterol; 8.1 g carbohydrates; .4 g protein; 206 mg sodium; 1 g fiber

shrimp with
kiwifruit-lime relish SERVES 4

Kiwifruit, lime juice, chiles, and cilantro make a tropical—and antioxidant-rich—accompaniment to simple seared shrimp; you can also use the relish to top grilled fish, or as a healthy dip with tortilla chips. Serve the shrimp and relish with black lentils and whole-wheat naan (Indian flatbread), as shown, or with brown rice and tortillas.

2 jalapeño chiles, finely chopped (ribs and seeds removed for less heat, if desired)

2 tablespoons fresh lime juice (from 1 to 2 limes)

4 kiwifruits, peeled and diced (page 39)

Coarse salt

½ cup finely chopped cilantro

20 large shrimp, preferably U.S. farmed, peeled and deveined (about 1 pound)

2 tablespoons neutral-tasting oil, such as canola or safflower

1 Stir jalapeños and lime juice together. Add kiwifruit, ¼ teaspoon salt (or to taste), and cilantro. Stir to combine.

2 Season shrimp with ½ teaspoon salt. Heat oil in a large skillet over high until shimmering. Add shrimp in a single layer and cook until pink on one side, about 3 minutes. Flip shrimp and cook until opaque throughout, about 2 minutes more. Serve with kiwifruit-lime relish.

per serving: 104 calories; .3 g saturated fat; 2.7 g unsaturated fat; 53.2 mg cholesterol; 11.3 g carbohydrates; 8.2 g protein; 462 mg sodium; 2.1 g fiber

paprika shrimp with walnuts SERVES 4

A cross-continental blend of flavors, this dish features a lively sauce that combines European paprika and sake or mirin (rice wine) from Japan. Turnips, popular in both European and Asian cuisines, add fiber, potassium, calcium, and vitamin C. Serve the shrimp over whole-wheat pasta or brown rice.

- 2 to 3 tablespoons neutral-tasting oil, such as canola or safflower
- 1 tablespoon minced peeled fresh ginger
- 1 ½ teaspoons paprika
- 3 tablespoons chopped walnuts
- 20 large shrimp, preferably U.S. farmed, peeled and deveined (about 1 pound)
- 1 ½ cups cubed (¼-inch) peeled turnips
- 1 tablespoon apple-cider vinegar or sherry vinegar
- 3 tablespoons sake or mirin (rice wine)

  Coarse salt and freshly ground pepper
- ¼ cup chopped fresh flat-leaf parsley (optional)

1 Heat oil in a large skillet over medium-high. Add ginger and paprika; cook, stirring, until fragrant, 20 to 30 seconds. Add walnuts; sauté, stirring, until lightly browned, 2 to 3 minutes.

2 Add shrimp; cook, stirring, until pink and opaque throughout, about 2 minutes per side. Stir in turnips, vinegar, sake, and 1 teaspoon salt; season with pepper. Continue to cook, stirring, until heated through, about 2 minutes. Stir in parsley, and serve warm.

per serving: 253 calories; 1.7 g saturated fat; 10.3 g unsaturated fat; 172 mg cholesterol; 6.4 g carbohydrates; 24.6 g protein; 204 mg sodium; 2.1 g fiber

brown rice with tofu, dried mushrooms, and baby spinach SERVES 6

Brown rice is the foundation of a simple, protein-filled vegetarian dish when it's paired with tofu. Spinach is "steamed" in the same pan for the ultimate in ease—and nutritional value.

1½ cups short-grain brown rice

2¾ cups water

½ ounce dried shiitake mushrooms (broken if large)

1 tablespoon finely chopped peeled fresh ginger

4 garlic cloves, minced

1 dried red chile, crumbled

Coarse salt

7 ounces (½ package) extra-firm tofu, drained and cut into ¾-inch cubes

3 ounces baby spinach

6 scallions, white and pale green parts only, finely chopped

¼ cup loosely packed cilantro leaves, finely chopped

2 tablespoons plus 1 teaspoon low-sodium tamari soy sauce

1½ tablespoons rice vinegar (unseasoned)

1 teaspoon toasted sesame oil

1 In a large saucepan, stir together rice, water, mushrooms, ginger, garlic, chile, and salt. Bring mixture to a boil; reduce to a simmer. Cover and cook until rice is tender and has absorbed all liquid; 45 to 50 minutes. Remove from heat.

2 Gently stir in tofu, and let stand, covered, 15 minutes. Stir in spinach. Cover, and let steam 3 minutes. Stir in scallions, cilantro, soy sauce, vinegar, and sesame oil. Serve immediately.

per serving: 247 calories; .3 g saturated fat; 2.7 g unsaturated fat; 0 mg cholesterol; 44.5 g carbohydrates; 9 g protein; 283 mg sodium; 3.8 g fiber

vegetable-rice bowl with miso dressing SERVES 4

Think of this recipe as a basic formula for making rice bowls, and then vary the beans (use canned ones to save time), squash, and greens, as desired.

FOR THE RICE BOWL

- 1 cup dried red azuki beans
  Coarse salt
- 2 cups short-grain brown rice
- 3¼ cups water
- ½ butternut squash, peeled, seeded, and cut into ½-inch-thick pieces (4 cups)
- 14 ounces (1 package) firm tofu, halved and cut into ½-inch-thick triangles
- ¼ pound mixed greens, such as kale, chard, and beet greens (8 cups), stemmed, leaves chopped

FOR THE DRESSING

- 1 piece (1 inch) fresh ginger, peeled and coarsely chopped
- 2 tablespoons plus 2 teaspoons white miso
- ¼ cup low-sodium tamari soy sauce
- ¼ cup water
- 1 tablespoon plus 1 teaspoon toasted sesame oil

FOR THE CONDIMENTS

- 2 tablespoons dried arame or wakame (seaweed)
- 1 daikon radish, peeled and finely grated (about ½ cup)
- 2 teaspoons ume plum vinegar or seasoned rice vinegar
- 8 umeboshi plums, halved and pitted (optional)
  Gomashio (sesame seeds dotted with salt) or toasted sesame seeds

1 Prepare the rice bowl: Place beans in a bowl; add enough water to cover by about 2 inches. Let soak overnight in the refrigerator. Drain beans, and rinse under cold running water; drain again. Transfer to a medium saucepan. Cover with water by about 2 inches, and bring to a boil. Reduce heat; simmer, stirring occasionally, until tender, about 30 minutes, seasoning with 1 teaspoon salt halfway through and adding more water, if necessary, to keep beans covered. Drain.

2 Meanwhile, place rice in another saucepan; add the 3¼ cups cold water and a large pinch of salt. Bring to a boil, stir once, and reduce heat. Simmer, covered, until rice is tender and has absorbed all liquid, 45 to 50 minutes. Remove from heat, and let stand (covered) 10 minutes.

3 Place the bottom basket of a large 2-tiered bamboo steamer in a wok or large pan filled with about 1 inch of simmering water (the water should just reach to bottom of basket; alternatively, use two pans fitted with steamer inserts). Carefully place squash slices in a single layer in bottom basket. Cover, and steam 10 minutes. Place tofu in a single layer in top basket, and top with greens. Cover, and carefully set atop bottom basket; steam until greens and squash slices are tender, 7 to 8 minutes more.

4 Meanwhile, make the miso dressing: Process ginger, miso, tamari, and the ¼ cup water in a food processor until smooth. With machine running, gradually add oil, and process until combined. Transfer to a small bowl.

5 Prepare the condiments: In a small bowl, cover seaweed with cool water. Let stand until soft, 10 to 15 minutes. Drain. Toss together daikon and vinegar in another bowl.

6 To serve, fluff rice with a fork and divide among four serving bowls; arrange beans, greens, tofu, squash, and seaweed on top, dividing evenly. Top each bowl with about 1 tablespoon daikon mixture and 2 plums. Drizzle with dressing, and sprinkle with gomashio.

per serving: 808 calories; 2 g saturated fat; 5 g unsaturated fat; 0 mg cholesterol; 142 g carbohydrates; 34 g protein; 1491 mg sodium; 18 g fiber

whole-wheat pizza with artichokes and pecorino SERVES 4

When you start with store-bought dough, homemade pizza comes together in minutes. Look for whole-wheat dough in the refrigerator section of health-food stores and some supermarkets. Frozen artichoke hearts are a convenient alternative to steaming fresh artichokes, and they retain much of their nutrients; if you use canned, rinse them well and let them drain. (Jarred, marinated artichokes are not recommended for this recipe.)

4 frozen artichoke hearts, thawed

1 tablespoon fresh lemon juice

1 tablespoon extra-virgin olive oil, plus more for baking sheet

1 pound whole-wheat pizza dough, room temperature

1 cup ricotta cheese, preferably fresh packed

2 plum tomatoes, thinly sliced crosswise

¼ cup pitted Kalamata olives, halved

3 ounces pecorino Romano cheese, shaved with a vegetable peeler

Coarse salt and freshly ground pepper

¼ cup packed fresh basil leaves

1 Thinly slice the artichoke hearts crosswise, then place in a small bowl. Add lemon juice, and toss to coat.

2 Preheat oven to 450°F. Lightly oil a baking sheet. Stretch dough to a 12-by-16-inch oval. Place dough on prepared sheet and brush with 1 tablespoon oil, making sure to coat edges well. Scatter spoonfuls of ricotta over dough. Top evenly with tomatoes, artichokes, olives, and three-quarters of the pecorino. Season with ¾ teaspoon salt (or to taste) and pepper.

3 Bake pizza until crust is browned and toppings are heated through, 20 to 25 minutes. Remove from oven. Sprinkle with basil and remaining pecorino, and serve immediately.

per serving: 579 calories; 9.7 g saturated fat; 9.8 g unsaturated fat; 46.9 mg cholesterol; 71 g carbohydrates; 28.4 g protein; 1307 mg sodium; 10.8 g fiber

stuffed swiss chard rolls SERVES 6

A relative of spinach and beets, Swiss chard offers fantastic antioxidant protection in the form of carotenoids, which help maintain eye health, boost immunity, and may even fight cancer. Here, chard leaves are rolled around a protein-rich quinoa-mushroom filling for an elegant entrée.

- 2 bunches Swiss chard (about 2 pounds), preferably red
- 1 cup quinoa
- 5 cups homemade or reduced-sodium store-bought chicken or vegetable broth
- 1 tablespoon unsalted butter
- 2 tablespoons extra-virgin olive oil, plus more for brushing
- 2 shallots, finely chopped
- 2 large carrots, peeled and cut into 1/8-inch dice
- 1 pound cremini mushrooms, stems removed, caps cleaned
- 1 pound fresh shiitake mushrooms, stems removed, caps cleaned

  Coarse salt and freshly ground pepper
- 2 tablespoons fresh marjoram leaves (or 1 teaspoon dried)
- 2 tablespoons Marsala (Italian fortified wine) or port wine

1 Preheat oven to 350°F. Prepare an ice-water bath. Bring a large pot of water to a boil. Blanch chard until tender and bright green, about 2 minutes. Using a slotted spoon or tongs, transfer chard to the ice bath; let cool, then transfer to paper towels and pat dry. Reserve leaves, being careful not to tear them. Cut off stem, making a V shape about 1 inch up from bottom of leaf. Chop stems into 1/4-inch pieces.

2 Meanwhile, place quinoa and 2 1/4 cups broth in a medium saucepan. Bring to a boil, and stir once. Reduce heat; simmer (uncovered) until quinoa is tender and has absorbed all liquid, about 15 minutes. Transfer quinoa to a large bowl; keep in a warm place.

3 Heat a large sauté pan over medium-high; add butter and oil. When hot, add shallots and carrots; cook, stirring, until shallots are translucent, about 1 minute. Add mushroom caps, chard stems, and 1/2 teaspoon salt; season with pepper. Sauté until vegetables are tender, stirring occasionally, about 8 minutes.

4 Remove 1 1/2 cups mushroom mixture from pan; add to quinoa. Reserve remaining mushroom mixture. Coarsely chop 1 tablespoon marjoram (or add 1/2 teaspoon dried); stir into quinoa.

5 Divide chard leaves into six portions. Form one portion into a 6-by-10-inch rectangle, overlapping leaves so there are no gaps. Place 1/2 cup quinoa mixture at a short end, then roll up chard, enclosing sides. Brush lightly with oil; place in an 8-inch baking dish. Repeat, making 5 more rolls. Bake until heated through, 5 to 10 minutes.

6 Heat remaining mushroom mixture over medium-high. Add Marsala; cook, stirring, until most of the liquid has been absorbed. Add remaining 2 3/4 cups broth; cook, stirring occasionally, until slightly thickened, about 6 minutes. Stir in remaining 1 tablespoon marjoram (or 1/2 teaspoon dried).

7 To serve, slice each chard roll in half; place in the center of a plate. Spoon the mushroom mixture around chard.

per serving: 258 calories; 2.4 g saturated fat; 6.4 g unsaturated fat; 5 mg cholesterol; 32.2 g carbohydrates; 12.6 g protein; 93 mg sodium; 6 g fiber

stuffed poblanos in chipotle sauce SERVES 4

Stuffed with quinoa, black beans, mushrooms, and corn, these peppers make a satisfying vegetarian main course. Poblanos are among the mildest chiles, although they still offer a nice zing. Chipotle chiles are smoked, roasted jalapeños, usually sold in cans with a spicy adobo sauce.

4 large poblano chiles

2 teaspoons plus 1 tablespoon neutral-tasting oil, such as canola or safflower

1 tablespoon chopped chipotle chile in adobo

1 garlic clove

Coarse salt and freshly ground pepper

½ cup packed cilantro leaves, coarsely chopped, plus more for garnish

⅓ cup quinoa

8 ounces small mushrooms, such as white button or cremini, trimmed, cleaned, and quartered

1 cup fresh or frozen corn kernels

1 can (15 ounces) black beans, drained and rinsed

4 ounces crumbled fresh goat cheese (1 cup)

1 Preheat oven to 475°F. On a parchment-lined baking sheet, rub poblanos with 2 teaspoons oil. Roast until slightly blackened and softened, 15 to 20 minutes, turning once. Remove from oven. When cool enough to handle, remove skins with paper towels. Use a paring knife to make a small slit in each chile, then carefully remove seeds (and discard), keeping stem end intact.

2 In a blender, combine chipotle, garlic, 1 teaspoon salt, and ¾ cup water; season with pepper. Blend until smooth. Add cilantro, and pulse once to combine.

3 In a small saucepan, bring ⅔ cup water to a boil. Add quinoa; return to a boil. Stir once, cover, and reduce heat to a simmer. Cook until quinoa is tender but still chewy and has absorbed all liquid, about 15 minutes. Fluff with a fork.

4 Meanwhile, in a large skillet, heat the remaining 1 tablespoon oil over medium-high. Add mushrooms and ½ teaspoon salt; season with pepper. Cook, stirring occasionally, until mushrooms are tender, about 5 minutes. Add corn and beans, and cook, stirring, until heated through, about 2 minutes. Stir in ½ cup cheese and the quinoa.

5 Spread chipotle mixture evenly in a 9-by-13-inch baking dish. Stuff peppers with filling, dividing evenly, and arrange in dish; dot with remaining ½ cup cheese. Bake until golden, 15 to 20 minutes. Remove from oven, and let cool in pan 10 minutes before serving.

per serving: 324 calories; 3.2 g saturated fat; 4.7 g unsaturated fat; 12.6 mg cholesterol; 49.5 g carbohydrates; 14.4 g protein; 910 mg sodium; 9.4 g fiber

whole-wheat spaghetti with herb-almond pesto and broccoli SERVES 6

A snappy almond-and-herb pesto is a fresh departure from the classic pine-nut-and-basil version. For an even more nutritious variation, add three tablespoons ground flaxseed to the pesto.

12 ounces whole-wheat spaghetti

1¼ ounces whole blanched almonds, toasted (page 53)

2 tablespoons finely grated lemon zest, plus ¼ cup fresh lemon juice (from about 3 lemons)

1 garlic clove

1 cup packed fresh flat-leaf parsley

½ cup packed fresh mint leaves

¼ cup packed fresh tarragon leaves

Coarse salt and freshly ground pepper

3 tablespoons extra-virgin olive oil

2 heads (2¼ pounds) broccoli, cut into small florets (about 6 cups)

3 tablespoons part-skim ricotta cheese

Lemon wedges, for serving

1 Bring a large pot of water to a boil. Cook pasta until al dente according to package instructions. Reserve ½ cup cooking liquid; drain pasta.

2 Pulse almonds in a food processor until finely ground. Add 1 tablespoon lemon zest along with the lemon juice, garlic, herbs, and ½ teaspoon salt; process until finely chopped. With machine running, gradually add 2 tablespoons oil and the reserved cooking water; process until pesto is smooth. The pesto will keep for 1 week in the refrigerator or up to 1 month in the freezer; store in an airtight container, covered with a thin layer of olive oil. To serve, bring the pesto to room temperature (never heat it), pour off extra oil from top, and stir in a little water, if necessary, to achieve the proper consistency.

3 Heat a large sauté pan over medium-high. Add remaining 1 tablespoon oil. When hot, add broccoli and 1½ teaspoons salt; season with pepper. Cook, tossing occasionally, until broccoli is lightly browned and crisp, 5 to 7 minutes. Add pasta and pesto; toss to coat.

4 Divide pasta among six bowls. Dollop with ricotta, and sprinkle with remaining 1 tablespoon zest, dividing evenly. Squeeze lemon wedges over tops, and serve immediately.

per serving: 345 calories; 1 g saturated fat; 7 g unsaturated fat; 3 mg cholesterol; 56 g carbohydrates; 16 g protein; 448 mg sodium; 14 g fiber

soba noodle, tofu, and vegetable stir-fry SERVES 4

Here's a spicy noodle dish that's packed with vegetables; covering the pan during cooking helps trap the steam so the vegetables soften more quickly (and retain their nutrients). Look for soba noodles made entirely of buckwheat flour; besides being gluten-free, they are more nutritious than soba made from whole-wheat flour.

8 ounces soba noodles (preferably 100 percent buckwheat)

2 tablespoons grapeseed oil

14 ounces (1 package) extra-firm tofu, drained, patted dry, and cut into ½-inch cubes

Coarse salt

2 red bell peppers, ribs and seeds removed, thinly sliced lengthwise

1 head (1½ pounds) broccoli, broken into small florets

1 head (1 pound) bok choy, trimmed and thinly sliced crosswise

4 garlic cloves, minced

½ teaspoon crushed red pepper flakes

3 tablespoons almond butter

2 tablespoons water

3 tablespoons rice vinegar (unseasoned)

2 tablespoons low-sodium tamari soy sauce

1 Bring a large pot of water to a boil. Cook soba noodles until tender according to package instructions. Drain, and rinse with cold water; drain again.

2 Heat 1 tablespoon oil in a large skillet over medium-high; add tofu and 1 teaspoon salt. Cook, tossing occasionally, until golden, 12 to 15 minutes. Transfer to a plate.

3 Heat remaining 1 tablespoon oil in same skillet over medium-high. Add bell peppers, broccoli, bok choy, garlic, red pepper flakes, and 1 teaspoon salt. Cover (pan will be very full), and cook, tossing occasionally, until vegetables are crisp-tender, 8 to 10 minutes.

4 Meanwhile, make sauce: In a small bowl, whisk together almond butter and the water, then whisk in vinegar and soy sauce.

5 Add reserved noodles, tofu, and sauce to pan with vegetables. Cook, tossing, until noodles are heated through, 2 to 3 minutes. Serve immediately.

per serving: 511 calories; 1.53 g saturated fat; 12.5 g unsaturated fat; 0 mg cholesterol; 67 g carbohydrates; 26.7 g protein; 670 mg sodium; 7.6 g fiber

whole-wheat pasta with lentils, spinach, and leeks SERVES 6

French green lentils, sometimes called *lentilles du Puy,* hold their shape well once cooked, making them particularly suited to salads and pasta dishes. Like other legumes, lentils are low in fat and are exceptional sources of folate, iron, and protein, plus other vitamins and minerals. Here, the lentils are combined with whole-wheat pasta shapes called *chiocciole* (snails), but you can substitute penne or any other short tubular shapes. If you like, grate or shave parmesan over the pasta just before serving.

- 2 cups (14 ounces) French green lentils
- 2 garlic cloves
- 1 dried bay leaf
- 1 pound tubular whole-wheat pasta, such as penne
- 2 tablespoons extra-virgin olive oil, plus more for drizzling
- 4 leeks (about 1¾ pounds), white and pale green parts only, sliced into ¼-inch rounds, washed well, and drained
- 1 teaspoon chopped fresh thyme
  Coarse salt and freshly ground pepper
- 8 ounces baby spinach

1 In a saucepan, combine lentils, 1 garlic clove, and the bay leaf. Add enough cold water to cover by 2 inches. Bring to a boil over medium-high heat. Reduce heat to medium-low, and simmer until lentils are tender, 20 to 25 minutes. Drain lentils, and discard garlic clove and bay leaf.

2 Bring a large pot of water to a boil. Cook pasta until al dente according to package instructions. Reserve 1 cup cooking liquid; drain pasta, and place in a large bowl.

3 Meanwhile, mince remaining garlic clove. In a large sauté pan, heat oil over medium. Add minced garlic, leeks, and thyme; cook, stirring occasionally, until leeks are soft but not browned, about 5 minutes. Add cooked lentils and 1½ teaspoons salt; season with pepper.

4 Add spinach and reserved pasta cooking liquid to pan; cook, tossing to wilt spinach, about 2 minutes. Pour mixture over pasta, and toss to combine. Serve immediately, drizzled with olive oil, if desired.

per serving: 579 calories; .7 g saturated fat; 4.1 g unsaturated fat; 0 mg cholesterol; 106 g carbohydrates; 24.6 g protein; 372 mg sodium; 19 g fiber

spinach pasta with corn, edamame, and green beans SERVES 4

Edamame contain as much protein per serving as eggs, milk, and meat, and are also a good source of iron, zinc, and B vitamins. Since the corn is not cooked, it's imperative that you use the freshest you can find. Serve hot or cold as a speedy, summery pasta dish.

1 pound short spinach pasta, such as shells or penne

2 cups (about 6 ounces) fresh green beans, trimmed

2 cups (about 8 ounces) frozen shelled edamame

2 ears of corn, shucked, kernels cut from cobs

2 garlic cloves, minced

3 tablespoons extra-virgin olive oil

Finely grated zest and juice of 1 lemon

1 cup loosely packed fresh basil leaves, torn

Coarse salt and freshly ground pepper

1 Bring a large pot of water to a boil. Cook pasta until al dente according to package instructions, adding the green beans and edamame 3 to 4 minutes before end of cooking. Drain pasta and vegetables, then place in a bowl.

2 Add corn kernels and immediately stir in garlic and oil. Add lemon zest and juice, basil, and ½ teaspoon salt; season with pepper, and stir to combine.

per serving: 824 calories; 2.9 g saturated fat; 12.8 g unsaturated fat; 108 mg cholesterol; 129 g carbohydrates; 35.6 g protein; 263 mg sodium; 20.2 g fiber

butternut squash curry **SERVES 4**

Rather than relying on store-bought curry paste, this dish uses a quick homemade version that's incomparably fresh and vibrantly flavored. For a thicker curry, mash some of the squash with the back of a wooden spoon.

1 cup long-grain brown rice

5 cups plus 1 tablespoon water

2 small butternut squash (2 pounds), peeled, halved lengthwise, and seeded

1 large onion, cut into large chunks

4 garlic cloves

1 tablespoon neutral-tasting oil, such as canola or safflower

1 teaspoon mustard seeds

1 teaspoon fennel seeds

¼ teaspoon ground coriander

1 piece (2 inches) fresh ginger, peeled and finely grated

2 tablespoons tomato paste

Coarse salt

¼ teaspoon crushed red pepper flakes

Cilantro, for garnish

Lime wedges, for garnish

1 Place rice in a medium saucepan. Add 2 cups water and bring to a boil; stir once, and reduce heat. Simmer, covered, until rice is tender and has absorbed all liquid, 35 to 40 minutes. Remove from heat; let stand 10 minutes (covered).

2 Meanwhile, cut solid sections of squash into large chunks and seeded sections into ¾-inch thick wedges. Puree onion, garlic, and 1 tablespoon water in a blender until smooth.

3 Heat the oil in a 4-quart pot over medium. Add the mustard and fennel seeds and the coriander; cook, stirring, until fragrant, 1 to 2 minutes. Stir in the onion paste and ginger. Cook, stirring often, until caramelized, 6 to 8 minutes.

4 Add tomato paste, and cook 1 minute, stirring and scraping bottom of pot, if needed. Stir in remaining 3 cups water, 2 teaspoons salt, and red pepper flakes. Add squash, and cover partially. Bring to a boil. Reduce heat, and simmer gently until squash is tender, 12 to 15 minutes.

5 Fluff rice with a fork, then divide among four bowls. Spoon curry mixture on top, and garnish with cilantro and lime wedges. Serve immediately.

per serving: 337 calories; .6 g saturated fat; 4.5 g unsaturated fat; 0 mg cholesterol; 70 g carbohydrates; 7.2 g protein; 1052 mg sodium; 7.6 g fiber

quick tomato sauce MAKES ABOUT 4 CUPS

This sauce tastes great over pasta, fish, or grilled chicken—and is packed with beneficial lycopene from the cooked tomatoes.

¼ cup extra-virgin olive oil

1 red onion, minced

8 garlic cloves, minced

2 cans (14 ounces each) diced tomatoes in juice

¼ cup plus 2 tablespoons dry red wine

1 teaspoon dried oregano, crumbled

1 teaspoon dried basil, crumbled

Coarse salt

1 In a medium saucepan, heat oil over medium. Add onion and garlic; cook, stirring frequently, until softened, about 7 minutes.

2 Stir in the tomatoes and their juice, wine, oregano, basil, and ¼ teaspoon salt. Simmer until lightly thickened, 8 to 10 minutes. Season with ½ teaspoon salt, or to taste. Serve immediately, or let cool completely before storing. The sauce can be refrigerated up to 5 days, or frozen up to 1 month, in an airtight container; thaw in the refrigerator and reheat in a pan over medium.

per 1/2-cup serving: 79 calories; 1 g saturated fat; 6 g unsaturated fat; 0 mg cholesterol; 3.1 g carbohydrates; .5 g protein; 107 mg sodium; .5 g fiber

spring barley risotto SERVES 4

High in iron, vitamins, and fiber, barley risotto is a nutritious (and quicker-cooking) alternative to a traditional risotto made with rice. This vegetarian dish also includes frozen peas, which are always available, easy to use, and contain nearly as many nutrients as fresh-picked. As a good source of chromium, peas also help control blood sugar levels.

2 tablespoons olive oil

1 cup pearl barley

2 leeks, white and pale green parts only, thinly sliced, washed well and drained

½ cup dry white wine (or water)

2 cups water

Coarse salt and freshly ground pepper

2 cups homemade or low-sodium store-bought vegetable broth

1 bunch asparagus (about 1 pound), tough ends trimmed, cut on the diagonal into 2-inch lengths

1 package (10 ounces) frozen peas, thawed

½ cup grated parmesan cheese

¼ cup packed thinly sliced fresh mint leaves, plus whole small leaves for garnish

1 In a large saucepan, heat oil over medium. Add barley and leeks; cook, stirring occasionally, until they begin to soften, 5 to 7 minutes. Add wine; cook, stirring, until evaporated, about 5 minutes. Add the water and bring to a boil; add ½ teaspoon salt and season with pepper to taste. Reduce heat; simmer, stirring occasionally, until liquid has been absorbed, about 10 minutes.

2 Add broth and continue to cook, stirring occasionally, until barley is tender and liquid is creamy, about 10 minutes. Add asparagus; cook until tender, about 5 minutes. Stir in peas and cook just until heated through. Remove from heat. Stir in parmesan and mint; season with pepper. Garnish with mint leaves, and serve.

per serving: 426 calories; 2.9 g saturated fat; 7.6 g unsaturated fat; 8.8 mg cholesterol; 62.4 g carbohydrates; 15.7 g protein; 465 mg sodium; 15.5 g fiber

swiss chard, mushroom, and quinoa salad SERVES 4

This main-course salad combines chard, mushrooms, and quinoa to form a satisfying vegetarian meal abundant with vitamins, minerals, and complete protein.

- 2 cups water
- 1 cup quinoa, rinsed and drained
- 1 tablespoon extra-virgin olive oil
- 1 pound Swiss chard, stems and leaves cut into ½-inch pieces (about 10½ cups), rinsed well, water still clinging to leaves

  Coarse salt and freshly ground pepper

  Pinch of crushed red pepper flakes

- 1 garlic clove, minced
- 12 ounces cremini mushrooms, trimmed, cleaned, and thinly sliced
- 2 teaspoons finely chopped fresh thyme
- 1 ounce shaved parmesan cheese (½ cup)

1 In a medium saucepan, bring the water to a boil. Add quinoa and reduce heat to a simmer. Cover and cook until quinoa is tender and has absorbed all liquid, about 15 minutes. Remove from heat. Meanwhile, heat 1 teaspoon oil in a large skillet over medium. Cook chard (stems and leaves), stirring occasionally, until wilted and tender, about 8 minutes. Add ¼ teaspoon salt; season with pepper. Add red pepper flakes, and toss to combine. Transfer to a platter.

2 Add remaining 2 teaspoons oil and the garlic to skillet. Cook over medium heat, stirring, until garlic is lightly golden, about 1 minute. Add mushrooms, and cook, stirring occasionally, until they start to release their juices, about 3 minutes. Add ½ teaspoon salt; season with pepper. Cook, stirring occasionally, until mushrooms are tender, about 5 minutes. Stir in quinoa; cook to heat through, about 1 minute. Stir in thyme; remove from heat.

3 To serve, divide chard among plates, and spoon quinoa mixture on top. Sprinkle parmesan over each portion.

per serving: 252 calories; 1 g saturated fat; 6 g unsaturated fat; 3 mg cholesterol; 38 g carbohydrates; 1 g protein; 666 mg sodium; 5 g fiber

walnut-crusted chicken breasts SERVES 4

Walnuts add a healthful dose of omega-3 fatty acids to bread crumbs, which keep the chicken moist. Roasting the chicken, rather than frying it, yields a crisp crust without adding much extra fat. If you don't have day-old bread, lightly toast fresh bread to use instead.

2 slices day-old whole-wheat bread

⅓ cup walnuts

2 tablespoons finely grated parmesan cheese

Coarse salt and freshly ground pepper

1 large egg white

4 boneless, skinless chicken breast halves (6 to 8 ounces each)

1 tablespoon grapeseed oil

Lemon slices, for serving

1 Preheat oven to 425°F. In a food processor, combine bread, walnuts, parmesan, and ¼ teaspoon salt; season with pepper. Process until fine crumbs form. Transfer to a shallow bowl. In another bowl, beat egg white until frothy.

2 Pat dry chicken with paper towels. Season chicken on both sides with ½ teaspoon salt, dividing evenly, and pepper. Dip each chicken breast into egg white to coat completely, then let excess drip off before dredging in crumb mixture, pressing to adhere.

3 Heat the oil in a large ovenproof skillet over medium until hot but not smoking. Cook chicken until lightly browned on one side, 1 to 3 minutes. Flip chicken and transfer skillet to oven. Bake until golden brown and cooked through, 8 to 12 minutes. Serve with lemon slices.

per serving: 331 calories; 1.9 g saturated fat; 9.6 g unsaturated fat; 101 mg cholesterol; 8.5 g carbohydrates; 44 g protein; 603 mg sodium; 1.6 g fiber

chicken breasts with fennel, carrots, and couscous SERVES 4

After the chicken is browned and the vegetables are sautéed, the meat is braised until fork-tender. Orange juice adds vitamin C and brightens the dish, but you can omit it and increase the chicken stock by half a cup.

1 cup water

2/3 cup couscous

4 boneless, skinless chicken breast halves (6 to 8 ounces each)

1¾ teaspoons paprika

Coarse salt and freshly ground pepper

2 tablespoons neutral-tasting oil, such as canola or safflower

1 fennel bulb, trimmed, cored, and thinly sliced

3 large carrots, peeled and thinly sliced

1 teaspoon ground cumin

2/3 cup dried apricots, preferably unsulfured, chopped

½ cup oil-cured pitted black olives, halved

½ cup fresh orange juice

½ cup homemade or reduced-sodium store-bought chicken broth

1 Bring the water to a boil in a small saucepan; add couscous, and stir to combine. Cover and let stand until tender, about 5 minutes, then fluff with a fork.

2 Pat chicken dry with paper towels. Rub chicken on both sides with ¾ teaspoon paprika and ½ teaspoon salt, dividing evenly; season with pepper. In a large skillet, heat 1 tablespoon oil over medium-high. Cook chicken until lightly browned, about 3 minutes per side; transfer to a plate.

3 Reduce heat to medium. Add remaining 1 tablespoon oil; when hot, add fennel and carrots. Cook, stirring occasionally, until vegetables are crisp-tender and lightly browned, 5 to 7 minutes. Add remaining 1 teaspoon paprika, the cumin, and ¼ teaspoon salt; season with pepper. Cook, stirring, until spices are fragrant, about 1 minute.

4 Add chicken and any accumulated juices from plate to skillet along with the apricots, olives, orange juice, and broth. Cover and simmer until vegetables are soft and chicken is cooked through, 12 to 15 minutes. Serve with couscous.

per serving: 492 calories; 1.4 g saturated fat; 8.9 g unsaturated fat; 99 mg cholesterol; 50 g carbohydrates; 46.5 g protein; 703 mg sodium; 6.5 g fiber

chicken with pumpkin-seed mole SERVES 6

This rich pumpkin-seed sauce, based on traditional Mexican moles, is made with green herbs, and is just as satisfying as cheese- or cream-based sauces but contains far less saturated fat and fewer calories. Serve the dish with rice for an authentic accompaniment.

3 boneless, skinless chicken breast halves (about 6 ounces each)

1 small serrano chile

1 small poblano chile

1 small white onion, cut into ¼-inch dice

2 garlic cloves

1 cup cilantro leaves, plus sprigs for garnish

½ teaspoon ground cumin

¾ teaspoon dried oregano, preferably Mexican

½ cup raw hulled pumpkin seeds (pepitas), toasted (page 57)

2 cups homemade or reduced-sodium store-bought chicken broth

1 tablespoon neutral-tasting oil, such as canola or safflower

Coarse salt

2 tablespoons fresh lime juice (from 2 to 3 limes)

1 Place chicken in a 4-quart pot, and add water to cover by 1 inch. Bring to a gentle simmer over medium heat, and simmer until chicken is cooked through, about 15 minutes. Remove from heat, and let stand 15 minutes. Transfer chicken to a plate, and tent loosely with foil. Discard water.

2 Roast both chiles directly over the flame of a gas-stove burner on high heat, turning with tongs, until blackened all over. (Alternately, place chiles under the broiler, turning often, until skin has charred.) Transfer the chiles to a bowl, and cover with plastic wrap. Let steam 15 minutes. Using paper towels, rub off skins, then remove stems, seeds, and ribs.

3 In a blender, puree roasted chiles, onion, garlic, cilantro leaves, cumin, oregano, toasted pumpkin seeds, and ½ cup broth to form a coarse paste.

4 Heat oil in a medium skillet over medium. Add chile paste, and cook, stirring constantly, until very thick, about 8 minutes. (Reduce heat if mixture begins to scorch.) Whisk remaining 1½ cups broth into paste until incorporated. Add ½ teaspoon salt and the lime juice.

5 Add chicken to sauce in skillet. Cook over medium-low heat, turning occasionally, until just heated through, about 5 minutes (do not let simmer, or sauce will "break," or separate).

6 With tongs, transfer chicken to a cutting board, let excess sauce drip back into pot, and slice in half crosswise. Divide chicken evenly among four plates, spoon sauce on top, and garnish with cilantro sprigs.

per serving: 294 calories; 2.6 g saturated fat; 10.5 g unsaturated fat; 67 mg cholesterol; 7.2 g carbohydrates; 36 g protein; 222 mg sodium; 2 g fiber

lemon chicken with avocado-corn salsa SERVES 4

Avocados in the salsa supply a generous portion of monounsaturated fat and fiber. If fresh corn is not in season, opt for frozen; it will taste better and have more nutrients than any "fresh" corn in the grocery store.

4 boneless, skinless chicken breast halves (6 to 8 ounces each)

¼ cup plus 2 teaspoons extra-virgin olive oil

2 tablespoons plus 2 teaspoons fresh lemon juice (from 1 to 2 lemons)

2 ears corn, husks and silks removed (or 1 cup frozen corn kernels)

2 teaspoons finely chopped red jalapeño chiles (ribs and seeds removed for less heat, if desired)

2 tablespoons minced peeled fresh ginger

½ cup canned black beans, drained and rinsed

½ red onion, finely chopped

¼ cup fresh lime juice (from 3 to 4 limes)

10 cherry tomatoes, quartered

2 firm, ripe Hass avocados, halved lengthwise, pitted, peeled, and diced

Coarse salt and freshly ground pepper

4 ounces baby arugula

1 Combine chicken with 2 tablespoons each oil and lemon juice in a shallow baking dish. Cover and marinate in refrigerator for 1 to 3 hours, turning once.

2 Working in a large bowl, stand each ear of corn on its flat end; shave off kernels with a serrated knife (to yield about 1 cup total).

3 Heat 1 tablespoon oil in a medium skillet over medium. Add corn kernels, chiles, and ginger; cook, stirring frequently, until softened, 3 to 4 minutes. Let cool.

4 Heat a grill (or grill pan) to medium (if using a charcoal grill, coals are ready when you can hold your hand 5 inches above grates for just 6 to 8 seconds). Grill chicken until lightly browned and cooked through, about 5 minutes per side. Remove from heat.

5 Stir together black beans, onion, corn mixture, lime juice, and 1 tablespoon oil. Add tomatoes, avocados, and ½ teaspoon salt (or to taste); season with pepper, and stir gently to combine.

6 Toss arugula with remaining 2 teaspoons each oil and lemon juice. Divide evenly among plates, and top with chicken and avocado-corn salsa. Serve immediately.

per serving: 524 calories; 5 g saturated fat; 4 g unsaturated fat; 68 mg cholesterol; 29 g carbohydrates; 34 g protein; 244 mg sodium; 11 g fiber

turkey cutlets with tomatoes and capers SERVES 4

Lower in saturated fat than chicken, turkey provides one of the leanest sources of animal protein. The nutrient-dense poultry also contains heart-healthy B vitamins and selenium. Round out this simple preparation with a side of steamed green beans.

4 turkey cutlets (about 4 ounces each)

Coarse salt and freshly ground pepper

2 tablespoons neutral-tasting oil, such as canola or safflower

1½ cups diced tomato (1 large)

12 caper berries or ¼ cup capers, rinsed and drained

1 Pat dry cutlets with paper towels and season both sides with ½ teaspoon salt, dividing evenly, and pepper. Heat 1 tablespoon oil in a large skillet over high until shimmering. Add 2 cutlets, and cook until golden brown on bottom, about 2 minutes. Flip and continue to cook until other side is golden brown, about 2 minutes more. Transfer cutlets to plates; reduce heat to medium, and repeat with remaining 1 tablespoon oil and 2 cutlets.

2 Add tomato to hot skillet. Cook, stirring, until juicy and just softened, about 2 minutes. Add caper berries, and stir to warm through; spoon mixture over turkey, dividing evenly, and serve.

per serving: 193 calories; .5 g saturated fat; 6 g unsaturated fat; 45 mg cholesterol; 2.7 g carbohydrates; 28.7 g protein; 601 mg sodium; .8 g fiber

grilled pork tenderloin and apricots with honey glaze SERVES 4

A mortar and pestle make easy work of crushing whole spices and peppercorns, but you can also use the bottom of a skillet or even the flat side of a chef's knife, pressing down firmly and working on a cutting board. Choose apricots that are ripe but still firm so they can hold up under the heat of the grill; brush the apricots and pork with the glaze as soon as they come off the heat. The glaze also tastes great on other grilled meats.

1 teaspoon coriander seeds

½ teaspoon whole black peppercorns

1 piece (2 inches) fresh ginger, peeled and thinly sliced

¾ cup honey

2 tablespoons apple-cider vinegar

Coarse salt and freshly ground pepper

2 pork tenderloins (about 1¼ pounds)

3 tablespoons neutral-tasting oil, such as canola or safflower

8 scallions

6 medium-ripe apricots (about 1 pound), halved and pitted

1 Coarsely crush coriander seeds and peppercorns. Toast in a small saucepan over medium heat until fragrant, shaking pan occasionally, 1 to 2 minutes. Add ginger, honey, vinegar, and ¼ teaspoon salt; cook, stirring occasionally, until bubbling rapidly, about 5 minutes. Remove from heat and let stand 15 minutes; strain into a small dish.

2 Heat a grill (or grill pan) to high (if using a charcoal grill, coals are ready when you can hold your hand 5 inches above grill for just 2 to 3 seconds). Sprinkle pork on all sides with ½ teaspoon salt, and season with ground pepper; brush with 1 tablespoon oil. Cook until browned, about 3 minutes per side. Move pork to indirect heat (or reduce heat to low if using a grill pan) and cook until an instant-read thermometer inserted in middle reaches 138°F, 10 to 12 minutes. Transfer to a cutting board; spoon 2 to 3 tablespoons of glaze over pork. Let rest 10 minutes before slicing.

3 Meanwhile, grill scallions until lightly charred and tender, about 3 minutes. Brush apricots with remaining 2 tablespoons oil. Cook, cut side down, until apricots are marked by the grill and release easily from the grates, about 3 minutes. Flip and cook until bubbling around the edges, skins pull away, and apricots are tender when pressed, about 2 minutes more. Dividing evenly, transfer to four serving plates, and drizzle glaze over each apricot half. Serve warm with pork and scallions.

per serving: 491 calories; 3.1 g saturated fat; 11.4 g unsaturated fat; 92 mg cholesterol; 61 g carbohydrates; 31.3 g protein; 537 mg sodium; 2.2 g fiber

pork tenderloin with sautéed beet greens and roasted beets SERVES 4

Roasting beets takes a bit longer than boiling them, but the time spent is well worth it for the resulting rich flavor. Using both the greens and the roots makes beets a great bargain.

- 2 bunches beets (3 to 4 pounds with greens), greens separated and chopped, washed, and drained with some water left clinging (about 9 cups greens)
- 2 pork tenderloins (about 1¼ pounds)

  Coarse salt and freshly ground pepper
- ¼ cup extra-virgin olive oil
- 2 teaspoons Dijon mustard
- 2 teaspoons plus 1 tablespoon red-wine vinegar
- 2 garlic cloves, smashed
- 2 tablespoons pine nuts, toasted (page 53)

1 Preheat oven to 400°F. Loosely wrap beets in a 12-by-20-inch piece of parchment, then wrap packet in foil. Place on a rimmed baking sheet and cook until easily pierced with the tip of a sharp knife, 35 to 45 minutes. When cool enough to handle, rub off skins with paper towels. Reserve 1 beet; halve and slice remaining beets.

2 Season pork all over with 2 teaspoons salt, dividing evenly, and pepper. Place on a rimmed baking sheet and roast until an instant-read thermometer inserted in middle reaches 138°F, 14 to 16 minutes. Transfer to a cutting board and let rest 10 minutes before slicing thinly.

3 Meanwhile, process the reserved whole beet with 1 tablespoon oil in a food processor until smooth. Pass through a fine sieve lined with cheesecloth into a small bowl (to yield 1 tablespoon plus 1 teaspoon juice); discard solids. Add mustard, 2 teaspoons vinegar, and 2 tablespoons oil; whisk to combine.

4 In a large skillet, heat remaining 1 tablespoon oil over medium. Cook garlic, stirring, until fragrant and golden, about 1 minute. Add beet greens and 1 teaspoon salt; season with pepper. Cook, stirring occasionally, until greens are wilted and tender, 2 to 4 minutes. Remove from heat, and discard garlic. Add sliced beets and remaining 1 tablespoon vinegar, and toss to combine. Sprinkle with pine nuts.

5 To serve, drizzle beet vinaigrette on each of four plates, dividing evenly, then top with pork and beet greens.

per serving: 553 calories; 4.3 g saturated fat; 18 g unsaturated fat; 111 mg cholesterol; 43.2 g carbohydrates; 44.6 g protein; 1208 mg sodium; 14.5 g fiber

steak with spicy papaya-carrot salsa SERVES 4

A papaya salsa with fiery Scotch bonnet chiles makes a colorful — and spicy — condiment for grilled steak. The salsa also goes well with grilled fish, particularly snapper. For less heat, seed the chiles before slicing them.

STEAKS

- 4 top round steaks (each ½ inch thick and 4 to 5 ounces)
- 2 teaspoons neutral-tasting oil, such as canola or safflower

  Coarse salt and freshly ground pepper
- 1 firm, ripe avocado, halved lengthwise, pitted, peeled, and cut into 8 wedges
- ¾ cup Spicy Papaya-Carrot Salsa (see right)

Heat a grill (or grill pan) to medium high (if using a charcoal grill, coals are ready when you can hold your hand 5 inches above grate for just 4 to 5 seconds). Rub the steaks all over with the oil; season with ¼ teaspoon salt, dividing evenly, and pepper.

Grill steaks 1 to 2 minutes per side for medium-rare. Transfer steaks to four plates. Serve with avocado and salsa.

per serving: 343 calories; 3.6 g saturated fat; 10.3 g unsaturated fat; 92 mg cholesterol; 7.5 g carbohydrates; 41.8 g protein; 134.5 mg sodium; 3.8 g fiber

SPICY PAPAYA-CARROT SALSA
MAKES ABOUT 3 CUPS

Chayote is a member of the gourd family, along with cucumbers, melons, and squash; it is mild tasting, with a crisp, pearlike texture. It is often used in salads and salsas, or baked and stuffed, like other squash. If you can't find one, you can substitute honeydew melon instead, adding it after the mixture has been cooked and allowed to cool.

- ¾ cup water
- 1 small chayote, peeled, seeded, and cut into ¼-inch dice
- 2 carrots, peeled and cut into ¼-inch dice
- ⅓ cup distilled white vinegar
- 1 or 2 fresh Scotch bonnet chiles, thinly sliced
- 1 teaspoon light brown sugar

  Coarse salt
- 1 large papaya (Mexican or Solo, about 1 pound), peeled, halved lengthwise, seeds removed, and cut into ½-inch dice (2½ cups)

Bring the water, chayote, and carrots to a boil in a medium saucepan. Add vinegar, chiles, sugar, and 1 teaspoon salt. Return to a boil. Reduce heat; simmer, partially covered, until chayote and carrots are tender, 20 to 25 minutes, adding papaya after 10 minutes.

Remove from heat; let cool slightly. Process one-third of mixture in a food processor; return to saucepan, and stir to combine. Season with more salt, if desired. Salsa can be refrigerated up to 2 weeks in an airtight container; let cool completely before storing. Serve cold, at room temperature, or warm (reheat over medium).

per serving: 16 calories; 0 g saturated fat; 0 g unsaturated fat; 0 mg cholesterol; 3.7 g carbohydrates; .4 g protein; 7.4 mg sodium; 1 g fiber

grass-fed beef stir-fry with broccoli SERVES 4

Grass-fed beef is leaner than beef raised on grain, which ultimately means it's lower in saturated fat. Here, beef is served over red quinoa, which adds protein and vitamins to the dish. Brown rice is another healthful option.

2 teaspoons neutral-tasting oil, such as canola or safflower

3 garlic cloves, minced

1 tablespoon finely julienned peeled fresh ginger

Pinch crushed red pepper flakes

½ pound boneless sirloin or tenderloin, cut into thin strips

1½ cups chopped broccoli

2 tablespoons low-sodium tamari soy sauce

2 tablespoons fresh orange juice

Heat oil in a medium sauté pan over medium-high. Sauté garlic, ginger, and red pepper flakes until just golden, stirring frequently, about 1 minute. Increase heat to high, and add beef and broccoli. Cook until beef is seared and broccoli is crisp-tender, turning strips once, 2 to 3 minutes. Stir in tamari and orange juice. Serve immediately.

per serving: 163 calories; 3.6 g saturated fat; 6.1 g unsaturated fat; 31.2 mg cholesterol; 2.6 g carbohydrates; 13.1 g protein; 535 mg sodium; .4 g fiber

SIDE DISHES

lentils with ginger, golden beets, and herbs SERVES 6

High-protein lentils are enlivened here by coriander, ginger, mint, and cilantro. For the best flavor, toast whole coriander seeds, then grind them to a fine powder. In a pinch, you can substitute a teaspoon of ground coriander instead of grinding your own. Beets add heart-healthy iron, potassium, and folate.

- 1 pound (about 6) golden or red beets, trimmed
- ½ cup water
- Coarse salt and freshly ground pepper
- 1 tablespoon plus 1 teaspoon extra-virgin olive oil
- ¾ cup (6 ounces) small lentils, such as French green or black beluga
- 6 thin slices peeled fresh ginger, plus 1 teaspoon finely grated
- ¼ red onion, finely chopped
- 2 tablespoons red-wine vinegar
- 2 teaspoons honey
- 1½ teaspoons coriander seeds, toasted (page 57) and finely ground
- ¼ cup coarsely chopped fresh mint, plus more leaves for garnish
- 2 tablespoons coarsely chopped cilantro, plus more leaves for garnish

1 Place beets, the water, and ¼ teaspoon salt in a baking dish. Cover with parchment, then foil, and bake until beets are tender when pierced with the tip of a sharp knife, 45 to 55 minutes. Let stand until cool enough to handle. Rub off skins with paper towel, then quarter beets and place in a small bowl. Toss with 1 teaspoon oil.

2 Meanwhile, combine lentils and sliced ginger in a saucepan, and cover with water by 2 inches. Bring to a boil. Reduce heat, and simmer gently. Cook, stirring occasionally, until lentils are tender, about 20 minutes. Drain; discard ginger. Transfer to a large bowl, and stir in ½ teaspoon salt.

3 Combine grated ginger, the onion, vinegar, honey, and ¼ teaspoon salt; let stand 15 minutes. Whisk in remaining 1 tablespoon oil and the ground coriander. Pour over lentils, and toss to coat. Season with pepper. Stir in chopped mint and cilantro. Arrange beet wedges on top of lentils. Garnish with herb leaves, and serve immediately.

per serving: 173 calories; 1 g saturated fat; 3 g unsaturated fat; 0 mg cholesterol; 28 g carbohydrates; 9 g protein; 383 mg sodium; 11 g fiber

ROASTED BRUSSELS SPROUTS WITH
PEAR AND SHALLOTS

GLAZED CARROTS WITH GINGER

roasted brussels sprouts with pear and shallots SERVES 4

Like other cruciferous vegetables, brussels sprouts contain glucosinolates, chemical compounds that have been shown to help prevent cancer. Partnering the little cabbages with pear gives this dish even more fiber, as well as a balance of sweet and savory flavors.

1 ripe, firm Bartlett pear, preferably red

1 pound brussels sprouts, trimmed and halved

3 shallots, quartered

4 sprigs thyme

1 tablespoon plus 1½ teaspoons extra-virgin olive oil

Coarse salt and freshly ground pepper

2 tablespoons fresh lemon juice

1 Preheat oven to 425°F. Core pear and cut into wedges. Place on a large rimmed baking sheet with brussels sprouts, shallots, thyme, oil, and 1 teaspoon salt; season with pepper. Toss to combine, and spread in an even layer.

2 Roast until brussels sprouts are tender and browned, 30 to 35 minutes, rotating sheet and tossing sprouts halfway through. Remove from oven; sprinkle with lemon juice, and toss to combine. Serve warm.

per serving: 124 calories; 1 g saturated fat; 4 g unsaturated fat; 0 mg cholesterol; 18 g carbohydrates; 4 g protein; 27 mg sodium; 5 g fiber

glazed carrots with ginger SERVES 4

Sweet meets spicy when parboiled baby carrots are sautéed with honey, ginger, and sliced hot red chile. Not to be confused with the type sold in bags at the supermarket, the baby in this recipe are young carrots with the tops still attached. If you can't find them, buy regular carrots; cut off the thick sections, then halve or quarter them.

Coarse salt

30 baby carrots (about ¾ pound), peeled and with 1-inch green tops intact

1½ tablespoons unsalted butter

1 tablespoon plus 2 teaspoons honey

1 piece (2 inches) fresh ginger, peeled and cut into thin matchsticks

1 fresh red chile, such as Thai bird or jalapeño, thinly sliced (ribs and seeds removed for less heat, if desired)

1 Bring a pot of water to a boil; add 1 tablespoon salt. Cook carrots until just tender, 3 to 4 minutes. Drain carrots; pat them dry with paper towels.

2 Melt butter in a large skillet over medium-high heat. Add the carrots, honey, and ginger; cook, turning carrots frequently, until browned and glazed, about 8 minutes. Add the chile, and continue to cook, stirring, until softened, about 1 minute more. Serve immediately.

per serving: 105 calories; 2.7 g saturated fat; 1.3 g unsaturated fat; 11.3 mg cholesterol; 16.4 g carbohydrates; 1 g protein; 46 mg sodium; 2 g fiber

kohlrabi and turnip slaw SERVES 4

These two members of the cabbage family deliver an interesting twist to standard coleslaw. Both kohlrabi and turnips offer fiber, iron, and vitamin C, and the thick kohlrabi leaves boast a high dose of cancer-fighting phytochemicals.

2 small kohlrabi bulbs (about 1 pound), leaves intact

1 turnip (about 8 ounces), peeled and quartered

3 tablespoons fresh lime juice (from 2 to 3 limes)

1 tablespoon neutral-tasting oil, such as canola or safflower

2 teaspoons honey

1 teaspoon toasted sesame oil

Coarse salt and freshly ground pepper

2 scallions, trimmed and thinly sliced

1 Separate stems from kohlrabi bulbs; trim off tough ends. Remove leaves from stems, and slice in half lengthwise, then thinly slice crosswise. Trim root end from bulbs and peel away tough outer layer; halve lengthwise. Shred kohlrabi bulbs (stem and root sections) and turnip in a food processor fitted with a shredding blade or on the large holes of a box grater.

2 In a bowl, whisk together lime juice, canola oil, honey, sesame oil, and 1 teaspoon salt; season with pepper. Add scallions, kohlrabi (leaves and bulb), and turnip to bowl; toss to coat. Let stand 15 minutes before serving.

per serving: 104 calories; .9 g saturated fat; 3.9 g unsaturated fat; 0 mg cholesterol; 15.5 g carbohydrates; 2.7 g protein; 543 mg sodium; 5.5 g fiber

steamed rutabaga and potato salad SERVES 6

A cross between a cabbage and a turnip, rutabaga also belongs to the *Brassica* family and contains some fiber and potassium along with vitamin C. Peel away the tough exterior of the root vegetable to discover hearty, firm flesh that's tasty and filling.

1 rutabaga (1 pound), peeled and cut into 2-inch pieces

1 pound red new potatoes, scrubbed, halved or quartered (to equal the size of the rutabaga pieces)

2 tablespoons white-wine vinegar

1 tablespoon Dijon mustard

Coarse salt and freshly ground pepper

2 tablespoons extra-virgin olive oil

2 celery stalks, halved lengthwise and sliced crosswise, plus ¼ cup coarsely chopped inner leaves

1 Fill a pot with 2 inches of water. Set a steamer basket (or colander) in pot. Bring water to a boil; place rutabaga in basket, and reduce heat to a simmer. Cover, and steam 5 minutes. Add potatoes, cover, and steam until vegetables are just tender when pierced with the tip of a sharp knife, about 15 minutes more.

2 In a large bowl, whisk together vinegar, mustard, and ½ teaspoon salt; season with pepper. Whisk in the oil until emulsified. Add vegetables to vinaigrette. Toss to combine; let cool, tossing occasionally.

3 Mix in sliced celery and celery leaves; season with more salt, if desired, and pepper to taste. Serve immediately.

per serving: 132 calories; .7 g saturated fat; 4.1 g unsaturated fat; 0 mg cholesterol; 20.2 g carbohydrates; 2.5 g protein; 250 mg sodium; 3.7 g fiber

KOHLRABI AND TURNIP SLAW

STEAMED RUTABAGA AND POTATO SALAD

carrot latkes MAKES 16

Latkes, traditionally served at Hanukkah, are typically panfried and topped with sour cream. This herbed carrot version eliminates much of the fat, requiring only a small amount of cooking oil and featuring drained low-fat yogurt as a topping. Be sure to squeeze all the juice from the onion to prevent the patties from falling apart.

- 1½ cups grated carrot (3 carrots)
- ¾ cup finely chopped celery (2 stalks)
- ½ cup finely grated onion (1 onion), squeezed of juice in cheesecloth or paper towels
- ¼ cup plain bread crumbs
- 2 large eggs, lightly beaten
- ½ cup packed fresh chervil leaves
  Coarse salt and freshly ground pepper
- 1 to 2 tablespoons neutral-tasting oil, such as canola or safflower
- ½ cup plain Greek-style yogurt (2 percent)

1 Combine the carrot, celery, onion, bread crumbs, eggs, chervil, 1 teaspoon salt, and ¼ teaspoon pepper in a bowl. Press a heaping tablespoon of the mixture between your hands to form a 2-inch patty, and place on a tray or baking sheet. Repeat with remaining mixture to form a total of 16 patties.

2 Heat 1 tablespoon oil in a large skillet over medium-low until simmering. Working in two batches, cook patties until golden brown, 3 to 4 minutes per side; transfer to a serving platter. Add remaining tablespoon oil between batches, if necessary. To serve, top each latke with a dollop of yogurt.

per 2-latke serving: 76 calories; .9 saturated fat; 1.9 g unsaturated fat; 58 mg cholesterol; 7.3 g carbohydrates; 5 g protein; 214 mg sodium; 3.2 g fiber

edamame and butternut squash succotash SERVES 6

Firm, buttery-tasting edamame stand in for lima beans in this all-American side dish. If you can't find fresh edamame, frozen work just as well.

1 small butternut squash
(1 pound), peeled, halved
lengthwise, seeded, and
cut into ½-inch pieces
(about 3 cups)

2 ounces green beans, sliced
on the bias into 1-inch pieces

2 teaspoons extra-virgin
olive oil

1 small onion, finely chopped

1 garlic clove, minced

½ cup homemade or reduced-
sodium store-bought chicken
or vegetable broth

1 cup fresh or frozen corn
kernels

1 cup fresh or frozen shelled
edamame

1 teaspoon coarsely chopped
fresh thyme

Coarse salt and freshly
ground pepper

1 tablespoon coarsely
chopped fresh flat-leaf
parsley

1 Fill a pot with 2 inches of water. Set a steamer basket (or colander) in pot; bring water to a boil. Place squash in basket and steam just until tender when pierced with the tip of a sharp knife, about 7 minutes. Transfer to a plate. Add green beans to basket; steam until crisp-tender, about 3 minutes. Transfer to plate.

2 In a large skillet, heat oil over medium. Add onion and garlic; cook, stirring occasionally, until soft and lightly golden, about 3 minutes. Add broth, and bring to a simmer. Add corn and edamame; cook, stirring occasionally, until brightly colored and crisp-tender, about 3 minutes.

3 Add thyme, along with steamed squash and green beans; cook until heated through, about 3 minutes, stirring to combine. Add 1 teaspoon salt (or to taste), and season with pepper; stir to combine. Sprinkle with parsley, and serve.

per serving: 104 calories; .3 g saturated fat; 1.7 g unsaturated fat; 0 mg cholesterol; 17.6 g carbohydrates; 4.4 g protein; 336 mg sodium; 3.7 g fiber

steamed broccoli with miso-sesame dressing SERVES 4

An outstanding member of the *Brassica* family, broccoli aids in detoxification, and steaming is the best cooking method for retaining the vegetable's potent nutrients. Miso, or fermented soybean paste, contains B vitamins, protein, and probiotics, which strengthen immunity.

2 heads broccoli (2 pounds), separated into florets (4 cups)

2 tablespoons dark miso

1 tablespoon plus 1½ teaspoons sesame seeds, toasted (page 57)

2 tablespoons fresh lemon juice

1 tablespoon plus 1½ teaspoons toasted sesame oil

¼ cup (2 ounces) drained silken tofu

2 to 3 tablespoons water

2 tablespoons minced red bell pepper (ribs and seeds removed), for garnish

1 Fill a pot with 2 inches of water. Set a steamer basket (or colander) in pot; bring water to a boil. Place broccoli florets in basket, and steam until bright green and just tender, about 5 minutes.

2 Meanwhile, mix together miso, sesame seeds, the lemon juice, and oil in a bowl. Slowly add tofu and 2 tablespoons water, stirring until combined; if dressing is too thick, add up to 1 tablespoon more water.

3 Transfer broccoli to a serving dish; drizzle with dressing, and garnish with red bell pepper.

per serving: 116 calories; .8 g saturated fat; 4.9 g unsaturated fat; 0 mg cholesterol; 8.4 g carbohydrates; 4.8 g protein; 261 mg sodium; 2.7 g fiber

sesame spinach SERVES 4

Blanching is a good way to cook vegetables so they retain most of their nutrients. In this Japanese preparation, spinach is quickly wilted in boiling water, then plunged into an ice-water bath to stop the cooking.

Coarse salt

2 pounds spinach (about 2 bunches), tough stems trimmed, washed, and drained

1 tablespoon plus 1½ teaspoons toasted sesame oil

1 tablespoon plus 1½ teaspoons low-sodium tamari soy sauce

1 tablespoon plus 1½ teaspoons rice vinegar (unseasoned)

1 tablespoon plus 1½ teaspoons mirin (rice wine)

3 tablespoons sesame seeds, toasted (page 57)

1 Prepare a large ice-water bath. Bring a large pot of water to a boil; add 1 tablespoon salt. Blanch spinach just until wilted, about 30 seconds. Drain in a colander, then set colander in the ice bath. When spinach is completely cooled, transfer colander to sink and drain again. Squeeze out excess water, then coarsely chop the spinach and place in a bowl.

2 In a small bowl, whisk together sesame oil, tamari, vinegar, and mirin until blended. Add dressing and toasted sesame seeds to spinach; mix to combine. The spinach mixture can be refrigerated, covered tightly, up to 2 days. Serve chilled or at room temperature.

per serving: 163 calories; .9 g saturated fat; 4.9 g unsaturated fat; 0 mg cholesterol; 11.6 g carbohydrates; 9 g protein; 533 mg sodium; 5.7 g fiber

baked plum tomatoes with herbed rice stuffing **SERVES 8**

Stuffed with brown rice, shallots, and fresh herbs, these tomatoes make a hearty and well-seasoned side dish for chicken or fish. They are also substantial enough to be the main course of a vegetarian lunch or light supper, served with a mixed-green salad. Here, the rice is boiled for ten minutes before being combined with the stuffing ingredients, to ensure it will be tender after baking. (Soaking the rice in water overnight would serve the same purpose.)

¼ cup brown rice

8 large plum tomatoes (about 1¾ pounds)

Coarse salt and freshly ground pepper

2 tablespoons finely chopped fresh basil, plus more, coarsely chopped, for garnish

2 tablespoons minced shallots

2 teaspoons grated parmesan cheese

1 teaspoon extra-virgin olive oil

¼ cup dry white wine

1 Preheat oven to 375°F. Bring a saucepan of water to a boil. Add rice, stir once, and return to a boil. Cook 10 minutes, then drain. Using a sharp knife, cut a very thin slice from bottom of each tomato so it can stand upright. Trim ⅛ inch from stem ends. Use a melon baller or small spoon to scrape the flesh, seeds, and juice from 6 of the tomatoes into a bowl. Repeat with the remaining 2 tomatoes, scraping pulp into a separate bowl.

2 Stand tomatoes in a small baking dish; sprinkle a pinch of salt into each. Add 1 teaspoon salt to reserved pulp of the 6 tomatoes along with finely chopped basil, the shallots, and rice; mix to combine. Fill tomatoes with rice mixture, gently tapping tomatoes to distribute evenly. Sprinkle parmesan over the tops and drizzle with the oil.

3 Add wine to the reserved pulp of 2 tomatoes, mix to combine, and pour into the bottom of the baking dish. Bake tomatoes until tops are golden brown and rice is tender, 45 to 60 minutes. Remove from oven. Serve immediately, garnished with coarsely chopped basil.

per serving: 50 calories; .2 g saturated fat; .7 g unsaturated fat; .4 mg cholesterol; 8 g carbohydrates; 1.3 g protein; 304 mg sodium; .9 g fiber

roasted fall vegetables SERVES 8

Eating fresh produce in a variety of colors is key to good health, and this autumn medley of carrots, butternut squash, rutabaga, parsnips, and shallots provides an abundance of vitamins, minerals, and other nutrients.

1 large butternut squash (1½ pounds), peeled, halved lengthwise, seeded, and cut into ½-inch wedges

1 pound carrots, peeled and cut into 2-inch lengths

1 pound parsnips, peeled and cut into 2-inch lengths

1 small rutabaga (1 pound), peeled, halved lengthwise, and cut into ½-inch wedges

1 pound shallots, peeled and halved if large

3 sprigs rosemary

3 tablespoons olive oil

Coarse salt and freshly ground pepper

1 Preheat oven to 450°F. Combine the vegetables and rosemary on a large rimmed baking sheet (or divide among 2 smaller sheets). Drizzle with oil, sprinkle with 1 teaspoon salt, and season with pepper. Toss to combine; spread in an even layer.

2 Roast until vegetables are tender and golden, tossing occasionally, 40 to 50 minutes. Serve warm or at room temperature.

per serving: 206 calories; 1 g saturated fat; 6 g unsaturated fat; 0 mg cholesterol; 31 g carbohydrates; 7 g protein; 775 mg sodium; 10 g fiber

savory stuffed sweet potatoes **SERVES 4**

Kale adds vitamin C and additional beta-carotene to the stuffing for sweet potatoes, while tofu contributes protein. For extra fiber, eat the skins. Round sweet potatoes work best; if you use oblong potatoes, trim along the top of each lengthwise instead of cutting off the top quarter.

4 large round sweet potatoes (10 to 12 ounces each), scrubbed

1 tablespoon plus 1 teaspoon olive oil

1 small onion, finely chopped

1 small garlic clove, minced

1 teaspoon finely chopped fresh rosemary

Coarse salt

¼ teaspoon crushed red pepper flakes

4 ounces kale, preferably Tuscan, trimmed and thinly sliced (about 2¼ cups)

3.5 ounces (¼ package) firm tofu, cut into ½-inch cubes

¼ cup water

1 Preheat oven to 375°F. Bake sweet potatoes on a parchment-lined baking sheet until tender but not completely cooked through, 55 to 70 minutes (depending on size). Remove from oven. When cool enough to handle, slice off the top quarter of each sweet potato; discard. Scoop out flesh, leaving a ½-inch-thick shell. Coarsely chop half of the flesh; reserve remaining flesh for another use.

2 Heat oil in a large skillet over medium-high. Add onion, garlic, rosemary, 1 teaspoon salt, and the crushed red pepper flakes; cook, stirring occasionally, until onion is softened, about 3 minutes. Add kale; cook, tossing occasionally, until kale has wilted, about 5 minutes. Stir in chopped sweet potato, tofu, and the water. Cook, stirring, until filling is heated through, about 1 minute.

3 Return sweet potato shells to baking sheet. Spoon filling into shells, dividing evenly. Cover with parchment, then foil, and bake until heated through, about 30 minutes. Remove from oven. Serve immediately.

per serving: 334 calories; .9 g saturated fat; 4.2 g unsaturated fat; 0 mg cholesterol; 63 g carbohydrates; 8.2 g protein; 650 mg sodium; 9.5 g fiber

sweet potato wedges with sesame-soy dipping sauce SERVES 6

Think of these roasted sweet potato wedges as a heart-healthy variation on French fries—without the frying. A sprinkling of sesame seeds and a tangy dipping sauce lend Asian flavors.

4 sweet potatoes (about 2 pounds), peeled and cut into ¾-inch-thick wedges

1 tablespoon plus 1 teaspoon extra-virgin olive oil

Coarse salt

2 tablespoons low-sodium tamari soy sauce

2 tablespoons rice vinegar (unseasoned)

¼ teaspoon toasted sesame oil

1½ teaspoons sesame seeds

1 Preheat oven to 425°F. Toss sweet potatoes with olive oil and ¼ teaspoon salt on a rimmed baking sheet. Spread in an even layer, and roast, turning halfway through (they should release easily from sheet), until tender and slightly browned, about 30 minutes.

2 Meanwhile, stir together tamari, vinegar, and sesame oil in a small bowl.

3 Transfer potatoes to a serving dish; immediately sprinkle with sesame seeds. Serve with dipping sauce.

per serving: 168 calories; .5 g saturated fat; 3 g unsaturated fat; 0 mg cholesterol; 32 g carbohydrates; 3 g protein; 309 mg sodium; 5 g fiber

wild and brown rice salad SERVES 4

Rice salads make nice gluten-free alternatives to pasta salads; like the latter, they can be served at room temperature or chilled. This fresh-flavored side uses three types of rice—wild, brown, and brown basmati—but any combination of rices would work well.

3 cups water

½ cup wild rice, rinsed and drained

Coarse salt and freshly ground pepper

¾ cup long-grain brown rice

½ cup brown basmati rice, rinsed and drained

1 tablespoon extra-virgin olive oil

1 tablespoon plus 1½ teaspoons balsamic vinegar

¼ teaspoon Dijon mustard

1 yellow bell pepper, ribs and seeds removed, cut into ½-inch pieces

½ red onion, finely chopped

2 celery stalks, cut into ½-inch pieces

½ English cucumber, quartered lengthwise and cut into ¼-inch slices

6 ounces cherry tomatoes, quartered

¼ cup coarsely chopped fresh cilantro

1 Bring 1 cup water to a boil in a saucepan; add the wild rice and ¼ teaspoon salt. Return to a boil; reduce to a simmer. Cover, and cook until rice is tender and has absorbed all liquid, 45 to 50 minutes. Remove from heat; let stand, covered, 10 minutes.

2 Meanwhile, combine 1¼ cups water, the long-grain brown rice, and ¼ teaspoon salt in another saucepan. Bring to a boil; reduce to a simmer. Cover, and cook until rice is tender and has absorbed all liquid, 35 to 40 minutes. Remove from heat; let stand, covered, 10 minutes.

3 In a third saucepan, bring remaining ¾ cup water, the basmati rice, and ¼ teaspoon salt to a boil. Reduce heat to a simmer. Cover, and cook until rice is tender and has absorbed all liquid, about 30 minutes. Remove from heat; let stand, covered, 10 minutes.

4 In a small bowl, whisk together the olive oil, vinegar, mustard, and 1 teaspoon salt; season with pepper.

5 Fluff all the rice with a fork, then transfer to a serving bowl. Add bell pepper, onion, celery, cucumber, tomatoes, and cilantro. Add dressing, and toss well to combine. The rice salad can be prepared up to 1 hour ahead and refrigerated, covered tightly. Serve at room temperature.

per serving: 177 calories; .5 saturated fat; 2.5 g unsaturated fat; 0 mg cholesterol; 34 g carbohydrates; 4 g protein; 151 mg sodium; 2 g fiber

cauliflower and barley salad with toasted almonds SERVES 4

Don't let the cauliflower's pale hue fool you into thinking it's less nutritious than more colorful vegetables; a member of the *Brassica* family, it contains powerful compounds that help detoxify the liver and fight cancer.

1 cup pearl barley

3½ cups water

Coarse salt and freshly ground pepper

¾ cup raw whole almonds, toasted (page 53) and coarsely chopped

½ head cauliflower, broken into small florets (2½ to 3 cups)

¼ cup extra-virgin olive oil, plus more for drizzling, if desired

3 ounces grated parmesan cheese (¾ cup)

1 cup coarsely chopped fresh flat-leaf parsley

½ lemon, for serving

1 Combine barley with the water and ½ teaspoon salt in a medium saucepan, and bring to a boil over high heat. Stir once and reduce heat to low; simmer, covered, until tender, about 30 minutes. Drain and let cool slightly.

2 Place barley in a large bowl, and add almonds, cauliflower, the oil, and ½ teaspoon salt (or to taste). Toss to combine. Stir in cheese and parsley; season with pepper. Squeeze lemon half over salad and drizzle with more oil just before serving, as desired.

per serving: 545 calories; 5.7 g saturated fat; 25.4 g unsaturated fat; 10.8 mg cholesterol; 49.2 g carbohydrates; 17.8 g protein; 534 mg sodium; 13 g fiber

quinoa and toasted-amaranth slaw SERVES 8

Amaranth is a small herb seed, not a cereal grain, that tastes a bit peppery and is rich in protein and high in fiber. Here, it is toasted until it pops, much like popcorn. The lemon juice is not only for flavor; it also keeps the apples from turning brown.

½ head red cabbage

¼ head green cabbage

1½ cups water

¾ cup quinoa, rinsed and drained

⅓ cup amaranth

2 Granny Smith apples

¼ cup plus 2 tablespoons fresh lemon juice (from 2 to 3 lemons)

1 tablespoon caraway seeds, toasted (page 57)

2 tablespoons extra-virgin olive oil

Coarse salt and freshly ground pepper

1 Shred red and green cabbages as thinly as possible on a mandoline (or on the large holes of a box grater).

2 Bring the water to a boil in a saucepan. Add quinoa; return to a boil. Stir once; cover, and reduce heat. Simmer until quinoa is tender but still chewy, about 15 minutes. Fluff quinoa with a fork; let cool.

3 Heat a small skillet over medium. Add half the amaranth; cover, and cook, shaking pan occasionally to prevent burning, until most of the amaranth has popped, 1 to 2 minutes. Transfer to a bowl, and repeat with remaining amaranth.

4 Slice the apples thinly on a mandoline (or grate on the large holes of a box grater, stopping at the core and rotating to slice the opposite side). Toss with the lemon juice in a large bowl. Add cabbages, quinoa, amaranth, caraway seeds, the oil, and 1 teaspoon salt (or to taste); season with pepper. Toss to combine. Serve at room temperature.

per serving: 176 calories; .7 g saturated fat; 4.1 g unsaturated fat; 0 mg cholesterol; 29.3 g carbohydrates; 4.9 g protein; 277 mg sodium; 5.1 g fiber

whole-wheat pasta salad SERVES 8

This version of pasta salad ditches the mayonnaise-based dressing for a lighter and brighter vinaigrette of flaxseed oil, lemon juice, and vinegar. It also incorporates ample fresh herbs, a variety of vegetables, and kamut pasta—a protein-rich whole-wheat pasta that contains healthy amounts of the antioxidants vitamin E and selenium. Other types of whole-wheat pasta can be used instead. The salad makes a great side for a potluck, but it works as a main course, too.

12 ounces kamut spiral pasta

1 small head broccoli (¾ pound), cut into small florets (3½ cups)

¼ cup flaxseed oil

¼ cup balsamic vinegar

2 tablespoons fresh lemon juice

1 tablespoon Dijon mustard

1 tablespoon honey

1 garlic clove, minced

Coarse salt and freshly ground pepper

2 pints cherry tomatoes, halved

½ cup pitted Kalamata olives, chopped

1 small head radicchio, cored and shredded (about 3 cups)

½ cup packed torn fresh basil

¼ cup packed fresh flat-leaf parsley

1 Bring a pot of water to a boil, and cook pasta until tender according to package instructions, adding broccoli 1 minute before end of cooking. Drain pasta and broccoli.

2 While pasta is cooking, whisk together the oil, vinegar, lemon juice, mustard, honey, garlic, and ½ teaspoon salt in a large bowl; season with pepper. Add drained pasta and broccoli, and stir to coat with dressing. Let cool.

3 Mix in tomatoes, olives, and radicchio; stir to combine. Season with more salt, if desired. Pasta salad can be refrigerated, covered tightly, up to 1 day. Let stand at room temperature 2 hours, and add basil and parsley before serving.

per serving: 292 calories; 1 g saturated fat; 8.6 g unsaturated fat; 0 mg cholesterol; 40.3 g carbohydrates; 7.6 g protein; 413 mg sodium; 4.5 g fiber

wheat berries with mixed vegetables SERVES 8

Wheat berries, the whole unprocessed wheat kernels, are most often ground to make whole-wheat flour. Like other grains, these kernels can also be cooked—as in this recipe—until they are tender yet pleasantly chewy. An excellent accompaniment to meat or fish, this dish is also substantial enough to serve as a meatless main course.

1 cup wheat berries

1 quart water

1 small head broccoli (¾ pound), cut into small florets (3½ cups)

2 teaspoons olive oil

1 yellow onion, diced

2 garlic cloves, minced

1 can (28 ounces) whole peeled tomatoes, drained and coarsely chopped

¼ cup finely chopped fresh oregano

1 large summer squash, quartered lengthwise and cut crosswise into ¼-inch slices

½ small eggplant, cut into ½-inch pieces

Coarse salt and freshly ground pepper

1 Bring wheat berries and the water to a boil; reduce heat. Simmer until tender, 40 to 50 minutes. Drain.

2 Meanwhile, prepare an ice-water bath. Fill another pot with water, and bring to a boil. Cook the broccoli until bright green and crisp-tender, 1 to 2 minutes. Transfer to the ice bath, and let cool.

3 Heat the oil in a large skillet over medium-low. Add onion and garlic; cook, stirring frequently, until translucent, about 5 minutes. Raise heat to medium, and add the tomatoes, oregano, squash, eggplant, and ½ teaspoon salt (or to taste); season with pepper; cook, stirring occasionally, until the vegetables have softened, about 15 minutes.

4 Add broccoli and wheat berries, and continue to cook just until heated through, about 3 minutes more. Serve immediately.

per serving: 141 calories; .3 g saturated fat; 1.3 g unsaturated fat; 0 mg cholesterol; 26.8 g carbohydrates; 5.9 g protein; 277 mg sodium; 6.3 g fiber

kale slaw with peanut dressing SERVES 8

Kale makes for a surprising alternative to cabbage in this sweet–sharp slaw. Curly kale, the most widely available, is used here; remove the tough stems and center ribs before slicing the leaves.

- 2 bunches kale (2 pounds), washed well and drained, stems and center ribs removed, leaves very thinly sliced crosswise (10 cups)
- 1 yellow, orange, or red bell pepper, ribs and seeds removed, halved crosswise and thinly sliced lengthwise
- 2 carrots, peeled and thinly sliced crosswise
- ½ cup roasted unsalted peanuts
- ½ cup neutral-tasting oil, such as canola or safflower
- ¼ cup apple-cider vinegar
- 2 tablespoons dark brown sugar

  Coarse salt

1 Toss together kale, bell pepper, and carrots in a large bowl. Puree ¼ cup peanuts, oil, and vinegar with the brown sugar and 1 teaspoon salt in a blender until smooth. Coarsely chop remaining ¼ cup peanuts.

2 Pour dressing over vegetables. Sprinkle peanuts on top, and serve immediately.

per serving: 221 calories; 1.6 g saturated fat; 15.5 g unsaturated fat; 0 mg cholesterol; 13.5 g carbohydrates; 4.4 g protein; 138.7 mg sodium; 2.5 g fiber

farro and mushroom dressing SERVES 8

A wholesome twist on a traditional Thanksgiving side, this dish uses farro, also known as emmer wheat, an Italian grain that is high in fiber, magnesium, and vitamins A, B, C, and E. Other grains, such as pearl barley, can be used instead; cook them according to package instructions.

2 cups farro

2 tablespoons neutral-tasting oil, such as canola or safflower

10 ounces cremini mushrooms, trimmed and thinly sliced

4 shallots, minced

4 celery stalks, minced

2 ounces smoked country ham, diced (optional)

2 tablespoons finely chopped fresh sage, plus more leaves for garnish

Coarse salt and freshly ground pepper

1 cup dry white wine (or water)

1 Place farro in a large saucepan and add enough water to cover by 3 inches. Bring to a boil; reduce heat to a simmer. Cook farro until tender, stirring occasionally, about 15 minutes; drain and return to pot.

2 Meanwhile, in a large skillet, heat the oil over medium-high. Add mushrooms, shallots, celery, ham (if using), 1 tablespoon sage, and ½ teaspoon salt; season with pepper. Cook, stirring frequently, until celery is crisp-tender, 2 to 4 minutes.

3 Add wine, and cook, stirring, until evaporated, 3 to 5 minutes. Add remaining 1 tablespoon chopped sage and the vegetable mixture to the farro; toss to combine. Serve immediately, garnished with extra sage leaves.

per serving: 263 calories; .7 saturated fat; 3.4 g unsaturated fat; 5 mg cholesterol; 40.7 g carbohydrates; 11 g protein; 359 mg sodium; 3.5 g fiber

swiss chard with olives SERVES 4

Aside from supporting your eyes, immune system, and heart, Swiss chard helps maintain bones and may protect against osteoporosis, thanks to high doses of vitamin K and magnesium as well as a healthy dose of calcium. Don't worry if your pan seems overcrowded with the chard; it will quickly wilt and lose most of its volume as it cooks. Cooking the stems a bit longer than the leaves will ensure they become perfectly tender.

- 2 small bunches Swiss chard (1¼ pounds), trimmed, washed, and drained
- 1 teaspoon extra-virgin olive oil
- 1 small yellow onion, sliced ¼ inch thick
- 2 garlic cloves, thinly sliced
- 1 jalapeño chile, finely chopped (ribs and seeds removed for less heat, if desired)
- ⅓ cup coarsely chopped pitted brine-cured olives, such as Kalamata (about 16)
- ½ cup water

1 Separate chard leaves and stems. Coarsely chop leaves; cut stems into 1-inch pieces.

2 In a large skillet or a Dutch oven, heat the oil over medium. Add onion, garlic, and jalapeño; cook, stirring occasionally, until onion is translucent, about 6 minutes.

3 Add chard stems, olives, and the water; cover and cook 3 minutes. Stir in chard leaves; cover and continue cooking until stems and leaves are tender, about 4 minutes more. Serve immediately.

per serving: 89 calories; .7 g saturated fat; 4.6 g unsaturated fat; 0 mg cholesterol; 9 g carbohydrates; 3.1 g protein; 584 mg sodium; 2.8 g fiber

DESSERTS

orange-walnut olive oil cake with sweet yogurt SERVES 8

Olive oil cakes are popular in Italy, where they are typically made with orange-flavored liqueurs. This version replaces the alcohol with orange juice (and zest), and calls for brown sugar instead of the more refined granulated variety. Use extra-virgin olive oil if you prefer a more pronounced fruitiness. This cake was made with an 8-by-2-inch round "professional" pan; the batter can also be baked in a standard 9-by-1½-inch cake pan.

½ cup olive oil, plus more for pan

1½ cups all-purpose flour, plus more for pan

1 cup walnuts

1 tablespoon finely grated orange zest, plus more for garnish, and ½ cup fresh orange juice (from 2 to 3 oranges)

2 teaspoons baking powder

1 teaspoon coarse salt

2 large eggs

1 cup packed dark brown sugar

1 cup plain Greek-style yogurt (2 percent)

2 tablespoons confectioners' sugar, plus more for dusting

1 Preheat oven to 375°F. Brush an 8-by-2-inch round cake pan with oil, then dust with flour; tap out excess. Line bottom with parchment; oil parchment. Pulse walnuts in a food processor until finely ground (do not overprocess).

2 In a large bowl, whisk together orange zest, flour, baking powder, salt, and ground walnuts. Make a well in the center of flour mixture and stir in eggs, brown sugar, orange juice, and the oil until just moistened; do not overmix.

3 Pour batter into prepared pan, and bake until a tester inserted in the center of the cake comes out clean, 40 to 45 minutes. Let cool in pan 10 minutes; turn out onto a wire rack to cool completely, top side up. Meanwhile, stir together yogurt and confectioners' sugar in a small bowl. Before serving, dust cake with confectioners' sugar, then slice into wedges. Pass sweet yogurt alongside. Garnish yogurt and cake slices with more orange zest, as desired.

per serving: 442 calories; 11.5 saturated fat; 11 g unsaturated fat; 55 mg cholesterol; 51 g carbohydrates; 8.5 g protein; 423 mg sodium; 2 g fiber

warm stone-fruit salad SERVES 4

The peaches and cherries in this quickly prepared dessert are a great source of vitamins A and C. Vanilla beans are available in many large supermarkets and most specialty food shops; you can substitute one teaspoon pure vanilla extract for the one-half bean used below (don't use imitation vanilla, which contains artificial ingredients).

½ vanilla bean, split lengthwise

1 star anise (optional)

¼ cup packed dark brown sugar

2 sprigs thyme, plus more for garnish

2 cups water

3 ripe peaches, halved, pitted, each cut into 6 wedges

2 cups pitted fresh or frozen (thawed) cherries (8 ounces)

1 cup part-skim ricotta cheese

1 In a large skillet, combine the vanilla bean, star anise (if using), sugar, thyme, and the water. Bring to a boil, and cook until lightly syrupy, about 6 minutes.

2 Add peaches and cherries, reduce heat to medium, and cook until the fruit is tender but not mushy and the liquid is syrupy again, 8 to 10 minutes. Shake the pan occasionally to prevent sticking, but don't stir, as this will break up the fruit. Remove and discard vanilla-bean pod, star anise, and thyme.

3 To serve, divide ricotta among 4 bowls; spoon fruit and syrup over cheese.

per serving: 215 calories; 3.1 g saturated fat; 1.8 g unsaturated fat; 19.2 mg cholesterol; 35.3 g carbohydrates; 8.6 g protein; 83 mg sodium; 2.7 g fiber

poached tropical fruit with sorbet SERVES 4

Chunks of kiwi, mango, and pineapple are poached in a spicy peppercorn-infused pineapple syrup, then served with sorbet. Kiwifruit and mango offer ample vitamin C; pineapple provides bromelain, an enzyme that aids digestion, reduces inflammation, and helps heal bruises.

2 cups unsweetened pineapple juice

¼ cup sugar

1 cup water

2 teaspoons cracked black peppercorns

½ pineapple, peeled, cored, and thinly sliced

2 mangoes, peeled and pitted (see page 193), thinly sliced

3 kiwifruit, peeled (see page 39) and cut into 8 wedges each

1 pint passionfruit sorbet

1 Combine pineapple juice, sugar, the water, and peppercorns in a small saucepan. Bring to a boil over high heat. Reduce heat to a simmer, and cook until syrupy, about 30 minutes. Remove from heat, and strain liquid through a sieve into a heatproof bowl. Discard solids.

2 Prepare an ice bath. Add the pineapple, mangoes, and kiwis to the poaching liquid, and let stand 15 minutes. Set the bowl in the ice bath; chill, stirring occasionally.

3 When ready to serve, divide chilled fruit among four dessert bowls, and spoon some poaching liquid into each. Add a scoop of sorbet to each, and serve immediately.

per serving: 347 calories; .3 saturated fat; .4 g unsaturated fat; 0 mg cholesterol; 88 g carbohydrates; 1.5 g protein; 43 mg sodium; 6.5 g fiber

WARM STONE-FRUIT SALAD

POACHED TROPICAL FRUIT WITH SORBET

roasted papaya with brown sugar SERVES 4

A sprinkle of cayenne pepper offers a bit of heat to complement the sweetness of the roasted fruit. Because they are petite, Solo papayas work best for halving into single servings; if you use Mexican papayas, quarter them instead.

2 tablespoons dark
brown sugar

¼ teaspoon ground ginger

2 papayas (Solo; 14 ounces
each), halved lengthwise
and seeded

¼ teaspoon cayenne pepper

1 lime, cut into 4 wedges,
for serving

1 Preheat oven to 450°F. Stir together sugar and ginger. Arrange papaya halves, cut side up, in a 10-by-13-inch baking dish. Sprinkle sugar mixture evenly over halves.

2 Bake, brushing papaya edges with melted sugar mixture (it will collect in well of fruit) two or three times, until mixture is bubbling and papaya edges are beginning to darken, 35 to 40 minutes.

3 Remove from oven, and sprinkle fruit with cayenne. Serve immediately with lime wedges.

per serving: 109 calories; .1 g saturated fat; .2 g unsaturated fat; 0 mg cholesterol; 28 g carbohydrates; 1 g protein; 9 mg sodium; 4 g fiber

sliced oranges
with candied hazelnuts SERVES 4

This Mediterranean-inspired dessert is a good source of two types of fiber—soluble, from the oranges, and insoluble, thanks to the hazelnuts. Look for orange-flower water at specialty grocers.

½ cup fresh orange juice, strained (from 2 to 3 oranges)

1 sprig rosemary, plus more for garnish

2 tablespoons mild honey, such as orange blossom

1 tablespoon orange-flower water

2 tablespoons coarsely chopped blanched hazelnuts

1 large egg white

1 teaspoon dark brown sugar
  Pinch of ground cinnamon

4 navel oranges, peel and pith removed

1 Preheat oven to 350°F. Stir together orange juice, rosemary, honey, and orange-flower water in a small saucepan. Bring to a boil over medium-high heat. Cook, skimming foam from surface with a slotted spoon, until mixture has reduced to ⅓ cup, 7 to 9 minutes. Let syrup cool completely.

2 Place chopped nuts in a small bowl. Whisk egg white in another bowl until foamy. Stir 2 to 3 tablespoons whipped egg white into the nuts (enough to coat nuts). Add brown sugar and cinnamon; stir to coat nuts. Transfer hazelnuts to a rimmed baking sheet, and spread in an even layer. Bake until dry, 5 to 7 minutes. Let cool completely.

3 Slice oranges into ¼-inch-thick rounds. Divide evenly among serving dishes. Drizzle orange-flower syrup on top; sprinkle with candied hazelnuts. Garnish with rosemary sprigs.

per serving: 146 calories; .2 g saturated fat; 2 g unsaturated fat; 0 mg cholesterol; 31 g carbohydrates; 3 g protein; 17 mg sodium; 4 g fiber

LEMON CREAM WITH BLACKBERRIES

FOUR-BERRY SALAD

lemon cream with blackberries SERVES 4

The "cream" in this dessert is actually pureed silken tofu, flavored with fresh lemon juice. You can make the puree, cover it, and keep it in the refrigerator for up to three days.

- 1 tablespoon finely grated lemon zest plus ¼ cup fresh lemon juice (from 1 to 2 lemons)
- ½ cup honey
- 1 cup (about 12 ounces) drained silken tofu
- 1 cup blackberries

1 In a blender, puree 2½ teaspoons lemon zest, the lemon juice, honey, and tofu until smooth, scraping down sides of blender with a flexible spatula as necessary. Refrigerate, covered, if not serving immediately.

2 To serve, divide lemon cream evenly among 4 bowls or serving glasses. Top each serving with blackberries and remaining ½ teaspoon lemon zest.

per serving: 180 calories; 0 g saturated fat; .1 g unsaturated fat; 0 mg cholesterol; 41 g carbohydrates; 4.4 g protein; 2.3 mg sodium; 2.4 g fiber

four-berry salad SERVES 4

Balsamic vinegar and brown sugar combine to make a tart, sweet dressing for all kinds of berries—a high variety ensures you'll get a range of antioxidants. Serve the salad as is or topped with chopped toasted nuts.

- 1 tablespoon balsamic vinegar
- 2 teaspoons dark brown sugar
- 1½ cups strawberries, hulled and halved (or quartered if large)
- 1 cup blueberries
- ¾ cup raspberries
- ½ cup blackberries
- 2 tablespoons small mint leaves, plus sprigs for garnish

In a medium bowl, whisk together vinegar and sugar. Add strawberries, blueberries, raspberries, blackberries, and mint leaves. Toss gently to combine, then divide among four bowls. Serve immediately, garnished with mint sprigs.

per serving: 113 calories; .5 saturated fat; 4 g unsaturated fat; 0 mg cholesterol; 18 g carbohydrates; 2 g protein; 4 mg sodium; 5 g fiber

individual sweet potato and apple soufflés SERVES 6

The flavor and texture of these miniature spiced soufflés are reminiscent of sweet potato pie, but with far fewer calories and much less fat.

1 large sweet potato (10 ounces), peeled and cut into 2-inch pieces

1 large apple (8 ounces), such as Granny Smith, peeled and cut into 2-inch pieces

1/8 teaspoon salt

1/2 teaspoon ground allspice

3 tablespoons sugar

1 large egg yolk plus 4 large egg whites

2 tablespoons all-purpose flour

1 Preheat oven to 400°F. Line a rimmed baking sheet with parchment paper. Arrange sweet potato pieces in an even layer on sheet, and cover with parchment, then foil. Bake 20 minutes. Add apple pieces, spreading evenly. Cover; bake until tender, about 20 minutes more. Transfer sheet to a wire rack. Uncover, and let cool completely, about 15 minutes.

2 In a food processor, puree sweet potato, apple, salt, allspice, and 1 tablespoon sugar until combined, adding 1 to 2 tablespoons water if necessary to achieve a smooth consistency. Pass through a medium sieve into a bowl. Stir in egg yolk and flour until combined.

3 With an electric mixer on medium-high speed, whisk egg whites until soft peaks form. Gradually add remaining 2 tablespoons sugar, beating until stiff, glossy peaks form (do not overbeat). Whisk one-third of the egg white mixture into the sweet potato mixture. Using a flexible spatula, gently fold in remaining egg whites.

4 Place six 6-ounce ramekins or custard cups on a rimmed baking sheet; divide puree evenly among dishes. Bake just until puffed and cooked through, about 14 minutes. Serve immediately.

per serving: 116 calories; .3 g saturated fat; .5 g unsaturated fat; 34 mg cholesterol; 24 g carbohydrates; 4 g protein; 113 mg sodium; 2 g fiber

berry grunt SERVES 8

A grunt, also called a slump, is a fruit dessert that's cooked on the stove and topped with dumpling batter, which steams in the cooking liquid. In this case, the filling consists of blackberries and raspberries, and the whole-wheat dumplings are flavored with cinnamon and ginger. Serve dumplings splashed with heavy cream, if desired.

FOR THE DUMPLINGS

- ½ cup whole-wheat flour
- ½ cup all-purpose flour
- 2 tablespoons plus 1 teaspoon sugar
- ¾ teaspoon baking powder
- Pinch of coarse salt
- ¼ teaspoon ground ginger
- ⅓ cup milk, room temperature
- 2 tablespoons unsalted butter, melted
- ⅛ teaspoon ground cinnamon

FOR THE FRUIT FILLING

- 4 cups raspberries (about 1½ pints)
- 3 cups blackberries (about 1½ pints)
- 2 tablespoons fresh lemon juice
- ½ cup sugar
- Pinch of salt
- Pinch of ground cinnamon
- 2 tablespoons water

FOR SERVING

- Heavy cream, for drizzling (optional)

1 Make the dumplings: Whisk together flours, 2 tablespoons sugar, the baking powder, salt, and ginger in a bowl. Stir together milk and butter, then stir into flour mixture until combined (do not overmix; dough will be stiff). In a small bowl, stir together 1 teaspoon sugar and the cinnamon.

2 Make the fruit filling: Gently fold together the raspberries, blackberries, lemon juice, sugar, salt, cinnamon, and the water in a large bowl. Transfer to a large straight-sided skillet. Cover, and bring to a boil over medium-high heat, gently stirring occasionally.

3 When fruit mixture is bubbling, drop 8 large dollops of batter on top using 2 spoons, spacing batter evenly. Sprinkle with the cinnamon-sugar mixture. Cover; reduce heat to medium. Cook until the dumplings are cooked through, about 15 minutes. Remove from heat; let cool slightly before serving, drizzled with cream, if using.

per serving: 175 calories; 2 g saturated fat; 1.3 g unsaturated fat; 8.5 mg cholesterol; 36.3 g carbohydrates; 3.2 g protein; 300 mg sodium; 7.6 g fiber

double dark chocolate and ginger biscotti MAKES ABOUT 1½ DOZEN

Dark chocolate, walnuts, and crystallized ginger combine in these incomparably good biscotti. Chocolate with at least 70 percent cocoa helps keep them rich but not too sweet.

- 1 cup all-purpose flour
- ⅓ cup unsweetened cocoa powder
- 1½ teaspoons baking powder
- ¼ teaspoon salt
- 1 large whole egg plus 1 large egg yolk
- ½ cup sugar
- 1 teaspoon pure vanilla extract
- ¼ cup neutral-tasting oil, such as canola or safflower
- ½ cup walnuts, coarsely chopped
- ½ cup (3 ounces) coarsely chopped bittersweet dark chocolate (at least 70 percent)
- ¼ cup finely chopped crystallized ginger

1 Preheat oven to 350°F. Line a large baking sheet with parchment paper. In a medium bowl, whisk together flour, cocoa powder, baking powder, and salt until well combined. With an electric mixer, beat egg, egg yolk, and sugar in another bowl until light and fluffy; beat in the vanilla and oil until well combined.

2 With the mixer on low, beat in flour mixture until combined. Mix in walnuts, chocolate, and ginger with a flexible spatula or wooden spoon (dough will be stiff).

3 With moistened hands, shape the dough into two logs, each about 6½ inches long, 1 inch thick, and 2 inches wide. Bake until set on top, about 25 minutes. Transfer sheet to a wire rack; let cool 30 to 40 minutes. Reduce oven temperature to 325°F.

4 Transfer logs to a cutting board. With a serrated knife, trim ends and cut each log on the diagonal into ½-inch-thick slices. Bake, cut side down, until crisp, about 20 minutes, flipping the biscotti and rotating sheet halfway through. Cool 5 minutes on the sheet, then transfer biscotti to rack to cool completely. Biscotti can be stored up to 1 week at room temperature in an airtight container.

per serving (one biscotto): 82 calories; 1 g saturated fat; 3 g unsaturated fat; 13.9 mg cholesterol; 9.9 g carbohydrates; 1.5 g protein; 49 mg sodium; .9 g fiber

CHOCOLATE-DIPPED PEARS

VANILLA-BEAN BAKED APPLES

chocolate-dipped pears **SERVES 4**

Petite and buttery-tasting, Forelle pears are ideal for dunking in chocolate, although any type of pear will be delicious, from a plump Bartlett to an elegant Bosc. Although it should be eaten in moderation, dark chocolate (with at least 70 percent cocoa) contains flavonoids that help lower blood pressure and reduce the risk of heart disease.

4 ounces dark chocolate (at least 70 percent), finely chopped

4 small pears, such as Forelle

1 Melt chocolate in a heatproof bowl set over (not in) a pan of simmering water, stirring until smooth. Let cool slightly.

2 Starting at bottom of each pear, use a melon baller or small spoon to remove core, leaving stem at top intact. Dip bottom three-quarters of each pear in chocolate. Transfer to a parchment-lined plate, and refrigerate until chocolate has set, at least 15 minutes (and up to 2 hours). Bring to room temperature before serving.

per serving: 265 calories; 7 g saturated fat; 0 g unsaturated fat; 0 mg cholesterol; 39 g carbohydrates; 3 g protein; 2 mg sodium; 5 g fiber

vanilla-bean baked apples **MAKES 4**

Apples are very versatile — they work well with a variety of nuts, spices, and natural sweeteners. Rome Beauty apples hold up especially well during baking. Here, pecans, vanilla, and dark brown sugar create a winning combination of flavors in skillet-baked apples, irresistible served warm from the oven.

4 thick-skinned, mildly sweet apples, such as Rome Beauty or McIntosh

3 tablespoons packed dark brown sugar

2 tablespoons unsalted butter, softened

½ large vanilla bean, halved lengthwise, seeds scraped and reserved

⅛ teaspoon salt

2 tablespoons finely chopped toasted (page 53) pecans, plus more for sprinkling

1 Preheat oven to 375°F. Using a cylindrical apple corer, core apples three-quarters of the way down. Arrange apples snugly in an ovenproof skillet or a loaf pan.

2 Stir together sugar, butter, vanilla-bean seeds, and the salt in a small bowl. Divide sugar mixture among apples (about 2 teaspoons each); sprinkle evenly with nuts. Bake until apples are soft, about 1 hour. Serve warm with pan syrup spooned on top.

per serving: 187 calories; 3.8 g saturated fat; 3.9 g unsaturated fat; 15 mg cholesterol; 28.8 g carbohydrates; .7 g protein; 66 mg sodium; 3.6 g fiber

strawberries with yogurt and pistachios SERVES 4

In this quick-assembly dessert, Greek-style yogurt is a rich and tangy stand-in for whipped cream. If you can't find Greek yogurt, follow the instructions on page 62 for straining regular yogurt.

1 large container (about 16 ounces) plain Greek-style yogurt (2 percent)

1 pound strawberries, hulled if desired

2 tablespoons plus 2 teaspoons honey

¼ cup unsalted roasted shelled pistachios, coarsely chopped

Divide yogurt and strawberries among four bowls. Drizzle with honey, sprinkle with pistachios, and serve.

per serving: 193 calories; 4.5 g saturated fat; 3 g unsaturated fat; 9 mg cholesterol; 24 g carbohydrates; 6 g protein; 17 mg sodium; 3 g fiber

berry crush SERVES 4

Berries, blended with ice and almonds, make a simple, refreshing dessert that is also packed with fiber and antioxidants. Raspberry and strawberry crushes are shown here (left to right), but blackberries and blueberries would work well, as would cut-up peaches or bananas.

4 cups berries, such as raspberries or hulled strawberries (halved or quartered if large)

1 cup ice cubes

¼ cup raw whole almonds, plus more, chopped, for garnish

¼ cup sugar

3 tablespoons milk

2 tablespoons almond-flavored liqueur, such as Amaretto

1 Place berries in an airtight container or plastic bag and freeze for 1½ hours.

2 Place half of the frozen berries in a blender. Add ice, almonds, sugar, milk, liqueur, and as many more berries as will fit. Blend until there is enough room to add more berries. Add remaining berries and blend until thick and smooth. Divide among four serving dishes. Garnish with chopped almonds and serve immediately.

per serving: 158 calories; .6 saturated fat; 4.2 g unsaturated fat; 1.1 mg cholesterol; 24.6 g carbohydrates; 3.2 g protein; 7 mg sodium; 4.1 g fiber

STRAWBERRIES WITH YOGURT AND
PISTACHIOS

BERRY CRUSH

oven-dried fruit with chocolate and toasted almonds SERVES 8

Oven-drying is a slow, gentle cooking process that uses dry heat to extract the water from fruit. Left in the oven for several hours at a low temperature, the fruit does not burn but shrinks and shrivels bit by bit as the water evaporates. As the outside of the fruit dries, the inside turns soft and chewy. Although pears, plums, and apricots are used here, any combination of stone fruit, berries, or other fruit can be dried in a similar way.

4 pears (1½ pounds)

4 plums (12 ounces)

4 apricots (12 ounces)

3 to 4 tablespoons honey

8 ounces dark chocolate (at least 70 percent)

1 cup raw whole almonds, toasted (page 53)

1 Preheat oven to 225°F, with racks in upper and lower positions. Core pears and slice ¼ inch thick. Pit plums and apricots, and cut fruit into ¾-inch wedges. Divide between two parchment-lined baking sheets. Drizzle fruit with honey, and toss to coat. Spread in an even layer.

2 Cook until the fruit is shriveled and slightly shiny but still chewy, rotating sheets from top to bottom and front to back halfway through, about 2½ hours. Remove from oven, and let cool completely. Dried fruit can be stored in an airtight container in the refrigerator for up to 3 days or in the freezer for up to 1 month (it thaws quickly).

3 Arrange the dried fruit on a platter and serve with chocolate and toasted almonds.

per serving: 385 calories; 6.2 g saturated fat; 7.9 g unsaturated fat; 3.5 mg cholesterol; 52 g carbohydrates; 5.8 g protein; 1.4 mg sodium; 7.8 g fiber

THE BASICS

TIP
Because most oils are sensitive to heat and light, refrigerate or store them in a cupboard, or other cool, dark place.

OILS

Cooking oils may increase the fat content of a dish, but not without enhancing flavor and, in many cases, offering a host of health benefits. In fact, incorporating the right oils (those low in saturated fats) into your cooking can help reduce cholesterol, prevent cancer, and even boost the health quotient of many ingredients. (Vitamins D and E, as well as lycopene, are absorbed better when paired with a fat.) Although organic varieties don't add any nutrients per se, they help you avoid toxic chemicals and pesticides. The following oils are best for cooking.

WALNUT OIL

With delicate roasted tones, walnut oil is considered by some to be the gold standard of culinary oils. It costs more than other oils, so use it sparingly. Because it has a relatively short shelf life, walnut oil should always be refrigerated. Walnuts contain omega-3 alpha-linolenic acid (ALA), as well as magnesium, potassium, and vitamin E.

HOW TO USE: Serve walnut oil cold or at room temperature to preserve its flavor. It is especially good drizzled on salads or over roasted vegetables.

OLIVE OIL

High in heart-healthy mono-unsaturated fats, olive oil contains antioxidant-rich plant compounds and has been shown to lower LDL ("bad") cholesterol. Virgin and extra-virgin olive oil generally boast greater antioxidant properties than the regular variety and are mechanically extracted without chemicals or added heat.

HOW TO USE: Heat can compromise the flavor and health benefits of higher-quality olive oils, so extra-virgin oil should be used only in salad dressings and for drizzling over soups and other dishes. Virgin oil works best for most other purposes. A good test for all oils: If it smokes, the heat is too high.

CANOLA OIL AND SAFFLOWER OIL

Canola and safflower oils are excellent for all-purpose use and are favorites of chefs and home cooks because of their neutral taste and tolerance to heat. Both are high in unsaturated fat, and low in saturated fat. Canola is higher in omega-3 fatty acids, which are essential for cognitive and heart health. Safflower is higher in omega-6 fatty acids; in moderate doses, these are also healthy for the heart. Look for high-oleic safflower and canola oils (these are higher in monounsaturated fat) that have been expeller-pressed.

HOW TO USE: Both are great choices for high-heat cooking and for baking.

FLAXSEED OIL

This rich, nutty-tasting oil is extracted from the seeds of the flax plant. Look for unfiltered varieties for more nutrients, and store in the refrigerator to preserve flavor. Like walnut oil, flaxseed oil is a great source of ALA, making it an excellent alternative for those who don't eat much fish. ALA appears to have anti-inflammatory properties and may also help lower blood pressure.

HOW TO USE: Flaxseed oil doesn't hold up to heat. Use it in uncooked dishes such as pesto or hummus.

PEANUT OIL

Derived from one of America's favorite snack foods, peanut oil's rich flavor is suitable for everyday use. High in monounsaturated fats, peanut oil contains the heart-friendly phytochemical resveratrol (also found in red wine). Resveratrol has antioxidant properties and may help prevent breast and other cancers.

HOW TO USE: Because of its tolerance for high heat (high smoke point), peanut oil works well for deep-frying and stir-frying.

GRAPESEED OIL

A by-product of winemaking, grapeseed oil has a clean flavor that shines in many dishes. It delivers big on vitamin E and flavonoids—antioxidants that may help reduce the risk of stroke and coronary disease. Manufacturers often use the harsh chemical hexane to extract the oil, so it's important to look for organic or expeller-pressed varieties.

HOW TO USE: It's ideal for sautéing because of its high smoke point. Grapeseed oil also makes a delicious salad dressing.

TIP
Store leeks and scallions in the refrigerator, but keep onions in a cool, dry place away from other fruits and vegetables that might pick up their flavor.

ALLIUMS

Compared with the many exalted foods in the produce aisle, onions, garlic, shallots, leeks, scallions, and chives don't tend to make health headlines. But alliums (this group's botanical name) have surprising nutritional value. These kitchen staples are all exceptionally rich sources of diallyl sulfide, a phytochemical that may reduce the risk of stomach and colon cancers. Perhaps the best news about onions and their kin is that they offer a low-calorie way to bring depth of flavor to dishes.

GARLIC

Garlic has long been considered one of nature's most effective health foods (particularly when eaten raw); now science has confirmed garlic's role in preventing cardiovascular disease by lowering blood pressure and reducing overall cholesterol levels, including short-term reduction of LDL ("bad") cholesterol, and inhibiting blood clotting. Garlic may also help ward off cancer by stimulating the body's white blood cells and neutralizing some carcinogens. Garlic also has strong antimicrobial properties.

HOW TO USE: Garlic's pungent taste makes it an ideal flavor enhancer. Serve raw in dips or vinaigrettes, sauté as a base for sauces and soups, or roast whole and spread the softened cloves on toasted bread or crackers as an appetizer.

LEEKS

Beloved by European chefs for their delicate flavor, leeks have thick white or pale green stalks with a slightly bulbous base and dark green tops. They are milder than onions and can be substituted for them in many recipes when a less intense flavor is desired.

HOW TO USE: Wash leeks thoroughly, as the many layers trap dirt and grit. Soak cut leeks in a bowl of cool water; lift them out, replace water, and repeat until no grit remains at the bottom of the bowl. Add leeks (white and pale green parts only) to soups and stocks—potato-leek soup is a classic. Or, for a standout side dish, try them steamed, sautéed, roasted, or braised, either on their own or drizzled with a vinaigrette.

SCALLIONS

Sometimes called green onions, scallions are actually baby onions picked before a large bulb has formed. Don't confuse them with leeks, or with spring onions, which have larger bulbs and appear only in May and June.

HOW TO USE: Use chopped scallions as a garnish, particularly for Asian dishes such as miso soup. Also try scattering a few over a bowl of brown rice and sautéed mushrooms.

CHIVES

The smallest of alliums, chives feature thin hollow stems that

LEEKS

GARLIC

SCALLIONS

CHIVES

SHALLOTS

ONIONS

have just a hint of onion flavor. The plant's small purple blossoms are edible as well, and have a more pronounced taste.

HOW TO USE: Mix chives into omelets, sprinkle on baked potatoes, incorporate into salads, or top soups as a garnish.

SHALLOTS

When the Crusaders brought shallots back to Europe from the Middle East in the 12th century, they were proclaimed a "valuable treasure." Shallots are supercharged with antioxidants, and they have been shown to effectively inhibit the growth of liver- and colon-cancer cells. The small copper-skinned bulbs have a milder flavor than larger onions and garlic.

HOW TO USE: Shallots are wonderful roasted whole with olive oil, salt, and a drizzle of balsamic vinegar, and when sautéed and tossed with braised greens. You can also use minced raw shallots in vinaigrettes and relishes.

ONIONS

Round or oval, with papery skin ranging in color from bright white to deep purple, all onions share similar health benefits. They contain potassium, fiber, and folate, as well as the flavonoid quercetin, which helps eliminate free radicals that may contribute to eye degeneration, the aging process, heart disease, and cancer.

HOW TO USE: When a recipe calls simply for "onions," use yellow globes; they are generally too sharp to serve raw, but they

become layered and sweet when cooked. Yellow onions also caramelize easily because of their high sugar content. White-fleshed Spanish onions have a crisp, juicy flavor that adds depth to sauces when cooked, and are equally delicious served raw atop a burger. Red onions are better raw, adding punch to salsas, salads, and sandwiches. The mild, sweet flavor of Vidalias makes them an excellent choice to serve raw in slaws and salads, though they're also tasty when grilled.

TIP
To preserve the flavor of fresh herbs, add them near the end of the cooking time or after cooking is complete.

HERBS

Fresh herbs are heralded for brightening the flavor of everything from soups to desserts. Less acknowledged, however, is their nutritional value. The aromatic leaves offer potent doses of antioxidants and vitamins. Eat them regularly to enhance a healthy diet that helps protect against cancer and heart disease.

ROSEMARY

Native to the Mediterranean region, rosemary has narrow leaves rolled so tight they resemble needles. Its soft pine-like fragrance endures better than that of most herbs when dried. In addition to having anti-inflammatory and tumor-fighting properties, rosemary's flavonoids may help keep LDL ("bad") cholesterol from oxidizing, preventing hardening of the arteries. The herb is also aromatherapeutic; research has shown its scent may improve alertness. Its antiviral, antifungal, and antimicrobial qualities make it great for treating sinusitis (along with oregano and thyme).

HOW TO USE: Flavor bread or crackers; season chicken and potatoes and other vegetables with rosemary before roasting them; or use in marinades for chicken or lamb.

OREGANO

A cousin of marjoram and thyme, oregano has small leaves that are flavorful fresh or dried. Gram for gram, oregano offers more antioxidants than any other herb, as well as most fruits and veggies.

HOW TO USE: Whisk minced oregano leaves into a salad dressing, or combine the herb with olive oil, lemon slices, olives, and capers to make a marinade for chicken or fish.

CILANTRO

Also known as fresh coriander, cilantro is featured in many Asian and Mexican dishes. Its main aroma component, decenal, has antibacterial effects, while cilantro's phytochemicals, including phthalides and terpenoids, possess anticancer properties. Cilantro's blood-sugar-lowering effects may help stave off or manage diabetes.

HOW TO USE: Stir into salsas and guacamole, or add to Asian soups and noodle dishes.

THYME

With powerful antimicrobial properties, thyme is known for mitigating asthma, bronchitis, and other respiratory complaints. It can even clear congestion and soothe sore throats. Its subtle, earthy flavor is extremely versatile and is used in cuisines all over the world; it pairs especially well with poultry, fish, and eggs.

HOW TO USE: Combine thyme with fresh parsley and bay leaves to flavor soups. Season chicken, fish, or vegetables with chopped leaves, or add them to omelets.

PARSLEY

PEPPERMINT

BASIL

OREGANO

ROSEMARY

THYME

SAGE

CILANTRO

BASIL

A staple of Italian cuisine, basil has a spicy fragrance with hints of anise. The herb contains phytochemicals, which help stimulate the immune system and block metabolic pathways linked to cancer development.

HOW TO USE: Combine basil with olive oil, garlic, pine nuts, and finely grated parmesan to make pesto; add to a sandwich; or toss torn basil leaves with sliced strawberries and add a drizzle of balsamic vinegar.

PARSLEY

Of this herb's 30 varieties, Italian (or flat-leaf) is a favorite because of its peppery flavor. In addition to vitamins A, C, and K, parsley contains the phytochemical polyacetylene, which helps reduce cancer risk. A sprig can also combat bad breath, thanks to its odor-absorbing chlorophyll.

HOW TO USE: Add parsley to mixed greens and dress with a simple vinaigrette, use it to garnish soups and main dishes, or put it in pesto in place of basil.

PEPPERMINT

Peppermint is among the most widely used of the 600 varieties of mint. Its refreshing flavor lends itself to both savory and sweet dishes; while menthol, an active terpenoid, triggers a cooling neurological sensation and could inhibit tumors by stimulating detoxifying enzymes. Peppermint also helps tame irritable bowel syndrome and offers small doses of vitamin A, calcium, and folate.

HOW TO USE: Because menthol breaks down with heat, raw mint offers greater health benefits. Try it in a salsa with cucumber or mango, or in pasta salad with peas, whole-wheat farfalle, olive oil, and grated parmesan. It is also delicious in iced tea and lemonade; add a sprig or two to each glass.

SAGE

A symbol of wisdom and longevity, sage has been valued for centuries for its culinary and medicinal qualities. In fact, its name is derived from the Latin word meaning "to heal." It has astringent and antiseptic properties, is thought to relieve the symptoms of menopause, and also aids in digestion. Its earthy, pungent flavor works well in hearty fall dishes such as stews, pastas, and roasts.

HOW TO USE: Season winter squash such as acorn or butternut with fresh or dried sage before roasting; or mix the herb into stuffing for turkey or other meats.

SPICES

Modern research is confirming what healers and traditional medicine practitioners have known for centuries: Many spices aren't merely flavorful—they're healthy, too. In general it's best to purchase whole spices and grind them as needed. Spices rarely go bad, but they do weaken over time. When stored in airtight containers, whole spices generally stay fresh for several years. Purchase them from a store with high turnover; this will usually ensure that they are fresher (if the spices come in a bottle, use by the "best by" date). Store in a cool, dark, and dry place to prolong potency, but try to keep spices where you'll see, use, and enjoy them.

CINNAMON

From the bark of a tropical evergreen, cinnamon stimulates the vital functions of the body. It counteracts congestion, aids circulation, eases nausea, and may be useful in the treatment of osteoarthritis and type 2 diabetes.

HOW TO USE: Use cinnamon in both sweet and savory dishes. Eating between ½ and 1 teaspoon of cinnamon a day may help reduce cholesterol levels and calm the stomach.

GINGER

For centuries, ginger has made a popular digestive tonic, appetite stimulant, and anti-nausea treatment—its active ingredients, gingerols and shogaols, help neutralize stomach acids. Research confirms ginger's anti-inflammatory properties; the spice shows promise in treating osteoarthritis and, topically, rheumatoid arthritis.

HOW TO USE: Ginger marries well with strong seasonings, such as curry powder. Yet it also works in milder preparations and even in desserts. Look for roots with smooth, shiny skin. You can refrigerate ginger wrapped well in plastic for up to three weeks, or freeze it for up to three months, slicing off what you need. Peel the thin outer layer, then grate, slice, or mince the fibrous flesh. The flavor and pungent heat tend to intensify during slow cooking, so be careful not to add too much in the beginning.

SAFFRON

This delicate, colorful spice derives from the dried red-orange stigma of a crocus flower. Since the threads are harvested by hand, saffron is the most expensive spice in the world. Its high price and intense flavor mean that saffron is used sparingly in most recipes. Crocetin, the carotene that gives saffron its deep orange color, has potent antioxidant and anticancer qualities.

HOW TO USE: The spice is used around the globe, in classic rice dishes such as Spanish paella, Indian biryani, and Italian risotto Milanese; it's also a key flavor-builder in bouillabaisse, a French seafood stew. Saffron can also be used to flavor teacakes, buns, and breads.

TURMERIC

Turmeric gives curry powder and mustard its deep yellow color. Rich in antioxidants, turmeric has long been prized in India for its

GINGER

SAFFRON

TURMERIC

CINNAMON

RED CHILES

CHILI POWDER

healing properties. Lately, turmeric has been the most newsworthy of spices; researchers have discovered that it may fight cancer, and that it contains a host of other healthy properties, including inflammation-fighting compounds called curcuminoids. Studies show that curcuminoids may help prevent Alzheimer's disease, joint inflammation, and carpal tunnel syndrome. Turmeric may also help reduce cholesterol and improve certain eye conditions, as well as heal skin infections.

HOW TO USE: Turmeric adds color and flavor to soups, marinades, and rice dishes. Eat the spice with healthy fats or combine with black pepper for better absorption.

RED CHILES AND CHILI POWDER

There are literally hundreds of types of chiles, ranging from mild to very spicy, and they are available fresh or dried in whole, crushed, or ground form. Chiles are particularly high in capsaicin, a carotenoid known for its anti-inflammatory and pain-relief properties. Capsaicin is used in skin creams to reduce pain, especially from osteoarthritis; it also has antioxidant properties and blood-thinning qualities. Some ground chile is made from just one type of chile, such as ancho chile powder or paprika. Others are a blend of chiles and other spices. Cayenne pepper, for example, is made of several types of red chiles, while most commercial chili powders contain chiles, cumin, oregano, paprika, salt, and garlic.

HOW TO USE: Fresh chiles may be diced and added to stir-fries, salsas, and other dishes. To reduce their heat, remove chile seeds and veins (although this is where most of the capsaicin is stored). When working with fresh chiles, wear gloves or wash hands thoroughly afterward to keep the capsaicin from burning the skin or eyes. Use red pepper flakes to spice up sautéed winter greens or pizza, and chili powder to add zest to chilis.

ALTERNATIVE SWEETENERS

Although they should also be consumed in moderation, natural sweeteners are an improvement over refined white sugar. Because it is typically refined at least six times, white sugar has little nutritional value. Consuming too much sugar can also contribute to obesity, diabetes, conditions like Crohn's disease, and elevated triglyceride levels (a risk factor for stroke and heart disease). The following natural sweeteners have their pros and cons. If you're diabetic or have health problems related to your diet, consult a dietitian to find the best option.

AGAVE NECTAR

Derived from the sap of the succulent agave plant, agave nectar (also called agave syrup) was once strictly used to make tequila. Recently, the nectar has gained popularity as a sweetener. With 60 calories in each tablespoon, it's not dietetic, but it's about 33 percent sweeter than sugar, so you can use less.

PROS: Easy to find in most supermarkets (look in the health-food section), agave nectar has a light, slightly fruity taste. Though research is still scant, agave appears to have a minimal effect on blood sugar and insulin levels.

CONS: Agave syrup is high in fructose; besides its triglyceride concerns, some research suggests that fructose doesn't suppress appetite hormones, so you may end up overeating.

HOW TO USE: Try agave nectar in coffee, tea, and baked goods. For the latter, you may need to reduce the liquid content in the recipe. Unfortunately, there's no foolproof equation, but experiment with a ¼-cup reduction for every cup of liquid sweetener. Lower baking temperature by 25 degrees.

HONEY

Once thought to be the food of the gods, honey has been used as a folk remedy for thousands of years, and for good reason—the golden nectar is loaded with health-promoting enzymes, minerals, prebiotics (which help feed bacteria), and antioxidants. It can help regulate digestion and ease an upset stomach, as well as soothe sore throats when added to tea. Choose raw honey over processed, as the high heat used during processing can destroy many of the beneficial compounds.

PROS: Honey contains minerals such as calcium, iron, and magnesium (though in very small quantities), as well as B vitamins. It's especially good for athletes, providing a quick energy boost and aiding muscle recovery. All honey has antibacterial properties, but it is believed that the less processed or cooked it is, the better.

CONS: Because all types of honey can contain spores that very young bodies can't tolerate, it shouldn't be given to babies until after their first birthdays. In addition, honey's glycemic index value is similar to that of sugar and (depending on the food it's partnered with) may elevate blood sugar quickly. Its high fructose content may be problematic for those with fructose-absorption issues.

AGAVE NECTAR

HONEY

MAPLE SYRUP

HOW TO USE: Drizzle raw honey onto fruit or yogurt (or just eat it by the spoonful). It is also excellent for baking, as it imparts a moist texture to cakes and breads. For the best results, look for recipes developed specifically for honey, as substituting honey for sugar can be tricky. However, if you want to try honey in your favorite recipe, follow the guidelines for baking with agave nectar (opposite), reducing the liquid and lowering oven temperature.

MAPLE SYRUP
While typically limited to the role of pancake and waffle adjunct, this boiled-down maple tree sap has a lot more to offer, particularly USDA Grade B syrup, which has a stronger flavor and more minerals. All maple syrup contains about 17 calories per teaspoon.

PROS: Low-tech and barely

processed, pure maple syrup is a good source of minerals, including manganese and zinc.

CONS: It has a very distinctive flavor, which limits its application.

HOW TO USE: Try drizzling a little syrup over yogurt as a dessert, or use it to sweeten fresh ginger tea.

STEVIA (not shown)
Made from an herb native to South America, stevia is extremely sweet and contains no calories. For many years the FDA approved stevia only as a supplement, not as a sweetener, citing "lack of safety evidence" to allow it for use as a food. More recently, the FDA has allowed rebiana, a sweetener derived from stevia, to be used in foods and beverages (commercially the sweetener is labeled Truvia). Look for pure stevia in liquid and powdered form in most health-food stores.

PROS: Because it's about 300 times sweeter than sugar, stevia is potent in minute quantities. In addition, some evidence shows that stevia may help lower blood sugar levels.

CONS: Some people find that stevia has a bitter aftertaste.

HOW TO USE: If you're interested in baking with stevia, consult specialty books or websites; since the herb's sweetness and volume are drastically different from that of sugar, there's no easy substitution formula. Stevia works well in hot beverages like coffee or tea, however. (The liquid and powder forms will dissolve; if you're using the fresh or dried leaf, let it steep and then strain it out.) Also try it for sweetening cold foods such as plain yogurt, salad dressing, or grapefruit. Because of stevia's extreme sweetness, start small and add gradually.

GLOSSARY OF TERMS

AMINO ACIDS

Amino acids are chemical compounds found in plant and animal proteins. There are 20 different types of amino acids. About half of these the body synthesizes (or creates); they are called nonessential amino acids. The rest—called essential amino acids—must be acquired from diet. The body uses both nonessential and essential amino acids to make proteins that are an integral element in repair and growth of body tissue, immune protection, and the transmission of nerve impulses.

ANTHOCYANINS

Anthocyanins are a large group of flavonoid pigments in the red-blue-purple range. Individual anthocyanins show promise as anti-cancer and anti-inflammatory agents.

ANTIOXIDANTS

Antioxidants help protect the body against free radicals—unstable molecules that can damage cells and cause cancer. A number of antioxidants are found in food while others are synthesized in the body. Many antioxidants come in the form of vitamins, such as vitamins A, C, and E, while others are phytonutrients, such as lycopene, beta-carotene, lutein, and selenium. Whole foods, such as fruits, vegetables, nuts, and grains, are among the best sources of antioxidants.

ARGININE

Also known as L-arginine, this amino acid is synthesized by most healthy adults. Arginine plays a crucial role in the body's ability to rid itself of ammonia. It also relaxes blood vessels (as nitric oxide) and may be useful in treating heart failure, erectile dysfunction, and vascular headaches.

ASTAXANTHIN

Astaxanthin is a carotenoid that produces a red pigment most commonly found in seafood (it gives salmon its dark pink color). It is a strong antioxidant, which may promote heart health by protecting arterial fat from oxidation.

BETA-CAROTENE

A member of the large carotenoid family, beta-carotene is a strong red-orange pigment, first discovered in carrots. It's used by the body mainly as a source of vitamin A, and it also functions as an antioxidant.

BETA-CRYPTOXANTHIN

Similar to beta-carotene, beta-cryptoxanthin is a carotenoid that can be converted in the body to vitamin A (although only about half as effectively as beta-carotene). In its pure form, it is a red pigment and an antioxidant.

BETA-GLUCANS

A group of sugars found in the cell walls of certain plants and fungi, beta-glucans help boost immunity and are used to fight cancer, diabetes, and cholesterol. Dietary beta-glucans are found in some mushrooms, bran, seaweed, and yeast cells.

BORON

Though little is known about its role in the body, boron may promote bone and joint health and increase estrogen levels in women. This trace element is found in all plant foods.

CAFFEOYLQUINIC ACID

An antioxidant and possible cancer inhibitor found in coffee, artichokes, and propolis, a resin created by bees from tree sap. Caffeoylquinic acid may inhibit cancer growth and reduce the risk of inflammatory and cardiovascular diseases.

CARBOHYDRATES

Along with protein and fats, carbohydrates are one of the main dietary components the body needs in order to function. Carbohydrates come primarily in the form of sugars, starches, and fiber (the latter can't be digested). Once carbohydrates are consumed, the digestive system converts the sugars and starches into sugar molecules, which enter the bloodstream and provide energy for cells and tissue. Whole, minimally processed foods, such as vegetables, fruits, whole grains, legumes, and low-fat dairy, are the best kinds of carbohydrates; the fiber in these foods is important for digestive health. It also helps slow sugar absorption, resulting in an even, sustained level of energy. Overly processed foods—including sugary cereals, white flour, and potato chips—have little fiber, and their starches and sugars rapidly turn into glucose in the body, spiking blood sugar, which can cause energy levels to quickly plummet. Excess glucose that the body doesn't need for immediate energy, or for future reserves in the form of glycogen (stored in the liver and muscles), turns to fat.

CAROTENOIDS

These fat-soluble plant pigments, ranging in color from yellow through orange to red, typically function as antioxidants; the body can even convert a few into vitamin A. The best-known carotenoid is carotene, from which the group gets its name.

CHOLESTEROL

A waxy fat compound, cholesterol is important for making some hormones and forming cell membranes. Cholesterol is found in animal foods and in the body, where the liver manufactures it from fatty foods. Cholesterol is transported through the body by molecules called lipoprotein: low-density lipoprotein (LDL) is known as "bad" cholesterol because it builds up on arterial walls and can lead to atherosclerosis; high-density lipoprotein (HDL) is considered "good" cholesterol because it helps move excess cholesterol from the arteries to the liver for disposal, and may protect against heart attack.

CYNARIN

Cynarin is a form of dicaffeoylquinic acid, which contributes to a sensation of sweetened taste after eating artichokes. Found in artichokes and echinacea, cynarin has been studied for its antioxidant, immuno-suppresant, and anti-microbial effects.

ELLAGIC ACID

This antioxidant has proved successful in prohibiting the growth of cancerous tumors in animal studies (although the research is still pending for humans). Ellagic acid is found mainly in strawberries, cranberries, raspberries, pomegranates, and walnuts.

ELLAGITANNINS

Found in fruits and vegetables, ellagitannins are phytochemicals that convert into ellagic acid when eaten.

ERGOTHIONEINE

An amino acid and an antioxidant, ergothioneine's purpose in the human body is still being studied. Ergothioneine is produced only by bacteria and fungi (it gets its name from the grain-loving ergot fungus) and obtained exclusively through diet.

FATS

Along with carbohydrates and protein, fats are one of the body's most basic nutrients. Just as amino acids make up protein molecules, so do fatty acids comprise fat molecules. Fats are considered to be saturated or unsaturated:

SATURATED FATS

Saturated fats are primarily found in animal products. In the diet, saturated fats tend to increase the body's production of LDL ("bad") cholesterol and reduce the production of HDL ("good") cholesterol. They have a higher melting point than similar unsaturated fats, and foods containing saturated fats (like butter) are often solid at room temperature.

UNSATURATED FATS

Unsaturated fats are mostly found in plant products, and they tend to lower the body's production of LDL ("bad") cholesterol. There are two main types of unsaturated fats:

Monounsaturated fats Found in olive oil and nuts, monounsaturated fats tend to increase the body's production of HDL ("good") cholesterol and reduce the production of LDL ("bad") cholesterol.

Polyunsaturated fats Polyunsaturated fats tend to reduce the body's production of cholesterol—both HDL ("good") cholesterol and LDL ("bad") cholesterol. Both omega-3 and omega-6 are polyunsaturated fats that have many health benefits. Omega-3 fatty acids are found in many types of cold-water fish, walnuts, and flaxseed; they are crucial to brain and heart health, and may reduce inflammation and lower risk of some chronic diseases (see page 356 for more information). Omega-6 fatty acids, which are also important to brain development, are plentiful in many types of vegetable oil, such as corn, soybean, and safflower. Unfortunately, many Americans get too many omega-6 fatty acids in their diets, and this imbalance may promote inflammation.

FIBER (SOLUBLE AND INSOLUBLE)

The indigestible portion of plant foods, fiber passes through the body without being absorbed. There are two main types: insoluble fiber, which does not dissolve in water and helps prevent constipation; and soluble fiber, which forms a gel in water, lowers cholesterol, slows the body's absorption of sugar, and has probiotic properties, thereby helping the immune system. Fruits, vegetables, whole grains, and legumes contain both types. Adequate consumption of fiber is associated with a lower risk of heart disease and type 2 diabetes.

FLAVONOIDS

A large group of plant-produced compounds (primarily pigments in the yellow and blue-to-red range), flavonoids may promote antioxidant and other beneficial responses in the body.

GAMMA-TOCOPHEROL

Gamma-tocopherol is a potent antioxidant that disables nitrogen free radicals, and is one of the eight compounds that make up the vitamin E group (see page 358).

GLUTATHIONE

The most important cellular antioxidant found in the body, glutathione prevents damage by carcinogens, neutralizes free radicals, and inhibits other kinds of toxic damage. It is essential to proper functioning of the immune, nervous, gastrointestinal, and pulmonary systems. Many foods contain glutathione, but a diet rich in fresh vegetables and fruits will help the body produce more of this powerful antioxidant.

INDOLES

Indoles are a group of alkaloid (bitter-tasting, nitrogen-based) compounds found in broccoli, cabbage, and other cruciferous vegetables. These phytonutrients are thought to be powerful cancer fighters. One variety, indole-3-carbinol, is believed to be particularly effective at fighting breast cancer.

ISOTHIOCYANATES

Also found in the cruciferous family of vegetables, isothiocyanates have been shown in animal studies to have anti-cancer properties.

LENTINAN

Lentinan stimulates the body's immune response, and recent studies suggest it can improve longevity and the quality of life for cancer patients. Found in shiitake mushrooms, lentinan is also being investigated for amplifying the immune response to pathogens.

LIGNANS

A group of chemicals found primarily in flaxseed, lignans are known as phytoestrogens—or plant-derived estrogen-like compounds. They may have antioxidant properties, although their role in human health is still being studied.

LIGNINS

Commonly found in trees and woody plants, lignins are a form of insoluble dietary fiber. Animal studies suggest lignins may have antiviral effects.

LUTEIN

One of the carotenoid pigments, *lutein* means "yellow." Lutein is an antioxidant important to eye health and is thought to protect the retina from the negative oxidative effects of light. It may also help prevent age-related macular degeneration.

LYCOPENE

A bright red pigment, lycopene is a member of the large group of carotenoids. This powerful antioxidant is primarily found in tomatoes, watermelon, and red grapefruit. Foods rich in lycopene appear to reduce the risk of prostate cancer.

LYSINE

This essential amino acid helps build protein in the body. It must be consumed through lysine-rich foods, such as beans, meat, and eggs.

MELATONIN

Melatonin is important to the body's daily biological rhythms and sleep patterns. A hormone synthesized by the body from the amino acid tryptophan, melatonin is also found in foods such as cherries, bananas, oats, and onions. Melatonin is produced by the pineal gland, the retina, and the skin; production of this hormone increases at night, particularly in a dark environment.

MINERALS

Whereas vitamins are organic (i.e., they contain carbon) and are produced by plants and animals, minerals are derived from inorganic substances, from the earth and water. Plants absorb these minerals, which are in turn eaten by animals. The body needs some minerals, such as calcium, in large quantities. Trace minerals, on the other hand, such as chromium, iron, selenium, and zinc, are needed only in small quantities each day.

CALCIUM

A nutritional mineral essential to bone health and growth, calcium is also required for muscle and heart function; when the body lacks calcium, it will draw calcium from the bones to support these vital functions. Deficiency may, therefore, result in fractures and diseases such as osteoporosis.

COPPER

A nutritional trace mineral that helps the body absorb iron, copper plays a role in brain development, immune function, and bone strength.

IRON

This trace mineral is required for transfer of oxygen to the body through the bloodstream, and is an important component of muscle cells and red blood cells. Sufficient iron is important to brain development and a healthy immune system. There are two main dietary forms of iron: heme (found in animal foods) and nonheme (found in plant foods). Heme iron is more readily absorbed by the body. An overdose of this mineral can be toxic, while deficiency may result in anemia and fatigue.

MAGNESIUM

A trace mineral, magnesium is essential for helping the body absorb and regulate calcium, making it crucial for bone health. Magnesium also helps regulate heart rhythms and reduce blood pressure. Deficiency has been associated with asthma, osteoporosis, cardiovascular disease, muscle spasms, and migraines.

MANGANESE

A nutritional trace mineral, manganese is required by enzymes involved in healing wounds, forming bone, and metabolizing food. Manganese also helps protect mitochondria (components of the body's cells that produce energy) from oxidative damage.

PHOSPHORUS

A nutritional mineral, phosphorus is essential to every cell in the body for energy production and regulation of the body's pH level. Phosphorus helps bone mineralization; 85 percent of the body's phosphorus is found in bone. Many foods contain phosphorus, and deficiency is rare.

POTASSIUM

A nutritional mineral that helps maintain the liquid balance between cells and their surroundings, potassium modulates nerve response and is necessary for muscle contraction. It is also essential for healthy brain and nerve function, the production of DNA and RNA, and the maintenance of normal blood pressure. Adequate potassium intake can reduce the risk of high blood pressure and stroke. Deficiency may result in muscle weakness, intestinal blockage, and heart rhythm irregularities.

SELENIUM

Selenium is a nutritional trace mineral that acts as a catalyst to recharge antioxidants and has a role in enzyme production. Some studies have shown a correlation between sufficient dietary selenium and a reduced risk of cancer and cardiovascular diseases. Adequate selenium is important to a healthy immune system, although large amounts can be harmful.

ZINC

A nutritional trace mineral, found in more than 200 enzymes, zinc has roles in the metabolism of RNA, DNA, and proteins. It is essential to the function of the immune system.

OMEGA-3 FATTY ACIDS

A type of polyunsaturated fat (along with omega-6 fatty acids), omega-3s are important to cardiovascular and neurological health. There are three types: ALA (alpha-linolenic acid), EPA (eicosapentaenoic acid), and DHA (docosahexaenoic acid). Of the three, ALA is considered an essential fatty acid; the body can't make it on its own, so it must be obtained through diet. Although the body can synthesize EPA and DHA, experts believe it's also best to consume these fatty acids through diet.

ALA

Found in flaxseed and other vegetable sources such as canola oil, alpha-linolenic acid in the diet reduces the incidence of coronary heart disease, according to studies.

DHA

Found in oily cold-water fish, docosahexaenoic acid is considered particularly important for fetal brain, neurological, and ocular development. There is also evidence that sufficient DHA in the diet lowers the risk of Alzheimer's disease.

EPA

Plentiful in oily cold-water fish, eicosapentaenoic acid is also believed to be particularly helpful in preventing heart disease.

PAPAIN

An enzyme found in papayas, papain helps break down proteins and aids digestion. It is an ingredient in some meat tenderizers.

PHYTONUTRIENTS

Phytonutrients, also called phytochemicals, include a wide range of plant compounds (*phyto* means "plant") that promote health. Some groups of phytonutrients currently being researched include carotenoids, phytosterols, and limonoids.

PHYTOSTEROLS

These compounds, found in plants, are similar to cholesterol. Phytosterols reduce cholesterol absorption from food, but since they may also reduce absorption of other compounds, and because some cholesterol absorption is important, they are best consumed as a natural ingredient in food.

POLYSACCHARIDES

These carbohydrate compounds are made up of groups of saccharides, or "sugars." Common polysaccharides with nutritional importance are glycogen (a storage form of carbohydrates), starches, and dietary fiber.

PREBIOTICS

Prebiotics are nondigestible foods that help feed beneficial bacteria (including PROBIOTICS, see below) in the intestinal tract. The most beneficial prebiotics are carbohydrate fibers called oligosaccharides, which are found in fruits, vegetables, whole grains, and legumes.

PROBIOTICS

Probiotic means "life-supporting," and these beneficial bacteria help improve overall health. Sufficient amounts of beneficial bacteria in the intestines are necessary to maintain a healthy immune system and aid digestion. Probiotics can be useful in treating intestinal disorders, protecting against candida infection, and reducing lactose in dairy products for those who have lactose intolerance. Bacteria, such as *Lactobacillus bulgaricus*, *L. acidophilus*, and *Streptococcus thermophilus*, are used to make yogurt and other fermented foods.

PROTEIN

Along with fats and carbohydrates, protein is a main component for fueling the body. Protein compounds are made up of chains of amino acids. "Complete" dietary proteins, such as quinoa, fish, eggs, meat, and cheese, contain all the essential amino acids, while "incomplete" proteins, such as grains, legumes, vegetables, and fruits, contain only some of them. The body breaks down the protein in foods into its amino acids and uses them as the building materials for all its cells, as well as for energy.

QUERCETIN

This flavonoid compound is found in plants, particularly onions, apples, and tea. Quercetin has antioxidant and anti-inflammatory properties, and may protect against some forms of cancer and provide relief for allergy sufferers.

RETINOL

Retinol is one of several retinoids, which are forms of vitamin A found in animal foods such as meats, eggs, and dairy products. Retinol is easier for the body to use than other retinoids.

TERPENOIDS

Terpenoids are a very large, diverse group of chemical compounds with widely varied effects in nutrition and herbal medicine. Terpenoids give cinnamon, ginger, eucalyptus, and cloves their aromatic qualities. Some terpenoids are used as building blocks for steroids and sterols in the body.

THIOPROLINE

This amino acid is created in some legumes and mushrooms when they are boiled. Thioproline is considered an effective nitrite-trapping agent, and may therefore play a role in preventing cancer.

VITAMINS

Organic compounds made by plants or animals, vitamins are essential for normal growth and promoting a healthy metabolism. Vitamins come in two varieties: fat-soluble and water-soluble. Fat-soluble vitamins, including A, D, E, and K, dissolve in fat and can be stored in the body's fatty tissue, so your body doesn't need a daily supply. Water-soluble vitamins, such as C and B complex, can't be stored; any excess is carried out of the body, so you need a fresh supply every day.

CHOLINE

A member of the B family of vitamins, choline is essential for keeping cell membranes healthy. Choline is required for proper brain and nerve function and plays a crucial role in the ability of cells to communicate with one another. Choline is also used to transport fat from the liver.

FOLATE

Folate plays an important role in cell division, growth, and red blood cell health. Also known as vitamin B_9, this water-soluble vitamin is important to fertility in both men and women, and critical during pregnancy and infancy. A deficiency can cause anemia and birth defects and is a risk factor for heart disease, stroke, and cancer. The synthetic form of folate, used in supplements and fortified foods, is called folic acid.

NIACIN

A water-soluble vitamin, also known as vitamin B_3 or nicotinic acid, niacin is found in foods and can be produced in the body from the amino acid tryptophan. Niacin is essential to cell metabolism and the production of energy, and important to DNA repair and cancer prevention. It also has an important role in the body's ability to manufacture fatty acids, steroids, and cholesterol.

PANTOTHENIC ACID

A water-soluble vitamin, also known as vitamin B_5, pantothenic acid is important to cell metabolism. It helps the body utilize fats, carbohydrates, and proteins. Pantothenic acid demonstrates antioxidant activity and has been studied as a means of reducing the pain of rheumatoid arthritis. Pantothenic acid is found in most foods.

RIBOFLAVIN

A water-soluble vitamin, also known as vitamin B_2, riboflavin is a bright yellow flavonoid. The antioxidant is important to cell metabolism and production of energy. Sufficient riboflavin may also combat migraine headaches.

THIAMIN

Also known as vitamin B_1, thiamin was the first water-soluble vitamin to be discovered. This antioxidant helps maintain proper nerve and brain function.

VITAMIN A

Vitamin A is fat soluble and part of a group of chemicals called retinoids. It is important to healthy cell growth, bone and skin health, reproduction, and the proper function of the immune system. The vitamin is also an essential part of the chemical mechanism of sight; a deficiency can cause night blindness.

VITAMIN B_6

Vitamin B_6 is a basic building block for many of the body's essential enzymes, as well as hemoglobin, niacin, insulin, and neurotransmitters. Also known as pyridoxine, this water-soluble vitamin is essential to cell metabolism of amino acids and glycogen, and important for maintaining healthy nerve, blood, and genetic function, as well as a strong immune system.

VITAMIN B_{12}

Vitamin B_{12} is produced by bacteria and found in animal foods. The water-soluble vitamin is essential for the production of DNA and RNA and is important for maintaining healthy red blood cells and the nervous system.

VITAMIN C

A water-soluble compound, also known as ascorbic (meaning "anti-scurvy") acid, vitamin C is a powerful antioxidant that protects the body's cells from free radicals. It helps to create enzymes that metabolize fats; produce collagen and connective tissues for muscles, bones, and blood vessels; and regulate iron absorption.

VITAMIN D

The name for a group of fat-soluble prohormones (chemical precursors to hormones), vitamin D helps the body to absorb and maintain calcium and phosphorus levels in the blood and is tied with increased serotonin production, which boosts mood. It is also important for healthy bones and teeth. Few foods naturally contain vitamin D, but our bodies can manufacture it if our skin is exposed to sufficient sunlight.

VITAMIN E

Fat-soluble vitamin E has strong antioxidant properties; in particular, it protects fat and cholesterol in the body against damage by free radicals. Consumed in its natural form, it may have a role in preventing cancer and nerve damage and reducing stroke damage. (The synthetic form of vitamin E is not as effective.) It may also serve to reduce cholesterol and enhance immunity.

VITAMIN K

Vitamin K is essential to normal blood coagulation. It helps maintain bone mass and may be a factor in slowing Alzheimer's disease. It is a fat-soluble vitamin that occurs in two main forms: phylloquinone, which is found in food, and menaquinones, which are found in food and produced by bacteria in the intestines.

ZEAXANTHIN

Similar to lutein, zeaxanthin is a common carotenoid pigment that is extremely beneficial for eye health. There is evidence connecting low levels of zeaxanthin in the blood with age-related macular degeneration. The best source of zeaxanthin is dark, leafy greens, such as collard greens, spinach, and kale.

EATING FOR YOUR HEALTH

It's no secret that eating healthy food does more than leave you feeling satiated and well nourished. When you choose wisely at mealtime, you'll increase your chances of living a vibrant, long life. A targeted dietary and lifestyle approach can help you prevent—or better control— conditions ranging from cancer to arthritis. Before you explore food-based prevention, make sure you get nutritional guidance. Research supports choosing whole foods over processed choices, limiting sugar and other refined carbohydrates, and emphasizing foods that reduce inflammation, which is the hallmark of many diseases. Here, you'll find dozens of foods shown to help prevent and control 11 chronic health problems. For each condition, there are foods backed by established research, along with suggested servings based on general approximations, while in the "Promising" section, we feature more preliminary studies.

ALLERGIES AND ASTHMA

OMEGA-3-RICH FOODS

Benefits: May help guard against and relieve asthma and allergies by taming inflammation and improving lung function. **Servings:** One or more servings daily of cold-water fish or flaxseed.

Promising:

Apples Eating apples elevates your levels of quercetin—an antioxidant that alters the immune response to allergic triggers—and may even enhance lung health and lower asthma risk.

Vitamin C-rich fruits Adults with low levels of vitamin C may be more asthma-prone. To replenish your supply of the immune-boosting antioxidant, indulge in juicy fruits like citrus, organic strawberries, and kiwifruit.

ALZHEIMER'S DISEASE

FISH

Benefits: Fish high in omega-3s may help lower Alzheimer's risk by reducing inflammation. **Servings:** 3 ounces of wild salmon, sardines, or other omega-3-rich fish at least four times a week. **Note:** Cutting back on saturated and trans fats is equally important for brain health.

SPINACH

Benefits: Folate, a B vitamin, may reduce Alzheimer's risk.
Servings: Two or three servings weekly.

BERRIES

Benefits: Berries help ease oxidative stress, an aging-related process associated with the onset of Alzheimer's and dementia. They can also reduce cholesterol, which has been linked to increased Alzheimer's risk. **Servings:** Three servings weekly.

Promising:

Black currants Like other berries, black currants offer anthocyanins and polyphenols (potent antioxidants known to preserve brain health as you age).

ARTHRITIS

OMEGA-3-RICH FOODS

Benefits: Omega-3 fatty acids help fight arthritis by easing inflammation.
Servings: Eat at least one omega-3-rich food daily, alternating fatty fish with freshly ground flaxseed.

Promising:

Low-fat dairy Since calcium can help keep your joints limber, eat three servings of low-fat dairy products like yogurt and cottage cheese each day. If you have dairy sensitivities, try to get your calcium intake from dark greens, tofu, beans, and almonds.

Onions Quercetin and vitamin C work together to stop inflammatory chemicals from wreaking havoc on joints. In addition to protecting against osteoarthritis, onions may also defend against rheumatoid arthritis.

Cherries An inflammation fighter, cherries may help decrease arthritis-related inflammation. Sour cherries, in particular, may help reduce chronic pain.

Pomegranates The red seeds contain compounds that may combat a host of inflammatory diseases, including arthritis. When the fruit's not in season, sip pomegranate juice to get the antioxidant and anti-inflammatory effects.

CANCER

LEAFY GREENS (Spinach, Kale, Collards)
Benefits: Abound with cancer-fighting vitamins, minerals, and phytochemicals.
Servings: Aim for 2 cups daily, a mix of raw and cooked.

BROCCOLI
Benefits: Contains chemicals that convert to isothiocyanates (shown in lab studies to stop tumors from forming) and indoles (associated with a reduction in hormone-related cancers); sulforaphane, another compound, may thwart the proliferation of breast-cancer cells. **Servings:** Four servings weekly, a mix of raw and cooked.
Note: When cooking broccoli, steaming helps seal in nutrients.

TOMATOES
Benefits: The carotenoid lycopene may shield cells from cancer-causing oxygen damage. Best known for preventing prostate cancer, lycopene may also help fend off both breast and pancreatic cancers. **Servings:** Four or more ½-cup servings weekly.
Note: Cooking tomatoes makes their nutrients more bio-available, particularly when cooked with healthy fat, such as olive oil.

BERRIES
Benefits: Fresh or frozen blueberries, blackberries, strawberries, and raspberries are high in fiber, vitamin C, and anthocyanins—antioxidants that counteract the effects of free-radical damage. **Servings:** 1 cup daily, fresh or frozen. **Note:** Seek out wild blueberries, which are especially high in antioxidants. Choose organically cultivated berries whenever possible.

Promising:

Mushrooms Maitake and shiitake mushrooms may help ward off cancer by revving up your immune system. Each variety contains an abundance of polysaccharides—molecules that help promote an increase in natural-killer-cell activity, which wipes out malignant cells. Add them to soups and stir-fries regularly.

Citrus Oranges and other citrus fruits deliver big on vitamin C, an antioxidant that helps guard DNA against free-radical damage and prevent cancer. Studies show that citrus may help lower the risk of lung cancer as well as stomach and esophageal cancers.

Pumpkin High in fiber, pumpkin provides two carotenoids (beta-carotene and alpha-carotene) that may protect against skin, lung, breast, bladder, and colon cancers. When autumn's over, look to canned pumpkin.

DEPRESSION

OMEGA-3-RICH FISH (Salmon, Sablefish, Sardines, Mackerel)
Benefits: The EPA and DHA omega-3 fatty acids in fatty cold-water fish have been shown to improve mood and emotions. **Servings:** One small serving (1 to 3 ounces) daily.

WHOLE GRAINS AND LEGUMES
Benefits: Slow-burning carbs (found in foods such as whole grains, legumes, and starchy vegetables) help the brain make serotonin, a mood-boosting chemical that has been detected at low levels in people with depression. **Servings:** Four or more servings a day. **Note:** Bananas and oats may help guard against depression by delivering tryptophan, an amino acid your body converts into serotonin.

Promising:
B-rich foods Depression is linked to a deficiency in brain-nourishing B vitamins, so make B-rich foods such as leafy greens, beans, peas, asparagus, and avocados part of your daily diet.

HEART DISEASE

WHOLE GRAINS

Benefits: Mop up artery-clogging cholesterol. **Servings:** Six daily servings (including ½ cup cooked grains, 1 slice bread, a small whole pita or tortilla, or 1 cup cooked whole-grain pasta). **Note:** Rich in a cholesterol-lowering fiber called beta-glucan, oats appear particularly powerful in protecting against heart disease.

FATTY FISH

Benefits: Omega-3 fatty acids in fish such as wild Alaskan salmon help improve triglyceride levels, stabilize heartbeat, lower blood pressure, curb heart-harming inflammation, and reduce stroke risk. **Servings:** Two to seven 3- to 4-ounce servings a week. **Note:** Include smaller fish such as sardines and anchovies.

NUTS (Walnuts, Almonds, Pistachios, Cashews)

Benefits: Plant sterols in nuts help stop your gut from absorbing cholesterol. **Servings:** A handful about five times a week. **Note:** A source of blood-clot-preventing omega-3s, walnuts also nourish your heart with vitamin E, fiber, potassium, and protein.

OLIVE OIL

Benefits: Antioxidants called polyphenols may prevent heart trouble by keeping LDL ("bad") cholesterol from oxidizing. Healthy fats and vitamin E also contribute to heart health. **Servings:** Use throughout the week for sautéing veggies or dressing salads. **Note:** Use extra-virgin olive oil, which contains more polyphenols.

BEANS

Benefits: Lower LDL ("bad") cholesterol and boost heart health by supplying the mineral magnesium, which helps to keep blood pressure in check, and folate, which decreases levels of homocysteine (an amino acid that raises heart-disease risk when it occurs at elevated levels). **Servings:** One daily (more if vegetarian); a serving may include ½ cup cooked beans or ⅓ cup hummus. **Note:** Include black, red, or azuki beans in your repertoire; research suggests that darker beans deliver more antioxidants.

Promising:

Grapes Grape skins contain resveratrol, a phytonutrient that may elevate your levels of HDL ("good") cholesterol. Choose organic grapes, as conventionally harvested grapes tend to be treated heavily with pesticides.

IRRITABLE BOWEL SYNDROME

Food sensitivities can play a role in agitating irritable bowel syndrome (IBS), so it's important to be aware of your own body's response to certain foods. The following have shown promise in helping to regulate IBS symptoms.

YOGURT

Benefits: Builds up the gut's supply of probiotics—friendly bacteria known to fight inflammation, thus reducing IBS-related gas, pain, and bloating—and helps food move through the intestine more quickly (particularly helpful for constipation). **Servings:** One serving daily. **Note:** Eat yogurt with prebiotics, including whole grains (such as oats), almonds, or bananas, which will help to feed the bacteria from the yogurt and make the probiotics more effective.

WHOLE GRAINS

Benefits: Reduce the time it takes for food to pass through the digestive system. **Servings:** Four or more servings daily. **Note:** To keep IBS in check, eat grains that contain both soluble and insoluble fiber (such as oats); choose whole grains and whole-grain products, such as breads, pastas, and cereals. Some IBS sufferers are particularly sensitive to wheat and gluten (found in wheat, rye, barley, and oats) and should not eat these foods.

BEANS
Benefits: Fiber-rich black, kidney, and pinto beans reduce the time it takes for food to pass through the digestive system. **Servings:** One serving daily. **Note:** Fiber can worsen gas and cramping for some IBS sufferers, so gradually increase your intake over the course of several weeks, and then assess whether your symptoms improve.

Promising:
Asparagus These green spears provide prebiotics—beneficial bacteria that stimulate the growth of stomach-soothing probiotics. When fresh is not available, go for frozen asparagus shoots.

Prunes Dried plums contain sugar alcohols that act as natural laxatives in the body. In addition to stimulating digestive health, prunes deliver antioxidants and help cool inflammation.

OSTEOPOROSIS

CALCIUM-RICH FOODS
Benefits: Keep bones strong. **Servings:** 8 ounces of low-fat yogurt provide 415 mg of calcium, and ½ cup of calcium-fortified tofu offers 204 mg.

MINERAL-RICH VEGETABLES
(Turnip Greens, Kale, Collards, Chinese Cabbage)
Benefits: Calcium fortifies bones; magnesium and potassium boost bone mineral density. **Servings:** 1 to 2 cups daily (best if steamed).

Promising:
Vitamin K-rich veggies A high intake of foods rich in vitamin K may help stave off bone loss and reduce risk of hip fractures, say a number of large-scale studies. Shown to work synergistically with vitamin D in preserving bone density, vitamin K is abundant in veggies like broccoli, kale, spinach, Swiss chard, and watercress.

PRE-MENSTRUAL SYNDROME

MAGNESIUM-RICH FOODS
Benefits: Foods such as cashews, almonds, halibut, dark leafy greens, and soybeans keep muscles from cramping. **Servings:** At least one serving daily.

CALCIUM-RICH FOODS
Benefits: In conjunction with vitamin D (best obtained from the sun or supplements), calcium may reduce risk of PMS. **Servings:** Three to four daily servings. **Note:** Load up on calcium by consuming low-fat dairy, sardines, salmon, almonds, dark leafy greens, and tofu.

Promising:
Sesame oil Used to stimulate energy in Ayurvedic medicine, sesame oil may help alleviate PMS-related fatigue. Drizzle 1 tablespoon of cold-pressed, uncooked oil atop your salad or stir-fry.

TYPE 2 DIABETES

BARLEY
Benefits: Boosts the body's ability to turn blood sugar (also known as glucose) into fuel for your cells. The grain also contains water-soluble fibers that help regulate blood glucose levels. **Servings:** At least six daily servings of whole grains, including barley. **Note:** Barley and oats contain beta-glucan, which helps guard against insulin resistance (a condition marked by diminished ability to remove glucose from the bloodstream).

CAROTENOID-RICH FRUITS AND VEGGIES (Tomatoes, Mangoes, Apricots, Cantaloupes, Sweet Potatoes, Spinach)
Benefits: Decrease inflammation and encourage the efficient use of insulin.
Servings: One or more servings daily.

LEGUMES
Benefits: Rich in water-soluble fiber that helps regulate glucose levels.
Servings: One or more servings daily (more if you're a vegetarian).

Promising:
Magnesium-rich foods Eating halibut, peanut butter, spinach, and other foods high in magnesium may help squash several diabetes risk factors, including high blood sugar, abdominal obesity, and excess blood fats.

Spices Cinnamon may help block the formation of compounds that contribute to damage caused by diabetes and aging. Turmeric (used in curry) may reduce the risk of type 2 diabetes; one study found that mice fed the spice were less likely to develop the disease.

VISION PROBLEMS

LEAFY GREENS (Kale, Bok Choy, Other Greens)
Benefits: Provide lutein and zeaxanthin, two carotenoids that form the yellow pigment in the central portion of the retina (known as the macula). **Servings:** At least one serving daily. **Note:** Eating green leafy veggies is essential for preventing age-related macular degeneration, the leading cause of blindness for older Americans.

OMEGA-3-RICH FISH
Benefits: Lowers age-related macular degeneration risk, as well as preventing dry-eye syndrome. **Servings:** Five or six servings (3 to 4 ounces) a week of oily fish such as wild salmon or sardines.

Promising:
Asparagus High in lutein, asparagus ranks among the plant world's best sources of vitamin E, an antioxidant linked with reduced risk of vision-clouding cataracts.

Eggs Eating one egg a day raises lutein and zeaxanthin levels in older adults. For extra protection against macular degeneration, crack an omega-3-enriched egg.

NUTRITIONAL INDEX

The following recommended serving sizes and nutritional information are based on the USDA's National Nutrient Database; the Dietary Reference Intakes (DRI) come from the National Academy of Sciences (1997 to 2004). The percentages are calculated for women between the ages of 31 and 50 who are not pregnant.

	FRUITS APRICOTS	BLACKBERRIES	BLUEBERRIES	RASPBERRIES	STRAWBERRIES	GRAPEFRUITS	ORANGES	KIWIFRUITS
per serving amount	1 cup raw (sliced)	1 cup raw	1 cup raw	1 cup raw	1 cup raw (whole)	1 large	1 large	1 cup (sliced)
calories	79	62	84	64	46	106	86	110
fat	.6 g	.7 g	.5 g	.8 g	.4 g	.3 g	.2 g	.9 g
fiber	3.3 g = 13% DRI	7.6 g = 30% DRI	3.6 g = 14% DRI	8 g = 32% DRI	3 g = 12% DRI	3.7 g = 15% DRI	4.4 g = 18% DRI	5.4 g = 22% DRI
other	Beta-carotene 1,805 mcg Potassium 427 mg = 9% DRI Vitamin C 16.5 mg = 22% DRI	Vitamin C 30.2 mg = 40% DRI Vitamin E 1.7 mg = 11% DRI	Vitamin C 14.4 mg = 19% DRI Vitamin E .84 mg = 6% DRI	Vitamin C 32.2 mg = 43% DRI Vitamin E 1.1 mg = 7% DRI	Vitamin C 84.7 mg = 113% DRI Vitamin E .42 mg = 3% DRI	Folate 33 mcg = 8% DRI Lycopene 3,768 mcg Vitamin C 114 mg = 152% DRI	Folate 55 mcg = 14% DRI Potassium 333 mg = 7% DRI Vitamin C 97.9 mg = 131% DRI	Potassium 562 mg = 12% DRI Vitamin C 166.9 = 223% DRI Vitamin E 2.6 mg = 17% DRI

	PAPAYAS	PEARS	VEGETABLES ARTICHOKES	ASPARAGUS	AVOCADOS	BEETS	BELL PEPPERS (RED)		CONTINUED
	1 medium	1 medium	1 cooked	8 spears cooked	1 cup (sliced)	4 cooked	1 cup raw (chopped)		
	119	103	64	26	234	88	46		
	.4 g	.2 g	.4 g	.3 g	21.4 g	.4 g	.5 g		
	5.5 g = 22% DRI	5.5 g = 22% DRI	10.3 g = 41% DRI	2.4 g = 10% DRI	9.8 g = 39% DRI	4 g = 16% DRI	3.1 g = 12% DRI		
	Folate 116 mcg = 29% DRI	**Potassium** 212 mg = 5% DRI	**Folate** 107 mcg = 27% DRI	**Folate** 179 mcg = 45% DRI	**Potassium** 708 mg = 15% DRI	**Beta-carotene** 42 mcg	**Beta-carotene** 2,420 mg		
	Vitamin A 167 mcg* = 24% DRI	**Vitamin C** 7.5 mg = 10% DRI	**Magnesium** 50 mg = 16% DRI	**Selenium** 7.3 mcg = 13% DRI	**Protein** 2.9 g = 6% DRI	**Folate** 160 mcg = 40% DRI	**Vitamin B6** .4 mg = 31% DRI		
	Vitamin C 188 mg = 251% DRI		**Potassium** 343 mg = 7% DRI	**Vitamin A** 60 mcg* = 9% DRI		**Iron** 1.6 mg = 9% DRI	**Vitamin C** 190.3 mg = 254% DRI		
	Vitamin E 2.2 mg = 15% DRI			**Vitamin K** 60.7 mcg = 67% DRI		**Potassium** 610 mg = 13% DRI			

* Based on a conversion of 1 retinol activity equivalents = 1 mcg retinol or 12 mcg beta-carotene

NUTRITIONAL INDEX

VEGETABLES (CONT.)

	BROCCOLI	BRUSSELS SPROUTS	CARROTS	KALE	MUSHROOMS (WHITE BUTTON)	MUSHROOMS (MAITAKE/HEN-OF-THE-WOODS)	MUSHROOMS (MOREL)	MUSHROOMS (PORTOBELLO)
per serving amount	1 cup cooked florets	1 cup cooked	1 cup raw (chopped)	1 cup cooked (chopped)	1 cup raw (whole)	1 cup raw (diced)	1 cup raw	1 cup raw (diced)
calories	55	56	52	36	21	22	20	19
fat	.6 g	0.8 g	0.3 g	0.5 g	.3 g	.1 g	.4 g	.3 g
fiber	5.1 g = 20% DRI	4.1 g = 16% DRI	3.6 g = 14% DRI	2.6 g = 10% DRI	1 g = 4% DRI	1.9 g = 8% DRI	1.8 g = 7% DRI	1.1 g = 4% DRI
other	**Calcium** 62 mg = 6% DRI **Folate** 168 mcg = 42% DRI **Potassium** 457 mg = 10% DRI **Riboflavin** .2 mg = 18% DRI **Vitamin C** 101.2 mg = 135% DRI	**Folate** 94 mcg = 24% DRI **Potassium** 495 mg = 11% DRI **Vitamin A** 61 mcg* = 9% DRI **Vitamin C** 96.7 mg = 129% DRI	**Calcium** 42 mg = 4% DRI **Vitamin A** 1,069 mcg* = 153% DRI **Vitamin C** 7.6 mg = 10% DRI	**Calcium** 94 mg = 9% DRI **Iron** 1.2 mg = 7% DRI **Vitamin A** 885 mcg = 126% DRI **Vitamin C** 53.3 mg = 71% DRI **Vitamin K** 1,062 mcg = 1,180% DRI	**Protein** 3 g = 7% DRI	**Protein** 1.4 g = 3% DRI **Vitamin D** 20.6 mcg = 412% DRI	**Protein** 2.1 g = 5% DRI	**Potassium** 313 mg = 7% DRI **Protein** 1.8 g = 4% DRI

	MUSHROOMS (OYSTER)	MUSHROOMS (SHIITAKE)	SPINACH	SWEET POTATOES	SWISS CHARD	TOMATOES	WINTER SQUASH (ACORN)	WINTER SQUASH (BUTTERNUT)	CONTINUED →
	1 cup raw (sliced)	1 cup raw	1 cup cooked	1 medium cooked	1 cup cooked (chopped)	1 large raw	1 cup cooked	1 cup cooked	
	28	24	41	103	35	33	115	82	
	.4 g	.3 g	.5 g	.2 g	.1 g	.4 g	.3 g	.2 g	
	2 g = 8% DRI	1.75 g = 7% DRI	4.3 g = 17% DRI	3.8 g = 15% DRI	3.7 g = 15% DRI	2.2 g = 9% DRI	9 g = 36% DRI	6.4 g = 26% DRI	
	Protein 2.9 g = 6% DRI	**Protein** 1.6 g = 3% DRI	**Folate** 263 mcg = 66% DRI **Magnesium** 157 mg = 49% DRI **Vitamin B6** .4 mg = 34% DRI **Vitamin C** 17.6 mg = 23% DRI **Vitamin K** 888 mcg = 987% DRI	**Beta-carotene** 13,120 mcg **Folate** 7 mcg = 2% DRI **Vitamin B6** .3 mg = 25% DRI **Vitamin C** 22.3 mg = 30% DRI **Vitamin E** .8 mg = 5% DRI	**Magnesium** 150 mg = 47% DRI **Vitamin C** 31.5 mg = 42% DRI **Vitamin E** 3.3 mg = 22% DRI **Vitamin K** 573 mcg = 636% DRI	**Folate** 27 mcg = 7% DRI **Iron** .5 mg = 3% DRI **Lycopene** 4,683 mcg	**Potassium** 896 mg = 19% DRI **Vitamin B6** .4 mg = 31% DRI **Vitamin C** 22.1 mg = 30% DRI	**Potassium** 582 mg = 12% DRI **Vitamin B6** .3 mg = 19% DRI **Vitamin C** 31 mg = 41% DRI	

* Based on a conversion of 1 retinol activity equivalents = 1 mcg retinol or 12 mcg beta-carotene

NUTRITIONAL INDEX

	GRAINS & LEGUMES BROWN RICE	OATS	QUINOA	BLACK BEANS	CHICKPEAS	KIDNEY BEANS	LENTILS	NAVY BEANS
per serving amount	1 cup cooked medium-grain	1/3 cup uncooked	1 cup cooked	1 cup cooked	1 cup cooked	1 cup cooked	1 cup cooked	1 cup cooked
calories	218	200	222	227	269	225	230	255
fat	1.6 g	3.6 g	3.6 g	.9 g	4.3 g	.9 g	.8 g	1.1 g
fiber	3.5 g = 14% DRI	5.5 g = 22% DRI	5.2 g = 21% DRI	15 g = 60% DRI	12.5 g = 50% DRI	11.3 g = 45% DRI	15.6 g = 62% DRI	19.1 g = 76% DRI
other	Manganese 2.14 mg = 119% DRI Vitamin B6 .3 mg = 23% DRI	Iron 2.4 mg = 13% DRI Magnesium 91 mg = 28% DRI Manganese 2.5 mg = 139% DRI Phosphorus 269 mg = 38% DRI Potassium 221 mg = 4.7% DRI Thiamin .4 mg = 36% DRI	Iron 2.8 mg = 16% DRI Magnesium 118 mg = 37% DRI Riboflavin .2 mg = 18% DRI Vitamin B6 .2 mg = 15% DRI Zinc 2 mg = 25% DRI	Folate 256 mcg = 64% DRI Niacin (B_3) .9 mg = 6% DRI Pantothenic acid (B_5) .4 mg = 8% DRI Protein 15.2 g = 33% DRI Riboflavin (B_2) .1 mg = 9% DRI Thiamin (B_1) .4 mg = 36% DRI	Folate 282 mcg = 71% DRI Niacin (B_3) .9 mg = 6% DRI Pantothenic acid (B_5) .5 mg = 9% DRI Protein 14.5 g = 32% DRI Riboflavin (B_2) .1 mg = 9% DRI Thiamin (B_1) .2 mg = 17% DRI Vitamin B6 .2 mg = 18% DRI	Folate 230 mcg = 58% DRI Niacin (B_3) 1 mg = 7% DRI Pantothenic acid (B_5) .4 mg = 8% DRI Protein 15.4 g = 33% DRI Riboflavin (B_2) .1 mg = 9% DRI Thiamin (B_1) .3 mg = 26% DRI Vitamin B6 .2 mg = 16% DRI	Folate 358 mcg = 90% DRI Niacin (B_3) 2.1 mg = 15% DRI Pantothenic acid (B_5) 1.3 mg = 25% DRI Protein 18 g = 39% DRI Riboflavin (B_2) .15 mg = 14% DRI Thiamin (B_1) .3 mg = 31% DRI Vitamin B6 .4 mg = 27% DRI	Folate 255 mcg = 64% DRI Niacin (B_3) 1.2 mg = 8% DRI Pantothenic acid (B_5) .5 mg = 10% DRI Protein 15 g = 33% DRI Riboflavin (B_2) .1 mg = 11% DRI Thiamin (B_1) .4 mg = 39% DRI Vitamin B6 .3 mg = 19% DRI

	PEAS	SOYBEANS	WHITE BEANS	NUTS & SEEDS / ALMONDS	PECANS	WALNUTS	FLAXSEED	PUMPKIN SEEDS	CONTINUED →
	1 cup cooked	1 cup cooked	1 cup cooked	1 ounce (about 23 whole)	1 ounce (19 halves)	1 ounce (14 halves)	1 tablespoon ground	1 ounce	
	134	298	249	163	196	185	37	158	
	.4 g	15.4 g	.6 mg	14 g	20.4 g	18.5 g	3 g	14 g	
	8.8 g = 35% DRI	10.3 g = 41% DRI	11.3 g = 45% DRI	3.5 g = 14% DRI	2.7 g = 11% DRI	1.9 g = 8% DRI	1.9 g = 8% DRI	1.7 g = 7% DRI	
	Folate 101 mcg = 25% DRI **Protein** 8.6 g = 19% DRI **Thiamin** (B1) .4 mg = 38% DRI	**Folate** 93 mcg = 23% DRI **Potassium** 886 mg = 19% DRI **Protein** 28.6 g = 62% DRI	**Folate** 145 mcg = 36% DRI **Niacin** (B3) .3 mg = 2% DRI **Pantothenic acid** (B5) .4 mg = 8% DRI **Protein** 17.4 g = 40% DRI **Riboflavin** (B2) .1 mg = 7% DRI **Thiamin** (B1) .2 mg = 19% DRI **Vitamin B6** .2 mg = 13% DRI	**Calcium** 75 mg = 8% DRI **Iron** 1.1 mg = 13% DRI **Magnesium** 76 g = 24% DRI **Protein** 6 g = 13% DRI	**L-arginine** .3 g **Protein** 2.6 g = 6% DRI **Vitamin E** .4 mg = 3% DRI	**ALA** (omega-3 fatty acid) 2.6 g = 234% DRI **L-arginine** .6 g **Protein** 4.3 g = 9% DRI **Vitamin E** .2 mg = 1% DRI	**ALA** (omega-3 fatty acid) 1.6 g = 154% DRI	**Magnesium** 168 mg = 53% DRI **Protein** 8.6 g = 19% DRI **Zinc** 2.2 mg = 28% DRI	

NUTRITIONAL INDEX

FISH, DAIRY, EGGS

	EGGS	YOGURT	RAINBOW TROUT	SABLEFISH	WILD ALASKAN SALMON
per serving amount	1 large hard-boiled	1 cup plain low-fat	3 ounces cooked farmed	3 ounces cooked wild	3 ounces cooked wild Coho
calories	78	154	128	212	118
fat	5.3 g	3.8 g	5 g	16.7 g	3.7 g
fiber	0 = 0% DRI	0 g = 0% DRI	0 g = 0% DRI	0 = 0% DRI	0 = 0% DRI
other	**Choline** 112.7 mg = 27% DRI **Folate** 22 mcg = 6% DRI **Potassium** 63 mg = 1% DRI **Protein** 6.3 g = 14% DRI **Vitamin A** 74 mcg* = 11% DRI	**Calcium** 448 mg = 30% DRI **Phosphorus** 353 mg = 33% DRI **Potassium** 573 mg = 8% DRI	**DHA** (omega-3 fatty acid) .4 g **EPA** (omega-3 fatty acid) .4 g **Niacin** (B3) 4.9 mg = 35% DRI **Pantothenic acid** (B5) 1 mg = 20% DRI **Protein** 19.5 g = 42% DRI **Vitamin B12** 5.4 mcg = 223% DRI	**DHA** (omega-3 fatty acid) .8 g **EPA** (omega-3 fatty acid) .7 g **Niacin** (B3) 4.4 mg = 31% DRI **Protein** 14.6 g = 32% DRI **Selenium** 40 mcg = 73% DRI **Vitamin B12** 1.2 mcg = 51% DRI	**DHA** (omega-3 fatty acid) .6 g **EPA** (omega-3 fatty acid) .3 g **Niacin** (B3) 6.8 mg = 48% DRI **Phosphorus** 274 mg = 39% DRI **Protein** 19.9 g = 43% DRI **Selenium** 32.3 mcg = 59% DRI **Vitamin B12** 4.3 mcg = 177% DRI

* Based on a conversion of 1 retinol activity equivalents = 1 mcg retinol or 12 mcg beta-carotene

PHOTO CREDITS

ANTONIS ACHILLEOS 71 (left), 136

SANG AN Front cover, 75 (left), 76 (left), 83, 87, 123, 124 (left), 141 (right), 142, 153, 158, 165, 218, 249, 261, 266, 274, 287, 303, 326 (left)

JAMES BAIGRIE 105 (right), 183, 200

CHRISTOPHER BAKER 88, 166

SIMON BROWN 91 (left)

EARL CARTER 52, 110, 135, 222, back cover (almonds)

JEAN CAZALS 114

LISA COHEN 291

CHRIS COURT 55, back cover (walnuts)

BEATRIZ DACOSTA 265

REED DAVIS 175 (left)

JOSEPH DELEO 343

STEPHANIE FOLEY 131

DANA GALLAGHER 157, 213, 338

RAYMOND HOM 54, 171, 229, back cover (pistachios)

LISA HUBBARD 91 (right), 284, 292

DITTE ISAGER 117, 118

RICHARD GERHARD JUNG 105 (left), 141 (left), 300, 308

JONATHAN KANTOR 288

JOHN KERNICK 180

YUNHEE KIM 20, 106, 124 (right), 184 (left), 242, 257, back cover (avocados)

RICK LEW 184 (right)

DAVID LOFTUS 23, back cover (broccoli)

RITA MAAS 18, 24, 97, 237, back cover (artichokes, brussels sprouts)

WILLIAM MEPPEM 38, 62, back cover (citrus, yogurt)

ELLIE MILLER 30, 70 (right), 150, 187, 233, 273, 296, 299, 322, 325, back cover (sweet potatoes)

JOHNNY MILLER 2, 9, 19, 21, 26, 31, 33, 39-41, 44-47, 49, 56-57, 61, 63-65, 68-69, 71 (right), 72, 79, 92-93, 101, 120-121, 127, 138-139, 145, 168-169, 192, 204-205, 209, 250, 269, 276-277, 280 (left), 307, 312, 316-317, 337 (right), 340-341, 345, 347, 349, 351, back cover (asparagus, beets, brown rice, dried beans, eggs, flaxseed, kale, kiwifruits, oats, papayas, pears, pumpkin seeds, quinoa, rainbow trout, sablefish, soybeans, Swiss chard, wild Alaskan salmon, winter squash)

MARCUS NILSSON 146, 162, 210, 245

HELEN NORMAN 109

KANA OKADA 195, 283

DEBORAH ORY 32, back cover (tomatoes)

VICTORIA PEARSON 6-7, 48, 304, back cover (green peas)

PERNILLE PEDERSON 102, 132

CON POULOS 53, 113, 241, 254, 334 (right), 360, back cover (pecans)

LARA ROBBY 196

MARIA ROBLEDO 230

TINA RUPP 36, back cover (apricots)

CHARLES SCHILLER 128

SCOTT & ZOË 221

KATE SEARS 76 (right), 188, 191, 270, 295

ANSON SMART 318

KIRSTEN STRECKER 161, 337 (left)

CLIVE STREETER 25, 29, back cover (carrots, spinach)

JONNY VALIANT 199

MIKKEL VANG 226, 311

LISA CHARLES WATSON 315

ELIZABETH WATT 84, 98, 225

WENDELL T. WEBBER 22, 214, 258, back cover (bell peppers)

ANNA WILLIAMS 70 (left), 75 (right), 234, 238

JAMES WORRELL 217

ROMULO YANES 4, 16, 27, 28, 34, 37, 42, 50, 58, 80, 94, 149, 154, 172, 175 (right), 176, 179, 203, 206, 246, 253, 262, 279, 280 (right), 321, 326 (right), 329-330, 333, 334 (left), back cover (berries, mushrooms)

INDEX